The Political Economy of Financial Market Regulation

The Political Economy of Financial Market Regulation

The Dynamics of Inclusion and Exclusion

Edited by

Peter Mooslechner
Helene Schuberth
Beat Weber

Oesterreichische Nationalbank, Austria

Edward Elgar
Cheltenham, UK • Northampton, MA, USA

Published by
Edward Elgar Publishing Limited
Glensanda House
Montpellier Parade
Cheltenham
Glos GL50 1UA
UK

Edward Elgar Publishing, Inc.
136 West Street
Suite 202
Northampton
Massachusetts 01060
USA

A catalogue record for this book
is available from the British Library

Library of Congress Cataloguing in Publication Data

The political economy of financial market regulation : the dynamics of inclusion and exclusion / edited by Peter Mooslechner, Helene Schuberth, Beat Weber.
p. cm.
Includes bibliographical references and index.
1. Finance—Social aspects—Congresses. 2. Financial institutions—Social aspects—Congresses. I. Mooslechner, Peter. II. Schuberth, Helene. III. Weber, Beat, 1970–
HG63.P64 2006
332—dc22

2006043871

ISBN-13: 978 1 84542 518 0
ISBN-10: 1 84542 518 9

Printed and bound in Great Britain by MPG Books Ltd, Bodmin, Cornwall

Contents

Contributors

Susanne Lütz is Professor for Political Regulation and Governance at the Open University in Hagen, Germany. She has conducted extensive research on financial market regulation, both from a global, multilevel and comparative perspective. Further areas of her academic work include governance approaches in the political economy, the politics of regulation in different economic sectors and policy analysis. She is author of *Der Staat und die Globalisierung von Finanzmärkten. Regulative Politik in Deutschland, Großbritannien und den USA* (Frankfurt a.M.: Campus, 2002) and has published articles in the *Journal of Public Policy, Comparative Political Studies, Journal of European Public Policy* and *German Politics*.

Peter Mooslechner is Director for Economic Analysis and Research at Oesterreichische Nationalbank and Lecturer in Economic Policy at the University of Economics, Vienna, Austria. His research interests concentrate on monetary and fiscal policy, financial markets and institutions, EU enlargement as well as on the history of economic development and economic thought. He has recently co-edited *Institutional Conflicts and Complementarities* (Kluwer Academic Publishers, 2004), *Economic Convergence and Divergence in Europe* (Edward Elgar, 2003), *Structural Challenges for Europe* (Edward Elgar, 2003), and *The Economic Potential of a Larger Europe* (Edward Elgar, 2004).

Tony Porter is Professor of Political Science at McMaster University in Hamilton, Canada. He is the author of *Globalization and Finance* (Polity Press, 2005), *Technology, Governance and Political Conflict in International Industries* (Routledge, 2002), and *States, Markets, and Regimes in Global Finance* (Macmillan, 1993), and coeditor with A. Claire Cutler and Virginia Haufler, of *Private Authority in International Affairs* (SUNY Press, 1999). His recent work on the regulation of global finance has appeared in single-authored and co-authored articles in *New Political Economy, Review of International Political Economy, Global Governance, Global Society,* and *Policy Studies Review*.

Vanessa Redak works at the Financial Markets Analysis and Supervision Division of the Oesterreichische Nationalbank. Her areas of research are: Financial market stability, financial market regulation, banking, Basel II, political economy. Recent publications include *Basel II, Procyclicality and Credit Growth* (in: Financial Markets Stability Report, No. 5, Oesterreichische Nationalbank, Vienna, 2003) with Alexander Tscherteu, and *Urban Development Projects: Modernising or Polarising Vienna?* (in: F. Moulaert, A. Rodriguez and E. Swyngedouw (eds), *Urbanising Globalisation. Urban Redevelopment and Social Polarisation in the European City*, Oxford University Press, Oxford, 2002) with A. Novy and J. Becker.

Stefan W. Schmitz studied economics, business administration and philosophy of science in Vienna and London (LSE). He obtained his Ph.D. from the Department of Economics at the University of Vienna. From September 1998 to June 2003 he worked at the Research Unit for Institutional Change and European Integration (ICE) at the Austrian Academy of Sciences as a research fellow before joining OeNB. He spent the summer semester 2000 at the University of Minnesota (Minneapolis) as Visiting Assistant Professor in economics and the summer 2002 at the DIW Berlin (German Institute for Economic Research) as Visiting Fellow. He published on monetary economics, industrial economics, and history of economic thought.

Helene Schuberth is economist at the Oesterreichische Nationalbank. She studied economics, history and political science in Vienna and Harvard. Her current research interests include monetary policy and theory, macroeconomic coordination and financial governance. She has published articles on monetary transmission, and monetary policy strategies. Recently, she co-edited a book on *Economic Policy under Uncertainty* (Edward Elgar, 2004).

Martin Schürz is economist at the Oesterreichische Nationalbank. He studied philosophy, political science and economics. His research interests include democratic theory and monetary policy. He has published as a co-editor two books on economic policy coordination in EMU (Kluwer Academic Publishers) and a further one on *Economic Policy under Uncertainty* (Edward Elgar, 2004).

Eleni Tsingou is a research fellow at the Centre for the Study of Globalisation and Regionalisation and a lecturer in international political economy at the department of Politics and International Studies of the University of Warwick, UK. She was educated at the Universities of

Oxford, George Washington and Amsterdam. Her research interests include private authority in the financial markets, the role of transnational financial policy communities in shaping practices of regulation and supervision, and the development of stronger patterns of accountability in financial governance. This work has developed into a series of articles and the book project *Non-state Actors and Financial Governance: Understanding Authority in the Financial Markets*. She is also working on a research project dealing with the emerging anti-money laundering regime *Global Governance and Transnational Financial Crime: Opportunities and Tensions in the Global Anti-Money Laundering Regime*.

Geoffrey R.D. Underhill is Chair of International Governance at the University of Amsterdam, and a member of the Amsterdam School for Social Science Research, accredited by the Royal Netherlands Academy of Sciences (KNAW). He has conducted extensive research and published widely on the political economy of international trade, the political economy of money and global financial markets, and global financial governance (most recently, see G.R.D. Underhill and X. Zhang, *International Financial Governance under Stress: Global Structures versus National Imperatives*, Cambridge University Press, 2003).

Brigitte Unger is professor of economics at the University of Utrecht. She has conducted extensive research and published widely on public sector economics and finance, institutional economics, macroeconomics, economic policy and international monetary economics. Her recent work on welfare state economics and institutional determinants of innovations has appeared in co-authored articles in the *Journal of European Social Policy* and the *European Journal of Social Science Research*. Her most recent research agenda includes work on criminal money.

Beat Weber is an economist at the international division of the Oesterreichische Nationalbank. He is co-editor of the quarterly social science journal *Kurswechsel* in Austria, author of several articles on financial markets and co-author of an introductory book on the stock market (*Boerse*, Europaeische Verlagsanstalt, 2000). His recent research projects are financial market regulation in Europe and financial literacy programmes.

Preface

At an international workshop organized at the Oesterreichische Nationalbank (OeNB) in the fall of 2004, a team of international academics and OeNB practitioners in financial market regulation were discussing recent regulatory reforms in financial governance. While central bankers when investigating the impact of financial market regulation typically analyse issues of economic efficiency in terms of monetary and financial stability, the workshop, by integrating insights from financial economics, political science and sociology, introduced a novel notion into the discussion on regulatory reform. The workshop participants investigated the dynamics of inclusion and exclusion in recent regulatory reform processes, such as Basel II, the Lamfalussy process, pension reforms, the proliferation of financial literacy programs and the deregulation of derivatives markets.

Based on the papers presented at the workshop the authors of this book analyse the process of designing financial governance as contested terrain. The resulting institutional set up involves inclusion and exclusion. In the economic area, exclusion means not to be able (or at least being severely restricted) to participate in overall welfare of society. In the political area, for instance in the area of financial regulation, exclusion refers to affected groups that are not permitted to contribute effectively to financial market regulation. This fact has important consequences for processes of inclusion and exclusion more broadly.

The contributions in this volume show that major parts of society who are affected by regulatory reform are excluded under current governance arrangements. As financial governance does not only affect the financial sphere but has wide impact on society, financial governance has to be embedded in broad legitimisation structures, encompassing the participation or representation of a variety of interests affected by it, if they are to be deemed democratically legitimate. Furthermore, inclusion also has to show substantive effects on governance outcomes. We hope that this volume opens the debate about the future of financial market regulation in this direction.

The insights of this book should prove useful to a broad range of readers such as political scientists, economists, financial market participants, regulators and economic policy makers in general in the EU but also around the world.

Last but not least, our thanks go to all the presenters and discussants at the workshop and to the contributors to the book, as well as to all who have helped to make the workshop and the book become reality – in particular to Brigitte Alizadeh-Gruber.

Peter Mooslechner, Helene Schuberth, Beat Weber, Vienna 2006

Financial Market Regulation and the Dynamics of Inclusion and Exclusion

Peter Mooslechner, Helene Schuberth and Beat Weber[1]

1. GLOBALIZATION AND FINANCIAL GOVERNANCE

Financial systems and the prevailing monetary landscape are the outcome of a cognizant political choice among a set of alternative options rather than the inevitable result of the force of economic logic that sorts out the most efficient from the less proficient arrangements in a Darwinian struggle (Kirshner 2003, p. 655). However, the latter narrative is fairly powerful. It creates the illusion that policy has no choice but to react in favor of the claims of financial capital, while controlling it is considered neither technically feasible nor desirable. This view is reasonably consistent with a recent wave of re-regulatory efforts to strengthen the stability of the financial sector. Regulatory arrangements such as Basel II or those in line with the Washington Consensus principles are – among many other available choices – the *liberal* response to financial crisis and to signs of unsustainability in the financial system (see Redak in this volume). In many cases, the reaction is not deregulation, but market-oriented re-regulation. The view that financial regulation inevitably converges toward a pro-market regulation model owes its vigor to the threat of exit of financial capital in globalized economies. Market-driven (re-)regulation is further supported by efficiency-related arguments. However, as pointed out by Grabel (2003), it might well be the case that the efficiency and legitimacy of policies forced by the vote of financial markets are deceptive in nature; they are more the result of a path-dependent self-fulfilling prophecy than the revelation of optimality.

However, if policy options are manifold and feasible (albeit in some ways restricted) in light of market logic, questions arise as to what

[1] The views expressed in this book are those of the authors and do not necessarily represent those of their employer.

mechanisms explain the prevailing policy choices taken. Can the claim that 'money is politics' (Kirshner 2003, p. 645) be maintained, that political forces are *the* dominant factor in shaping regulation given worldwide convergence toward a liberal mode of financial governance? An influential approach explaining the driving factors behind the recent wave of reform attempts in financial governance mechanisms stresses the role of non-state and private actors in emerging transnational policy processes and the migration of political authority to supranational levels, which increasingly share elements of authority with their member states in regulatory reform. Competing and overlapping structures have emerged, with formal and informal interrelationships between public and private bodies, networks and webs which appear to be as complex as and similar to medieval times (Cerny 2005). Thus the inherently multi-level nature of finance precipitates multi-level institutional processes and practices. This has been associated with a change in the logic of democratic accountability in democracies which are restricted to the nation-state level. In key areas of policymaking, multi-level governance by supranational, private, technical and popular sources of authority has undermined traditional nation-state based mechanisms of democratic accountability (such as elections and legislation), while in procedural terms the public sector still plays a key role in setting standards (Porter 2001 and in this volume). In global finance, the state has gone particularly far in willingly accepting the shift of regulatory competences to private institutions, as indicated by the evolving mechanisms of self-regulation and co-regulation in financial governance (for example in the form of codes of conduct).

2. POLITICAL ECONOMY OF FINANCIAL REFORM

Theoretical explanations of the recent financial governance trends described above are manifold but can mainly be condensed into two broad lines of research: economic theories and political economy theories of regulatory reform.

One influential strand of literature among the economic theories of the political economy of financial governance focuses on efficiency-related explanations of reforms in financial governance (for a critique, see Underhill in this volume). In these approaches, as a rational decision maker the state aims for optimal governance which safeguards financial stability and provides underpinnings for the successful operation of markets. The high degree of involvement of experts and 'committees of wise men' in regulation would safeguard the scientific, non-interest-based optimal resolution of policy dilemmas concerning alternative forms of regulation in different market settings. But regulatory modes change with time and political proclivity. The International Monetary Fund, to give a prominent example, favors the sequential and cautious liberalization of capital accounts today, while ten years ago it considered instantaneous and full liberalization to be the essential ingredient in successful development strategies for transition and emerging economies. What is considered optimal is bound to change repeatedly. Furthermore, in the recent past, financial crises have occurred too often to regard efficiency-related explanations of regulatory reform as truly convincing and viable.

In his investigation of regulatory responses to financial crises in the United States in the 20th century, Jonathan Macey (1998) argues that the reform measures taken did not so much reduce the financial sector's exposure to risk, but benefited those specific interest groups and constituencies which lobbied more effectively than others. Hence, the economic theories of the political economy of financial reform have been particularly challenged by political economy theories of regulatory reform which view governance as an outcome of conflicting interests. They devote special attention to the state-market relationship. Rather than being separate or even opposed units (as is usually assumed in the literature), in many cases states are observed to form alliances with private actors in financial liberalization (see Lütz in this volume) and to drive globalization toward neoliberal outcomes. As argued by Cerny (2005), this is not accompanied by a retreat of the state but by the role of the state as an enforcer of rules which is perceived to follow the trends of financial globalization. But why has the state become a facilitator of global processes rather than a protector of national incumbents? Is it because the state is simply overburdened in controlling the forces set free by liberalization, as it is faced with conflicting pressures and the ad hoc tactics of many actors? Or can it be explained as a consequence of a conscious strategy bringing about the transformation of an interventionist into a competitive and/or regulatory state that requires regulatory standards which favor dominant market participants? While it is easier to identify the private sector's interests in terms of economic benefits due to specific regulations, state interests are difficult to scrutinize and impossible to generalize across regulatory fields and regions. One major drawback of the political economy theories of financial governance is that they limit their analysis to describing regulation as an outcome of various actors forming coalitions against others, without further deconstructing the substance of interests followed by those actors. With this focus on procedure rather than substance, crucial questions remain unanswered: Are the actors' interests purely economic or also political, social and cultural? Do governance outcomes stem from the unintended consequences of actors' decisions (Streeck 2003) taken under fundamental uncertainty about economic, political and distributional effects? Is there a causal influence of ideas and discourse in the formulation of policies? By which instruments – formal (procedure) and informal (values) – is authority exercised?

3. INCLUSION AND EXCLUSION IN FINANCIAL GOVERNANCE

The contributions in this volume do not investigate all of these issues, but they share a common perspective of analyzing the political economy of regulatory change. This allows us to address the entire spectrum of questions raised above. The authors examine governance arrangements in the financial sphere as the outcome of political economy conflicts which are linked to inclusive and exclusive processes.

Financial governance is understood as the definition, application and enforcement of the rules of the game (Kjaer 2004) in financial systems. This comprises formal and informal rules and can be enacted by private as well as public actors. The process of designing financial governance is contested terrain. The resulting institutional setup involves inclusion and exclusion. In the existing literature, exclusion refers to individuals who are prevented from participating in certain activities of society. Two aspects seem relevant for our purposes: In the economic area, exclusion refers to an inability (or at least a severely limited ability) to participate in the overall welfare of society. In the political area, for instance in financial regulation, exclusion refers to affected groups that are not permitted to contribute effectively to financial market regulation, which has important consequences for the broader processes of inclusion and exclusion. Whereas exclusion is a relatively straightforward concept, inclusion is more ambivalent. It can imply active participation, but at the same time it can imply passive integration, absorption, or even exploitation.

These processes are investigated in light of recent regulatory changes at the global level, such as Basel II or the governance of derivatives markets, with special emphasis on how these changes are implemented in the European Union. In particular, the contributions in this volume shed light on issues arising from the application of features from an Anglo-Saxon context (self-regulation, financial literacy, privatization of pensions, etc.) in the entirely different institutional setting of continental Europe and the conflicts involved.

The authors ask whether the inclusive mechanisms and processes of regulatory change observed are, as often portrayed, substantial enough to offset exclusionary tendencies (Porter 2001 and in this volume), and whether the recently evolving mechanisms of multi-level governance, which entail multiple levels of public-sector and private authority, offer an alternative to national public authority in terms of democratic legitimacy.

In the following paragraph, the demands on democratic legitimacy in financial governance are first discussed, in particular in areas where formal authorization is not available or of disputed value – as in the international sphere. Based on these normative legitimacy criteria, the procedural and substantive prerequisites of inclusion in financial governance arrangements that effectively increase societal participation are then reviewed and contrasted with phenomena of inclusion and exclusion in practice. Before this discussion, the few available studies on the distributive effects of finance are summarized. These studies are rare because financial matters undoubtedly have a sizable impact on everyday life, but the channels through which these mechanisms are exercised are often meandering, difficult to grasp and beyond the awareness of the general public. Knowing these effects is decisive, as financial governance is exclusively associated with efficiency most of the time and with pursuing the sole objective of preserving financing stability. The latter is in fact a common global concern, as crisis contagion exerts negative spillover effects throughout the world and the macroeconomic costs are high, sometimes even severe and long-lasting. Moreover, the subject matter requires sophisticated technical expertise which is not easily accessible to the general public. Both features add to the popular understanding that standards of financial regulation are preferably set by expert institutions, with accountability being exercised vis-à-vis the overall financial sector at best.

Financial Structure and Distribution of Income and Wealth

Impact studies on financial governance typically examine how financial services are affected, or they look at its consequences for efficiency in terms of financial stability, growth or macroeconomic volatility (e.g. Goodhart 2005, OeNB 2003). But different regulatory regimes have distinct distributive effects which go far beyond the narrow scope of the financial sector itself. Most of the case studies presented in this volume describe regulatory reform initiatives that set off a transformation of European financial systems toward arm's length financing, for instance through the promotion of private pensions and the emergence of a European market for corporate control. In the following an overview is given of the channels through which the changes in the financial structure have an impact on income and wealth distribution.

One might think of at least four different channels by which financial structure can impact the distribution of income and wealth (Mooslechner 2003). First, a direct and most dominant channel is the way in which corporate governance modes have an impact on resource allocation among shareholders and other stakeholders. Financial structures leading to the adoption of a focus on shareholder value creation in firms restrict the ability to transfer resources from profitable sectors to less profitable ones. In an established market for corporate control, the increased attention to short-term profitability in an attempt to increase return on equity will distribute income from other stakeholders to shareholders (de Jong 1997). While supporters of an active market for corporate control claim that takeovers will direct corporate assets toward more efficient uses, Shleifer and Summers (1988) argue that shareholders' gains result less from increased efficiency than from the ability of managers to breach the 'implicit contracts' of stakeholders (such as employees). As employment perspectives of employees with industry-specific skills are not adequately protected, they are vulnerable to a 'breach of trust' which aims to distribute wealth to shareholders at the expense of the firm's long-term performance. This 'breach of trust' hypothesis is also supported by Deakin et al. (2002).

A second and closely related channel through which financial structure impacts income and wealth distribution can be derived from the idea of institutional complementarities, according to which different models of market economies are constituted by a broad set of complementary and mutually reinforcing institutions such as industrial relations, innovation and training systems, as well as financial structure (Hall and Soskice 2001). A change in one institutional pattern will set changes in motion in other subsystems (for a critique, see Streeck 2003 or Schuberth and Schürz 2004). Convergence toward a market-based financial system should thus alter industrial relations and the way in which conflicts of interest between social partners are orchestrated. Centralized and coordinated wage bargaining enables more equal outcomes from a macroeconomic perspective. In general, the bargaining power of trade unions, consumers and pensioners will probably decline vis-à-vis financial investors (see Schmitz in this volume, who investigates this phenomenon in the case of private pensions). Furthermore, given the dispersion of corporate control across countries, territorially based bargains become less effective (Underhill 2002). Though causality is difficult to establish and the determinants of income distribution are manifold, it can be observed that bank-based economies generally demonstrate more equal income distribution than market-based systems. The most recently available Gini coefficients for countries classified as more bank-based vary from 0.25 to 0.27, while those categorized as market-based had a much higher Gini coefficient, ranging from 0.31 in

Australia to 0.37 in the United States.[2]

Third, the secondary distribution of income is affected inasmuch as the emphasis on shareholder value creation has an impact on how risk sharing is organized in society. Typically, households in a financial system dominated by market-based financing bear a greater share of risk than in bank-based systems, where intermediaries absorb and pool risks for households (Allen and Gale 2001). Fourth, and closely related to the last two points, is the role of the hegemony of ideas in creating support for shareholder value orientation and exerting a negative impact on distribution. The latter is the most indirect – but nevertheless equally important – transmission channel. Market-based instruments for retirement savings or health care provision are not only promoted through pecuniary incentives via fiscal measures and/or the propagation of higher expected yields among risk-averse households. They are also advertised by means of a hegemonic discourse that generates an attitude of self-responsibility, self-interest and self-determination (Schürz in this volume), norms that institute the moral superiority of the distributive outcomes of the market over those of the redistributive welfare state (Bourdieu 1998). Thus, financial governance is exercised through formal as well as informal channels, via values and the promotion of ideas. The transformation of the European financial system toward an Anglo-Saxon system might eradicate the prevailing welfare arrangements and make the principle of social solidarity less acceptable in society (Salacuse 2002). Therefore, as exemplified in the most recent regulatory reform initiatives at the European level, financial governance shapes the political, social and cultural sphere. Considering its impact on distribution, one would suspect that these initiatives need to be embedded in broad legitimation structures.

Democratic Legitimacy

One influential view in economic policy circles and supervisory authorities considers the financial governance of non-state actors to be exclusive expert terrain where satisfactory legitimacy is achieved if clear statutory objectives such as financial stability and transparency requirements are fulfilled. This kind of output legitimacy is considered sufficient if the goal of policy is to find a solution capable of improving the conditions of all individuals and groups in society. In contrast, a policy with redistributive consequences can only be legitimated by voters

[2] Bank-based: Finland, Germany, Sweden, Denmark and Austria. Arm's length (or market) based: Australia, Ireland, United Kingdom and the United States. See Luxembourg Income Study Key Figures (www.lisproject.org/key/figures/).

or their elected representatives (Majone 1997). As the perception of the existence of distributive effects in financial regulatory reform is minimal or even non-existent, this influential view considers output legitimacy to be a sufficient prerequisite for democratic legitimacy. However, any policy with redistributive impact requires input legitimacy, that is, the incorporation of social groups in financial governance.

While the focus on input legitimacy is important, it also has its problems and limitations. In order to avoid the inherent limits of restricting the analysis to either input or output legitimacy, the contributions to this volume simultaneously look at inclusion and exclusion from a narrow (procedural) and a broader (substantive) perspective. The narrow perspective examines major elements of input legitimacy: Who is part of the decision-making bodies, whose voice is heard, who is excluded, who is finally assigned which tasks, and what are the mechanisms by which inclusion and exclusion take place? From a substantive perspective, these procedural aspects are linked with the economic, social, political and cultural effects of the specific regulatory measures taken. This is crucial as the interests of actors are sometimes vague or opaque and often subject to change.

A conceptualization of financial governance based solely on procedure lacks decisive linkages between developments in the political (in the areas of policy, polity and politics), economic and social spheres. From a procedural perspective only, accountability and legitimacy are expected to increase with the number of actors involved in multi-level decision-making, for instance by including non-governmental organizations in the process or by increasing transparency (Wolf 2002). However, if the decisions taken have negative distributive effects on those who never have a chance of inclusion, or if the decisions promote a discourse of anti-solidarian values which help to reconstruct the perception of interests and thus feed back into politics, the picture changes (Schürz in this volume). Equally subject to further consideration is the view that in light of recent re-regulatory efforts a retreat of the state is not observable. Hence public national interests should be well represented and democratic legitimacy secured if deliberation on regulatory reform is restricted to the national technocratic elite. National experts and representatives of national authorities are incorporated in formal and informal international, multi-level expert networks. These constitute epistemic communities that share a similar cognitive and normative orientation toward key objectives. Expert networks are often seen as a quasi-experimental device able to promote deliberative problem-solving within society (Bohmann 2004). However, by these mechanisms, national representatives have probably become more distant from the instruments that have traditionally ensured democratic accountability at the domestic level.

Even more contested is the legitimacy of private, supranational and independent agencies, which is beyond the reach of public opinion, parliaments and electorates. Ironically, the decision to delegate policies to independent institutions, agencies and private associations is often taken specifically in order to increase legitimacy. In fact, the recent changes in global financial regulation are often portrayed as an inclusive process: Governance is now less exercised by imposing a centralized set of administrative procedures from an organized hierarchy, a powerful political authority, but rather by a decentralized, sometimes self-regulatory system of codes, rules and standards developed through deliberation and consultation in a variety of dispersed and often informal institutions and networks (for a discussion, see Porter 2001 and in this volume). Strengthening the role of non-state actors in decentralized public-private policy networks is supposed to improve the input legitimacy of governance (Wolf 2002). But a mere focus on procedural aspects without taking account of the substantive features regarding the precise social and economic impact of reforms taken may send misleading signals concerning the legitimatory quality of the process.

The Dynamics of Inclusion and Exclusion in Recent Financial Regulatory Reform

The contributions in this volume explore the consequences of these considerations in a series of detailed case studies on the most recent developments in financial governance reform. From these studies, several common themes and patterns emerge.

In financial services research, the term ‘financial exclusion’ has taken hold to designate the lack of access of certain groups of society to basic infrastructure in the financial field. But – as the authors of this volume demonstrate – financial governance arrangements can also produce far broader effects through their impact on the real economy and on public discourse concerning issues of political economy. Far from being a technical affair optimized for the benefit of all, different financial governance arrangements have different distributional effects. From the perspective of democratic legitimacy, decision-making on policies with distributional effects should involve the broad-based participation of those affected by it wherever possible.

As has been shown by a growing body of literature and as underlined in the contributions to this volume, however, the setting and administration of financial governance arrangements are characterized by narrow participation mainly consisting of experts from national administrations, independent regulatory agencies and industry representatives. While reform in financial governance arrangements has been a widespread and ongoing phenomenon in recent years, its sometimes large distributional consequences have not been accompanied by a broadening of the interests represented in their definition.

The emerging picture is rather clear: Power in the political sphere shapes economic outcomes, and economic power translates into political power. Political exclusion and economic exclusion are correlated. This is underlined by the analyses undertaken by Lütz, Redak, Schmitz, Tsingou, Underhill and Weber in this book. On this account, a lack of inclusion seems to be the main problem from the viewpoint of democratic legitimacy, but things are not that simple.

Criticism regarding a lack of representation can endanger the legitimacy of governance processes and market expansion projects. Therefore, one recurring strategy in international financial governance arrangements is to selectively include some of the voices of those formerly excluded from the governance polity. A recent example of this in the domain of international financial governance is the foundation of the G20, which Porter (2001) describes as a reaction of the leading industrial countries to criticism about the exclusionary character of G7-led financial governance. In a case study on Basel II, Vanessa Redak shows that the elaboration of the framework was based on far broader participation and more open consultation than its predecessor, Basel I. Similarly, Beat Weber emphasizes the consultation and transparency provisions attached to the regulatory reform process in the Lamfalussy procedure used in implementing the European Union's Financial Services Action Plan. But these steps toward greater formal transparency and the broadening of membership by public consultation procedures have not resulted in increased visibility or weight for views which oppose the approaches favored by industry and regulatory expert circles up to now. This can be interpreted as an example of the ambivalent nature of inclusion. Because the process is ambivalent, the inclusion of new actors in the decision-making process does not automatically result in policy changes. In addition to factors such as limited voting power, a lack of resources and other asymmetries limit the influence of new ideas. Hegemonic ideas can survive, leaving policies unchanged and turning the inclusion of new actors into a mere legitimacy-enhancing measure. Being included in formerly exclusive governance bodies also makes these groups (jointly) responsible, e.g. for promoting existing governance arrangements which continue to produce economic exclusion. Aspects of this can be identified, for example, in processes to ensure the 'democratic accountability' of the EU's financial services legislation process, as Weber shows in his case study.

While this points to the possible coincidence of formal political inclusion and economic exclusion, the opposite is also observable: Political exclusion can go hand in hand with economic inclusion.

Governance arrangements exclusively dominated by industry and administrations can be instrumental in economic inclusion strategies. For instance, governance reform may be essential to enabling the inclusion of new groups when it comes to opening up new markets through regulatory reform. Schmitz's examination of efforts to promote private pension schemes by devising regulations which included guarantees for customers (which were withdrawn as soon as they became applicable) traces the pitfalls included in this process for beneficiaries in the case of private pensions. Another example is the handling of the problem of 'financial exclusion', as explored by Martin Schürz in his case study: Experience in the United States and United Kingdom has shown that a well-developed financial market can go hand in hand with widespread financial exclusion – for example leaving fewer people with access to the financial system. Debates about this problem have led to reform efforts which aim to transform the groups concerned into financial services consumers. Educational efforts are envisaged to increase the ability of the excluded to become included, but research highlights that at least some of those excluded do not regard access to the official financial system as their main problem. More importantly, exclusion seems to result from both a lack of resources among the excluded and from certain deficiencies on the supply side of the financial sector (see Schürz in this volume). Their exclusion as customers in the financial sector seems to be related to exclusion in other areas of society, among them governance processes regarding control over the distribution of resources and the regulation of the financial system.

Currently, exclusion from decision-making sometimes does not give rise to widespread complaints. This is because finance is considered the exclusive terrain of experts, pointing to widespread exclusion through expertise. In financial governance matters, asymmetries in expertise are common, as expert knowledge represents a normative framework. After events of crisis and change, this attitude is sometimes subject to revision. For instance, greater public awareness of the costs of financial crises borne by taxpayers may give rise to demands for the greater inclusion of public concerns and representatives in rule-making for crisis prevention and negotiations about burden-sharing.

These aspects of the dynamics of inclusion and exclusion highlight the risks of using these terms as elegant disguises for 'good' and 'bad'. One important lesson to be drawn from the contributions in this book is that when assessing governance processes, one has to look at the various dimensions of inclusion and exclusion simultaneously.

4. STRUCTURE OF THIS VOLUME

The volume is divided into two parts. Part I discusses conceptual and theoretical issues of financial governance in an attempt to conceptualize governance as an outcome of conflicting interests which repeatedly produce inclusion and exclusion. Part II presents case studies on the most recent issue areas.

In the first contribution, Geoffrey **Underhill** surveys the most important approaches of governance theory from mainstream economics and political economy. He criticizes the predominant tendency to see the market and state as dichotomous. Markets are politicized entities, and political actors have economic motives. In order to capture these aspects more effectively, Underhill calls for a view of political authority and markets as analytical parts of an integrated ensemble of governance, the state-market condominium. Within this condominium, significant changes have occurred in recent times. Above all, the state has become more a facilitator of economic internationalization than a protector of broad domestic interests. Drawing conclusions for the International Financial Architecture, Underhill calls for a redesign in order to facilitate access to the policy process for interests which are currently excluded, arguing that there must be a greater role for democracy in governing international finance. Indeed, enhancing political legitimacy is both necessary and possible: While economic theories of governance deny this, the state-market condominium model sees room for a variety of governance mechanisms which are compatible with market processes.

Susanne **Lütz** takes a closer look at the dynamics within and triggered by this condominium. According to Lütz, preferences and power relationships between states and market actors are key variables. In recent times, they have increasingly joined forces and sometimes forged modernization coalitions in order to promote domestic financial reform. These coalitions are heavily influenced by the changing international landscape.

The dynamics of ‘uploading’ and ‘downloading’ as well as imitation and learning take place within an environment of international regulatory competition. Institutional legacies and the contingencies of politics yield the result that there is no common international pattern concerning the details of regulatory models. Globalization in financial regulation is a selective process which exhibits features of multi-level governance.

Part II presents case studies on the most recent issue areas, addressing the topics of financial market integration in the European Union under the Lamfalussy process, Basel II, the regulation and promotion of pension funds, the international derivatives market and the proliferation of financial literacy programs. Special emphasis is placed on the issue of how inclusion and exclusion are organized in the process of setting up regulation. With its focus on political financial sector reform in the European Union, this section sheds light on issues arising from features of the Anglo-Saxon model (liberalization, financial literacy, privatization of pensions, etc.) in the entirely different institutional setting of continental Europe.

In asking "Who Governs?" Brigitte **Unger** critically evaluates the financial governance debate. In her view, power relations are not addressed in an adequate way. In an effort to bring power back into the debate on financial governance she elucidates seven approaches that might be useful for exploring who governs financial markets, among them the concept of hegemony and epistemic community governance.

Tony **Porter** provides an empirical assessment of the claims surrounding global finance: Critical views highlight the exclusionary aspects of finance and sometimes portray it as a unified actor which is able to force its will upon people globally. The supportive view tends to portray the globalization of finance as a process which brings benefits to all by promoting openness and competition. One way to assess this debate is to look at the ways in which private-sector actors are organized in global finance. Porter's preliminary finding is that there is an impressive amount of organizing going on in finance, but the organizational structure shows features of regional and sectoral dispersal. While it would certainly be premature to draw firm conclusions about the political influence of finance from these studies, it does open an avenue for empirical research.

The EU has seen a wave of financial integration efforts since the turn of the millennium. In applying insights derived from the analytical frameworks elaborated by Geoffrey Underhill and Susanne Lütz, Beat **Weber** contextualizes these developments in political and economic changes on the global and European scale. Looking at the dimensions of policy, politics and polity of financial governance in the EU, Weber presents significant evidence of exclusion. While the legislative initiatives taken by the EU have effects which transcend the financial sector, the policy process and the polity responsible for decision-making is dominated by the interests of financial market firms.

In the US, the problem of financial exclusion has been a recurring topic in policy debates on the financial sector for quite some time. Martin **Schürz** investigates the recent wave of efforts to increase the financial literacy of the US public. Financial education initiatives are officially labeled as a tool to tackle the financial exclusion of the poor, but the sparse empirical evidence available does not indicate that such initiatives can make a meaningful contribution toward this goal. A lack of education and knowledge is not a major cause of the problem, nor do literacy efforts seem to make much difference to the outcomes. The fact that financial literacy initiatives are increasingly put forward can be interpreted as an attempt to legitimize economic exclusion by blaming the lack of knowledge among those excluded. By appealing to hegemonic values, above all individual responsibility, decisive distributional issues are cast in the shadows.

Over-the-counter (OTC) derivatives have gained prominence in the past 15 years. Eleni **Tsingou** traces the extent to which the governance of OTC markets has become a policy issue and explains that two elements have prevailed in policy debates: (i) OTC derivatives are just another type of financial instrument and do not require special treatment, and (ii) best practice (as defined by the private sector) and private mechanisms of monitoring are both sufficient and effective. The governance of OTC markets essentially takes the form of monitored self-regulation and self-supervision. Yet derivatives arguably merit greater attention because they carry leverage and are increasingly used not just to hedge against risk, but also to embrace risk. In this context, the paper argues that the governance arrangements of OTC markets show the way in which the functions of regulation and supervision are changing: Governance is shared among a transnational policy community of public and private-sector parties, and private interests are internalized in financial policy processes.

In an analysis of Basel II, one of the best-known recent regulatory reforms in financial governance, **Vanessa Redak** focuses on the relationships between public and private agents. In this respect, Basel II gives a mixed picture. Whereas private agents – like rating agencies – expect an increase in their authority, the discretion of public supervisory authorities will also increase, at least in some respects. Furthermore, Basel II is an example in which private industry representatives have become more important, as their concerns have been internalized in the new regulatory framework. In contrast, the influence of labor and consumer groups is largely absent in the Basel II process, despite the fact that the reform will have a significant impact on the economy as a whole.

One of the most prominent changes in financial markets in recent years has been the growing importance of private pension funds in the provision of social security. After a few years of disappointing yields as well as episodes of mismanagement and fraud, the high hopes held toward these vehicles in the 1990s have given way to a more critical view of pension funds. Particular attention is increasingly turning toward their governance structures and the question of how much this industry operates in the interest of its alleged beneficiaries. Stefan W. **Schmitz** examines these issues in a case study on Austria, a country in which private pension schemes have been given a boost by the government only recently, therefore making the country a likely candidate for featuring 'state-of-the-art' governance provisions. In an analysis of recent developments in the sector, Schmitz concludes that incentive structures to protect beneficiaries' interests against the shareholders in Austrian pension funds are rather weak and expose them to considerable economic and political risks. It remains unclear whether it is at all possible to eliminate this problem, thus highlighting the limitations of privatizing old-age provision.

5. CONCLUSION

Financial governance can be interpreted as a 'state-market condominium' consisting of experts delegated by industry, national administrations and independent regulatory agencies. The precise effects of this situation on inclusion and exclusion have rarely been explored. Financial markets are gaining unprecedented importance, extending their reach and thereby affecting more areas of life than ever before. These changes – both in the reach of the financial sector and in the polity responsible for its governance – suggest that the question of who is in and who is out is a central theme in understanding current processes in this area. The concept of inclusion and exclusion is intended to cope with the interconnected processes of change occurring in the economic and the political sphere of financial governance.

Obviously, the linkages between exclusion in the political and economic spheres are important. However, one has to be very careful about simply reacting to them with a call for more inclusion. Inclusion is a double-edged sword which can have either a substantial or a merely symbolic meaning. When democratic legitimacy is reduced to a vague notion of inclusion, it can be employed to legitimate situations with important exclusionary aspects. For this reason, inclusion and exclusion should be viewed not only from a procedural but also from a substantive perspective. The latter enriches a purely procedural analysis with an investigation of the economic, social, political and cultural effects of the specific regulatory measures taken.

While the current trend toward a more market-oriented framework in financial governance is often justified to include new groups in previously unexplored market niches, this inclusion does not provide for any participation of the targeted groups apart from their role as (passive) consumers. Substantial inclusion would require the ability to take part in framing the workings of market processes, thus participating in the decision as to how and under what terms one would like to be included. The fact that participatory inclusion rarely exists under current governance arrangements points to significant exclusion in this area and a definite need to develop modes of inclusion in order to make it more widespread and substantial.

REFERENCES

Allen, Franklin and Douglas Gale (2001), 'Comparative Financial Systems: A survey', Wharton School Center for Financial Institutions Working Paper 01-15.

Bohmann, James (2004), 'Deliberative Democracy as an Institutional Mode of Inquiry: Pragmatism, Social Facts and Normative Theory', in Peter Mooslechner, Helene Schuberth and Martin Schürz (eds), *Economic policy under uncertainty. The role of truth and accountability in policy advice*, Cheltenham, UK and Northampton, MA, USA: Edward Elgar, pp. 40–62.

Bourdieu, Pierre (1998), The Essence Of Neoliberalism, *Le Monde*, December, available at http://www.analitica.com/biblioteca/bourdieu/neoliberalism.asp

Cerny, Philip G. (2005), 'Power, markets and accountability: the development of multi-level governance in international finance', in Andrew Baker, David Hudson and Richard Woodward (eds), *Governing Financial Globalization. International political economy and multi-level governance*, London: Routledge, pp. 24–48.

De Jong, Henk W. (1997), 'The governance structure and performance of large European corporations', *Journal of Management and Governance*, **1** (1), 5–27.

Deakin, Simon, Richard Hobbs, David Nash and Giles Singer (2002), 'Implicit Contracts, Takeovers, and Corporate Governance: In the Shadow of the City Code', ESRC Centre for Business Research Working Paper 254, Cambridge, UK: ESRC Centre for Economic Research.

Dingwerth, Klaus (2004), 'Democratic Governance beyond the State', Global Governance Working Paper No 14, December.

Goodhart, Charles A.E. (2005), 'Financial Regulation, Credit Risk and Financial Stability', *National Institute Economic Review*, **192** (1), 118–27.

Grabel, Ilene (2003), 'Ideology, Power and the Rise of Independent Monetary Institutions in Emerging Economies', in Jonathan Kirshner (ed.), *Monetary Orders: Ambiguous Economics, Ubiquitous Politics*, Ithaca: Cornell University Press, pp. 25–52.

Hall, Peter A. and David W. Soskice (eds) (2001), *Varieties of Capitalism. The Institutional Foundations of Comparative Advantage*, Oxford: Oxford University Press.

Kirshner, Jonathan (2003), 'Money is politics', *Review of International Political Economy*, **14** (4), 645–60.

Kjaer, Anne Mette (2004), *Governance*, Cambridge: Polity Press.

Macey, Jonathan (1998), 'Regulation and Disaster: Some Observations in the Context of Systemic Risk', in Robert E. Litan and Anthony M. Santomero (eds), *Brookings-Wharton Papers on Financial Services*, Brookings Institution Press, pp. 405–25.

Majone, Giandomenico (1997), 'Independent Agencies and the Delegation Problem: Theoretical and Normative Dimensions', in Bernard Steunenberg and Frans van Vught (eds), *Political Institutions and Public Policy. Perspectives on European Decision Making*, Dordrecht: Kluwer Academic Publishers, pp. 139–56.

Mooslechner, Peter (2003), 'The Transformation of the European Financial System – A Brief Introduction to Issues and Literature', OeNB Workshop Series No 1.

OeNB (2003), 'Finance for Growth', *Focus on Austria*, 1/2003.

Porter, Tony (2001), 'The Democratic Deficit in the Institutional Arrangements for Regulating Global Finance', *Global Governance*, 7, 427–39.

Salacuse, Jeswald W. (2002), 'European Corporations American Style? Governance, Culture and Convergence', paper presented at a conference hosted by the John F. Kennedy School of Government, April 11–12.

Schuberth, Helene and Martin Schürz (2004), 'Paradoxes of Financial Governance in U.S. Capitalism', in I.D. Salavrakos (ed.), *Aspects of Globalisation, Regionalisation and Business*, London: London Metropolitan University, pp. 141–57.

Shleifer, Andrei and Lawrence Summers (1988), 'Breach the trust in hostile takeovers', in Auerbach (ed.) '*Corporate Take-overs: Causes and Consequences*', University of Chicago Press: London and Chicago, 33–68.

Streeck, Wolfgang (2003), 'Taking Uncertainty Seriously: Complementarity as a Moving Target', OeNB Workshop Series No 1.

Underhill, Geoffrey (2002), 'Global Integration, EMU, and Monetary Governance in the EU: the political economy of the "stability culture"', in Kenneth Dyson (ed.), *European States and the Euro*, Oxford: Oxford University Press, pp. 31–52.

Wolf, Klaus Dieter (2002), 'Contextualizing Normative Standards for Legitimate Governance beyond the State', in Jürgen R. Grote and Bernard Gbikpi (eds), *Participatory Governance*, Opladen: Leske und Budrich, pp. 35–50.

PART I

THE THEORY OF FINANCIAL MARKET GOVERNANCE AND THE PROBLEM OF INCLUSION AND EXCLUSION

1. Theorizing Governance in a Global Financial System

Geoffrey R.D. Underhill*

Although the word 'governance' has been recorded as part of the English language since the 1300s,[1] it has only recently entered the vocabulary of policy studies and political economy. In the absence of systematic research into the matter, one may suggest that certainly since the work of Rosenau and Czempiel in 1992,[2] the term has found a consistent place in the international relations and political economy literature.[3] If the concept did not exist, it would certainly need to be invented. It attempts to capture the idea that not all political and/or regulatory authority is exercised through the formal decision-making channels or formal institutions of government. This is particularly true of the international domain, where there is no formal agreement on overarching patterns of political authority, no govern*ment*. At the domestic level many governance functions have traditionally been assumed by private or other non-state actors which lie outside official constitutional and party systems, and at the global level non-state actors and authority abound as the process of global economic integration proceeds.[4] This has long been the case in the process of financial governance.[5] In other words, the concept of governance indicates that the common assumption that formal state institutions of 'sovereign' entities have a monopoly on the exercise of political authority requires adjustment. If concepts require adjustment, it is likely that the practices based on these concepts will, too.

This article aims to assess the literature on a range of contemporary concepts of governance, how they have been applied to the financial and

* My thanks to Emile Yesodharan for his research assistance in preparing this article.

[1] The Compact Edition of the Oxford English Dictionary (1971), Vol. 1, p. 319.

[2] Rosenau and Czempiel (1992).

[3] For a useful survey of various definitions and approaches to governance, see van Kersbergen and van Waarden (2004).

[4] See Higgott, Underhill and Bieler (2000); Cutler, Haufler and Porter (1999).

[5] See Moran (1984), Coleman (1996).

monetary domain in an age of global integration, and how we might take them further. It is not intended as a comprehensive review of theories of governance as such, but more as a demonstration of how contrasting explanations might lead us to different ideas concerning what is to be done. The focus is on how concepts of governance attempt to account for the nature of authority across levels of analysis, the range of actors involved, their interaction as agents in producing outcomes, and the relationship between political authorities and the dynamics of market institutions and structures in an increasingly globalizing financial and monetary space.

The article argues that theories of governance derived from the economics literature tend to focus to a fault on the interaction of rational actors and on achieving optimal patterns of economic transactions and on preventing market failure under assumptions of (multiple) equilibrium, with insufficient attention to the broader goals of governance and to understanding the necessary role of political authority and institutions. They represent a narrow conception of governance which assumes that the principal goal of governance is market-based efficiency, as if the functioning of the market were the end purpose of governance. While institutional economics provides some indications for overcoming these limitations, this potential has not yet been realized. Governance is also about objectives concerning the *norms* underpinning the broader social and political stability without which markets are unable to function. Furthermore, competitive market systems are one, if important, way of achieving some of the goals of governance, not the other way around.

On the other hand, 'political' theories of governance focusing on the international domain have long tended to overplay the role of formal government at the domestic level, and of state-to-state cooperation at the international level. This underplays the importance of private actors in emerging transnational policy processes, and more contemporary accounts are correcting this imbalance.[6] There have long been clues as to how to overcome this in the policy studies literature at the domestic comparative level, but this requires adaptation to fit the circumstances of global integration. However, there is further need to theorize how non-state actors relate to processes of (domestic or international) governance in which states and concepts of sovereignty still play a vital role – how states and markets should be conceptualized as integral elements of a broader process of governance.

Furthermore, improved thinking about financial and monetary governance in an integrating world leads us to some possible reflections

[6] See Hall and Biersteker (2002); also the pioneering works cited in Footnote 3 above.

concerning what is to be done. More integrated concepts of governance focusing on the embeddedness of the state and the market as institutions in the broader structures of society lead us to expect that as the global market emerges, pushed largely by political processes altering the structures of markets, we should also anticipate changes in the nature of governance and in the form of states in particular. Changing actor preferences in a situation of integration are central to this equation. In stylized terms we may adopt two policy approaches to such changes. First, we might allow events to take their course, as has tended to happen in global financial governance. This has led to an *ad hoc* crisis-response adaptation of global financial architecture and the norms of governance alternating with painful and costly financial and monetary crises. Second, we might adopt a more proactive approach, as occurred at the domestic level in the post-depression/post-1945 period. This should lead us to conclude that an increasing number of functions normally provided at the domestic level will need to be provided at the international level if financial markets are to work successfully and if a broad range of economies and citizens are to benefit from a liberal financial system. This is likely to render financial and monetary crises far less frequent and certainly far less central to the progress of the reform process.

'ECONOMIC' THEORIES OF GOVERNANCE

Theories of governance stemming from the economics literature tend to focus on regulatory and related arrangements for the governance of markets at either the domestic or the international level. The starting point for this bundle of theories is that markets are 'created and maintained by institutions', in contrast to neo-classical assumptions.[7] Indeed the term 'governance' is not always explicitly recognized in the theories themselves, but they typically offer, or argue for, solutions to public policy dilemmas in relation to the governance of economic transactions, which is surely an aspect of governance. In this sense there are often important normative aspects to this group of theories. Here the article will discuss economic theories of regulation and regulatory competition (i.e. dealing with issues of market failure), public goods/economics approaches, and transaction cost/institutional economics approaches. Care will be taken to relate these approaches to the increasing global integration of market structures and the

[7] See van Kersbergen and van Waarden (2004), p. 146.

correspondingly increasing uncertainties concerning the locus of authority across levels of analysis.

Economic theories of regulation and of regulatory competition emerged out of the work of Arrow, Bernstein, Peltzman, and Stigler, among others.[8] Their work merges with the contemporary law and economics[9] and financial regulation literature.[10] Key concepts presented in this broad range of literatures include market failure and the provision of public goods (usually seen as inherently normative 'welfare economics' approaches to the problem), and their critique in the form of regulatory competition and regulatory capture approaches (which are presented as positive theories). Let us deal briefly with each.

Market failure is central to broader concepts of economic regulation but is perhaps particularly relevant to financial regulation given the frequency of financial crises and their consequences. Market failure in a financial market context might include herd behavior, informational asymmetries concerning either public-sector macroeconomic policies or private-sector disclosures which can be related to herd behavior, moral hazard and adverse selection in investor behavior, or outright fraud and criminal activity. Wherever large amounts of money are to be made, and the preferences of many market agents with different levels of resources and capacities exist, the interplay of human passions is unlikely to lead to solely equilibrium outcomes, however high the possibility of such might hypothetically be.[11]

Over the past hundred years, attempts to deal with these problems of market failure have led to increasing intervention by financial authorities at the domestic level, particularly in terms of financial market supervision. Here one may distinguish between the more interventionist post-depression/post-war approaches to regulation and supervision (on-site inspection, interest rate ceilings, credit controls, etc.) and more recent innovations such as disclosure and informational requirements on the part of financial institutions marketing their products, and also in terms of standards of information concerning government policies, e.g. interest rate and bond market trends. The seminal experience was the Great Depression, but subsequent banking and financial crises have led to further refinements. Many of the policy measures involve official oversight of essentially self-regulatory arrangements carried out by private market players and associations. As the post-depression/post-war

---

[8] See, for example, Bernstein (1955), Stigler (1971) and Peltzman (1976).

[9] Bratton and McCahery (1996).

[10] Goodhart et al. (1998).

[11] Goodhart et al. (1998) covers these issues very well.

order of public control and repression of financial market forces gave way to more market-oriented structures and regulatory polices, the latter have required consistent adaptation, and cross-border market integration has implied more developed cross-border cooperation among public and private authorities. Conflict of interest questions have been important to the debate, and financial and corporate governance scandals have fuelled the impression that despite common rules established by political authorities, interested parties cannot entirely be trusted to implement the rules in line with broader public interest concerns.

The literature in general argues that public authorities provide public goods for the efficient functioning of markets, thus resolving a range of collective action problems. Most important is financial supervision at the level of individual institutions, to prevent imprudent individual responses to market incentives, and systemic monitoring to prevent individual transactions from aggregating into systemically adverse outcomes such as collective herd behavior. Regulatory restrictions may be imposed on the behavior of investors and financial institutions in order to pre-empt adverse outcomes, and a potential tradeoff between stability and innovative behavior is often noted. Finally, debt workout procedures and deposit or other forms of financial system insurance are specified to prevent panic in the event of bank or other financial failure. At the international level authorities cooperate or international institutions step in to prevent forms of regulatory competition which might lead to a race to the bottom. They also seek to provide cooperatively some of the public goods normally associated with the domestic level, resolving conflicts among different regulatory approaches. Needless to say, given the existence of govern*ment* at the national level and its general absence at the international level, the provision of public goods for the efficient and stable functioning of markets remains very incomplete despite extensive cross-border market integration and the cross-border strategies of firms in the sector.

Economic theories thus view successful governance as a matter of providing underpinnings for the successful operation of markets. If one indulges in the details of these theories, they as mentioned offer clear guidance for the resolution of policy dilemmas concerning alternative forms of regulation in different market settings. They allow for a broad debate on the effects of more versus less intervention on the part of public authorities and for a clear understanding of the incentives for different sorts of agents in particular regulatory and institutional settings. Transaction cost approaches and institutional economics may help us determine when market-based interactions will result in an acceptable outcome, and when more hierarchical arrangements are required or when institutions may be more efficient, and how this relates to economic performance.[12]

These approaches to governance carry with them a number of problems. They say very little about preferences/preference formation and actual decision-making processes. Policies are seldom neutral in their impact, and a range of alternatives is most often available. Economic theories can tell us about incentive structures for particular forms of regulation or policy, but little about why some actors prefer certain governance options (more/less institutionalized, more/less liberal) when they do. They can often tell us what we *should* choose given certain norms and preferences in terms of outcomes, but not *how* outcomes *actually* occur. Economic theories of governance assume a process of rational decision-making wherein agents aim at optimizing a typically narrow (and in terms of theory, necessarily so restricted) definition of their self-interest, and wherein their interaction in the 'market for regulation' leads to an optimal system of governance. Such theories famously do little to allow for differential political resources, the differential institutional capacities and access potential of the respective players, or the role of institutional inertia and stickiness with respect to vested interests (possible exception of Stigler and theories of regulatory capture). In short, the rent-seeking activity of private market agents or official institutions (as conceived of by Stigler), their preferences in terms of openness versus official protection or intervention, and how one set of interests succeeds in prevailing over another, are poorly explained. There is little on how the preferences of public versus private actors might either differ from or relate to each other, and why. The basic 'contestability' of market structures (e.g. enforcement of competitive relations versus more oligopolistic 'club' structures, regulatory segmentation versus open competition; restrictions on market access or product innovation versus freedom for firms) is given little credence. How is it that apparently sub-optimal policies are consistently adopted, policies which do not make sense in terms of economic theories of governance? Why do economic agents consistently support outcomes which have little to do with textbook models of market competition? In short, economic theories of governance are not very realistic when it comes to explaining outcomes in terms of policy and market structure, and why different outcomes occur.

Most importantly, economic theories of governance assume that the functioning of market competition and efficiency are the only or at least the most central concern of governance. If this were true, then much of

[12] See Coase (1937) and North (1990).

the fabric and institutions of contemporary society are unlikely to have come into being. While there is a more or less latent utopianism in many economic theories of governance which tends toward normative preferences of precisely this kind, generations of arguments in favor of competitive markets as the principal arbiters and feature of our social existence and interaction have failed to lead to market outcomes free of political and other socially based preferences. Despite arguments which advocate markets as natural to human behavior, there is little historical evidence of systems of transactions based on perfect competition. If everything we experience were 'commodifiable', this might be true, but one may apologize for the suspicion that contentment among human beings is unlikely to be the outcome.[13] There is more to life than transactions and their alleged efficiency or otherwise, and choice among governance alternatives unavoidably involves normative preferences as well as contrasting technical mechanisms. Certainly, financial systems are central to economic development processes, and their success or their dysfunction can have a direct and often negative impact on social and political stability at the domestic or the global level. Broader thinking about their governance may prevent some of the mistakes which have stemmed from reliance on theories which see successful financial and monetary systems as principally requiring a successful competition-based pattern of market interaction.

Perhaps one might explain the point with reference to historical practice. Abstract theories were always capable of determining the need for resolving collective action problems and overcoming potential market failures. Economic theory has long argued in the abstract concerning the potential for instability versus equilibrium, and the requisite conditions for each. But economic theories of governance did not become a growth industry until the manifest failure of the market in the post-1918 period – see Keynes's reflections in *The Economic Consequences of the Peace*. Economic theories of governance and discussions of the desirable level of state intervention emerged when *there was political pressure to do something far more radical.* Economic theories of governance in the financial and monetary domain therefore have a historical context for

---

[13] One cannot resist here a reference to the classic work by Karl Polanyi, *The Great Transformation* (1944), who argued that the breakdown in international society and security of the Depression and Second World War was intimately related to utopian attempts to create a society based almost entirely on the commodity relationships of the market; humankind reacted in sometimes ugly ways to the instability and negative consequences of the system. The perceived failures of laissez-faire also led directly to the plans laid at Bretton Woods, where monetary and financial governance was deliberately subjected to public oversight and market forces were repressed in favor of outcomes generated through public policy.

their emergence, and the questions they examine cannot be separated from this context. The imperfections of the market were not discovered through abstract theorizing, but through practical experience and social and political disaster. One might say much the same thing about more contemporary crisis-related debates concerning the reform of global financial architecture. One would think that human beings could do better than that. In the absence of a consistent relationship between greed and financial market structures, they can.

We must therefore confront fully the 'Bretton Woods' question of the relationship between the international availability of finance and the pressures for economic adjustment on national economies. Put less technically, we must think systematically about the relationship between the needs of domestic social and economic stability, compensation for the losers in dynamic market processes, and the need for political legitimacy of governance arrangements at the domestic and the international level. The difference between today and the post-war golden age is that then the worry was balance of payments crises and the maintenance of exchange rate stability in a context of national control of capital flows. Today we have globally integrated capital markets wherein the US can apparently sustain a huge and growing current account deficit due to ongoing and favorable access to capital markets. At the same time, a number of emerging market countries with relatively robust macroeconomic performance indicators compared to a number of the advanced economies find that crises suddenly cut them off from global capital markets and render them unable to finance their far more modest debt problems.

POLITICAL ECONOMY THEORIES OF GOVERNANCE[14]

We can use the emergence of the post-war discipline of (international) political economy as a proxy for political economy theories of governance. These theories, to which full justice concerning the available variety cannot be done here, emerged from comparative politics, policy studies at the domestic, EU, and international levels, and international relations scholarship. They assume that markets and their structures are basically contestable, that power, preference, and institutional variables interact to produce outcomes, and that the state and the market are both embedded in the broader political economy or social whole.

The revival of political economy approaches to the understanding of governance has its roots in the world view of the classical political

[14] This section draws on Krätke and Underhill (2005).

economists, which preceded the disciplinary social sciences as we know them today. The classical political economists were responsible for a number of crucial innovations which have affected a range of the contemporary social sciences, such as the notion of 'economic laws' or dynamics and a long-run staged evolution of human societies during which the basic features of economic, social, and political life changed in relation to each other.

The Classical Tradition

Classical political economy (CPE) focused on the new social and economic order of modern (mercantile, later industrial) capitalism as it emerged. Its virtues and associated ideas of political and economic freedoms had to be propagated and defended against the prevailing ideas of the ancien regime and absolute monarchy, and its prerequisites had to be created and defended (e.g. private property rights; freedom of entrepreneurship; trade-oriented national and international monetary systems; a financial system free of restraints on 'usury'; and new forms of private enterprise, e.g. 'limited liability' and joint-stock ownership). All had to be constructed, institutionalized, and enforced together with the basic institutions of the modern state, which associated itself with emerging capitalism through new forms of taxation, public money and, last but not least, the public debt. Classical political economists therefore shared an overtly political conception of their science.

The movement may be regarded as beginning with the mid-18th century 'Physiocrats' in France.[15] They were the first to see a political economy as a circular flow of production, employment, and consumption oiled by money as a medium and corresponding to social and political interdependence among different constituents of the economy. They also gave birth to the idea that the best prices were likely to emerge if individuals were allowed to compete freely, revealing a self-regulating natural order. The central place of manufactures and commerce in the political economy was a crucial development of the Scottish Enlightenment. David Hume made a central contribution concerning the role of money in the circular economic flow of commerce and price levels (the quantity theory of money), and its international payments dimensions (the price-specie flow mechanism of the Gold Standard).[16] Adam Smith's seminal contribution was in understanding that high levels of specialization in the division of labor in industry and a developed system of commerce lay at the root of greater productivity, and therefore

---

[15] See Landreth (1976, pp. 24–9).
[16] See Hume ([1752] 1970).

greater levels of wealth and prosperity for all.[17] Furthermore, Smith developed a number of key arguments in favor of enforcing market mechanisms: As individuals pursue their own best interests motivated by greed, they unwittingly realize an important public good – a more productive and innovative society with a broader division of labor, and more for all. Competition would lower prices and free resources for investment. In this way he argued against the restrictive practices which institutionalized the privileges of the powerful and impaired adjustment to economic change: the craft guilds in the labor market which controlled the quantity and price of labor in crucial activities for their members' benefit (often through inherited membership), and against royal and other commercial monopolies set by political fiat. Despite this optimistic doctrine, Smith remained skeptical about the power of commercial interests and argued that intervention was needed to ensure that the restrictive practices and self-interested behavior of the commercial classes was curbed and regulated to ensure market-based outcomes and benefits.

This fully integrated approach, wherein the social, political, economic and indeed normative aspects of governance were conceptualized as interrelated, is precisely what contemporary economics has lost. While David Ricardo's aim was still holistic, his now familiar techniques of deductive economic reasoning under strict and highly abstract assumptions linked up with Jeremy Bentham's 'utilitarian calculus' in moral philosophy: People are assumed to be rational and to pursue a self-interested agenda of 'utility maximization' in interaction with others, an effort carried further by John Stuart Mill. Liberal ideas concerning harmony of interests and economic equilibrium combined with the new 'science' in a heady idealism which often conflicted with observable realities.

Marx's revolutionary critique of classical political economy was a turning point. He used political economy's holistic approach against itself, arguing that the circular dynamics of the economy and the social and political interdependencies which accompanied them were inherently conflictual: The dynamics of the system would tend toward its own destruction, not long-run equilibrium. This stimulated supporters of the liberal thesis to intensify the attempt to employ 'pure science', removed from the complexities of history and socio-political interaction, to demonstrate irrefutably the underlying harmony of the system. This generated 'Economics' as opposed to the older and now discredited term 'Political Economy'. The utilitarian calculus fostered the 'marginal revolution' based on (often highly algebraic) marginal utility analysis as

[17] See Smith ([1776] 1937), Book I, Chapters 1–3.

a sort of anatomy of market transactions, including Leon Walras' mathematical 'general equilibrium model' demonstrating in the abstract that interdependent economic flows could result in a long-run balance between demand and supply factors, and Alfred Marshall's neo-classical *Principles of Economics* (1890). Political economy was purified, and professional economists often forgot about history, politics, and the conflicts of social life. The new orthodoxy also implied the emergence of a *separate* study of society (sociology) and of politics (political science and international relations). These separate disciplinary tracks have been maintained to this day.

Contemporary Revival

How is the tradition of classical political economy relevant to theorizing governance today? The heritage appears split between (i) those who claim 'laws' of economic interactions as natural laws of 'rational behavior' and (ii) those who focus more upon the historical, transient and contested, hence *political* nature of economic processes. Political economy informs us not to take 'economic man' for granted, but to study the relationships which lie behind the division between private interests and the public or 'common' good. Individuals and economic relationships, thus 'laws', are in fact highly contestable, generated by society through social and political interaction, not as assumed by mainstream economics. Governance is difficult to think of in relation to optimality or equilibrium: It stems from the messiness of political and social conflict.

Political economy theories of governance are thus preoccupied with the study of the interaction between (socio-)political and economic processes. The tradition understood that systems of production changed symbiotically with patterns of governance and the structure of society. The 'inter-action' between states and markets is a misleading formula if each represents a competing logic: power on the one side, rational exchange behavior on the other. Private property and market exchange also involve power structures underpinned by the political and social arrangements maintained through our institutions of governance. Understanding how and why markets are politically made and determined, as well as how and why states are made up of and determined by peculiar economic institutions of their own making, allows political economists to overcome the oversimplified state-market divide.

In the post-war period social science began a rapid and, a political economist must argue, rather exaggerated process of specialization, and much concerning the interrelationships and shared heritage of these subjects was lost. The re-emergence of political economy approaches to governance refers to re-integrating what had been somewhat arbitrarily split up: Though specialization was in the laudable pursuit of better expertise, it had important opportunity costs for our understanding of the world around us. Furthermore, as the global economy became increasingly integrated, the traditional distinction between the study of things international and things domestic began to break down. As the political and economic domains stubbornly revealed themselves to be closely interdependent, there was a re-examination of disciplinary specialization.

One might begin with the work of Richard Cooper (an economist, as it happens), [18] who was particularly influential in inducing scholars to consider the observable fact of *interdependence* and what it meant for our understanding of the world around us. Increasingly, foreign affairs and international governance would be understood by political scientists in relation to the tensions between domestic considerations and relations with other states and their own domestic dynamics. This blurred the levels of analysis distinction through the work of a range of foreign policy specialists (for example James Rosenau).[19] Furthermore, there was a debate among international relations scholars in the late 1960s about 'transnational relations', wherein *inter*national was placed in opposition to the more sophisticated concept of *trans*national relationships (see also the introduction to this volume). Interdependence among states and their societies[20] was central to this debate, highlighting the role of both *non*-state and *sub*-state actors of a private or public nature in governance processes. Such concepts greatly expanded the empirical terrain on which the debate could take place.

There were disputes about basic assumptions of agency and method. Cooper's article was an early application of methodologically individualist rational choice to the political economy of interdependence, an application which became particularly influential when international relations scholars and political scientists began building on game theory and transaction cost economics of Nobel Prize winner Ronald Coase[21] and others. Axelrod's innovative use of game theory and Keohane's use of transaction cost logic were particularly useful examples, as was Mancur Olson's application of his own public goods approach in his *Rise and Decline of Nations*.[22] These more formal and quantitative rational choice contributions under the 'positive political economy' label represent a growing direct overlap of neo-classical economics and

[18] Cooper (1968).
[19] Rosenau (1967).
[20] Keohane and Nye (1977, pp. 8–11).
[21] Coase (1960).
[22] Axelrod (1984), Keohane (1984), Olson (1982).

international political economy (IPE) where concepts of power and institutions can coexist with concepts of rational self-interest.[23]

Meanwhile, 1970s monetary turbulence, the rise of the Euromarkets, and the expansion of international trade signaled a transformation at domestic and international levels. Governance in the trade and financial domain was becoming more difficult in practical terms and had anyway always been highly charged politically, both *within* and *among* states in the system. This proved fertile ground for interdisciplinary sectoral research projects combining economics, international relations and political science scholars, e.g. the team under Andrew Shonfield at the Royal Institute for International Affairs (Chatham House) which included Susan Strange, perhaps the most renowned of the entire IPE 'revival' generation.[24] B.J. Cohen represented one of the rare cases of an economist who came in from the cold of the dismal science – producing his seminal *Organizing the World's Money* (1977).[25] A healthy literature on emerging cooperative governance through 'international regimes' in various issue areas emerged.[26]

Discussions of governance in comparative and international political economy began increasingly to overlap in an increasingly integrating world. Robert Gilpin, who began as a specialist in French public policy, built on the economic historian Charles Kindleberger's 'hegemonic stability' hypothesis[27] to explain the apparent threat to liberal economic regimes represented by the new protectionism and monetary instability.[28] Further contributions from comparative political economists followed, including Peter Katzenstein's *Between Power and Plenty*[29] on diverse national responses to the 1970s oil shocks, and the work of Peter Gourevitch and John Zysman.[30] Comparative specialists recognized that the phenomenon of deepening European and global integration forced them to reassess their approach to their subject, linking the crisis of welfare states variously to systemic or national level developments: The debates about corporatism and the role of organized interests in governance processes were forced to 'go global'.[31] Comparativists were also busy analyzing the difficulties of developing political economies at the domestic level (the 'developmental state' debate) as global integration

[23] Alt and Schepsle (1990), Rodrik (1997).
[24] Shonfield, Curzon et al. (1976) and Susan Strange (1976). For a critical assessment and further development of the work of Susan Strange, see the 21-chapter volume edited by Verdun and Lawton (2000).
[25] Cohen (1977).
[26] Starting with Keohane and Nye (1977) and Krasner (1983), among others.
[27] Kindleberger (1973).
[28] Gilpin (1987).
[29] Katzenstein (1978).
[30] See respectively Gourevitch (1986) and Zysman (1983).
[31] See Greenwood and Jacek (2000).

pressures mounted.[32] While some IPE specialists had always anchored global generalizations in specific sectoral and indeed country cases, IPE and comparative political economy (CPE) approaches to governance needed each other as much as ever, coming together in a synthesis through the work of scholars such as Philip Cerny.[33]

The radical tradition in international political economy must not be neglected, especially as it kept alive assumptions about the interdependent nature of the political and economic domains. Indeed, over time the radical and the 'orthodox' have moved closer together.[34] Considerable innovation occurred with the emergence of the 'French Regulation' school led by economist Michel Aglietta and including well-known scholars such as Robert Boyer and Alain Lipietz.[35] Robert Cox's 'neo-Gramscian' approach,[36] resolutely post-structuralist in its theory, has been embraced in whole or in part by a sizable proportion of IPE specialists.

IPE and CPE scholarship focusing on governance is now rich and varied. Different perspectives and scholars emphasize different aspects of the normative agenda, and much of the underlying debate is ultimately about values, not simply analysis and research tools.[37] Yet mainstream (international) economics and (international) political economy accounts of governance remain in mutual neglect or even denial. Hardly anyone, perhaps with the remarkable exception of the pioneer Susan Strange, has ever complained.[38]

WHITHER THE DEBATE ON GOVERNANCE AND GLOBAL FINANCIAL ARCHITECTURE?

Political economy approaches to governance remain in touch with their roots in classical political economy. Unlike their equivalents in economics, they are in search of the linkages between the economic and the social, the political and the market. They demonstrate that the inclusion of political and social variables, in particular the interaction of social constituencies in the policy process across levels of analysis, can help us explain governance outcomes in a globally integrating economic

[32] See Evans and Stephens (1988).
[33] On the state in the global economy, see Cerny (1990); on finance, see Cerny (1993).
[34] The influence of radical political economy on Cerny's work is a good example of the ways in which radical insights have affected a range of scholars.
[35] Aglietta (1979). The school is covered well in Noël (1987).
[36] See Cox (1987 and 1996).
[37] See Chapter 1 of Strange (1988).
[38] Cf. Strange (2002) and especially her classic article (April 1970).

space. These approaches to governance are also increasingly resisting disciplinary straightjackets and reaching across boundaries toward economics and, in particular, their classical roots. Research into social and economic interdependence across political boundaries threw into question the assumptions regarding levels of analysis in comparative politics and international relations. It threw open the question of actors and issues (who, and what issues, were [or should be] important in explanations?). By examining the constraints of economic structure and the impact of political interaction on the changing economic scene, it highlighted the role of structure versus agency in this process of transformation (for an account of these theoretical issues, see the Introduction to this volume). This all underpinned a move away from a focus on 'government' toward a focus on the looser concept of 'governance'[39] representative of the discipline's field of enquiry.

In other words, the emergence of political economy was a re-awakening and re-linking with the broad if not always coherent tradition of social science scholarship from the French Physiocrats onward, via Smith, Marx, Keynes, Polanyi, and the pioneers of the contemporary period. This welcome ecumenism has become characterized by a concern with how the pieces of the global puzzle fit together: the social, the normative, the formal and institutionalized, the public and the private, the local and the global. This requires specialized research employing diverse techniques but based on a broad understanding of the nature of political authority and underlying socio-economic structures in a variety of settings.

It is arguable that despite this welcome diversity in *approach*, the political economy of governance has come to settle around a set of core questions and empirically verifiable assumptions concerning the nature of the social whole. Given arguments about roots, a useful starting point is Adam Smith himself,[40] who was strongly aware of how, historically, the evolving ways in which who gets what, when, and how lends form and substance (sometimes rather unpleasant) to society and to its more formal institutions of governance, and who has power over whom. In this he shared much with his eventual critic, Marx. Smith observed that there was an ongoing tension between the private interests of individuals and the needs of the wider community – a tension between the pursuit of self-interest and the public good. This leads to the first core issue: How is this tension to be resolved in particular issue areas? One might disagree or not with Smith's market-based proposal, but his core question remains

---

[39] As noted at the outset of this article, a concept overcoming the gap between formal and informal frameworks of 'government', well outlined in Rosenau and Czempiel (1992).

[40] See Skinner (1970), Heilbroner (1986).

relevant in our increasingly transnational political economy, with the lines of institutionalized authority becoming more blurred all the time.

This point leads to a crucial second core assumption which focuses enquiry – that there is a systematic and reciprocal relationship between the political and the economic domains: Systems of production and exchange are deeply embedded and indeed underpin the evolving characteristics of our societies. Building on classical political economy's concern with history, there follows a third: that over time there is a systematic but not always linear relationship between the changing ways in which societies organize production and exchange on the one hand, and emerging patterns of governance on the other.

These core issues can be formulated in contemporary terms. We now have a market-based social system, indeed an increasingly global one, but not always the carefully contrived conditions Smith recommended. The market, particularly in the monetary and financial domain, has furthermore proven less stable, less equal, and less harmonious in operation than he and many of his successors thought would be the case. Power in governance processes is clearly not the preserve of the formal political institutions which pretend to monopolize it, particularly states – private market power is very much part of the pattern of governance we experience. The core issues noted above all focus on the reciprocal relationship between economic structures of the market and political authority (loosely defined) in the ongoing and accelerating process of global governance,[41] where formal political authority is today largely represented by the state. This means we should focus on the *contemporary relationship between political authority and the market* in this period of global economic integration and changing forms of governance: What do we think states and governance are, what do we think a market is, and how, if at all, are they/should they be related? The central focus on the contemporary state-market relationship leaves ample room for normative concerns such as who should get what and how, the appropriate nature of governance, and guidance as to how we might improve the global (monetary and financial) order.

If the relationship between political authority and markets is the core question in theorizing governance, the argument here is that the discipline must move beyond mere invocation in terms of dealing with it. For too long, scholars have either merely invoked the interrelationship in terms of mutual effects (i.e. economic liberal or realist approaches), or assumed it. Either way, the relationship has not been adequately conceptualized. Politics and markets, as most IPE/CPE literature insists, are interdependent, but their interdependency is usually depicted as a simple

[41] The point made so long ago by Strange (1976b).

dichotomy: governance versus markets, each following contrasting and antagonistic logic (political power versus rational, self-interested action) and pulling in opposite directions. In the conventional view, states and markets are ruled by contrasting values, and the processes in each domain remain distinct. This tug-of-war between politics and markets is deeply rooted in the 19th century disciplinary split between economics and political science. Accordingly, the dichotomy view, still prevailing in contemporary political economy, does not fully overcome the conceptual divide between politics and economics, nor the weaknesses of economic theories of governance. In fact, it at least unintentionally reproduces their unhappy divorce.

This 'dichotomy' view has a number of disadvantages. First, it is based upon formulas that lack explanatory accuracy through empirically inaccurate analytical differentiation. To invoke 'markets' as an abbreviation for the structure and logic of development of contemporary economies is wide of the mark. Modern capitalist economies are structured by firms – which internally are not markets, but power hierarchies.[42] Furthermore, modern economies comprise a variety of markets, among them the markets for 'fictitious commodities' such as human labor, land or natural resources, money and capital. These are also essentially social power structures which yield a range of potential conflicts requiring political resolution (e.g. between employers and employees, land owners and land users, creditors and debtors, investors and capital users). These are not 'markets' in the abstract but distinct or specific markets and market systems as social entities.

On the other hand, states and associated patterns of governance at the international level, as political economists should see them, are economic *organizations* of a peculiar, political kind and origin. They have acquired a series of 'monopolies' which are either directly economic (power of taxation, monopoly of monetary issuance) or central to modern economic life, like the 'monopoly of legitimate violence' and the 'monopoly of law'. States are in this sense the institutions which act as a forum to settle the political conflicts generated in the social domain of the market. Cooperative international governance seeks to extend this to areas where direct state authority is uncertain.

Secondly, the state-market dichotomy explains a number of phenomena rather poorly. For instance, why have persistent predictions of a 'retreat of the state'[43] and race-to-the-bottom regulatory competition failed to materialize under the pressures of global market integration? Or again, why do some economies display an outstanding adaptive capacity

[42] See Williamson (1975), who recognizes the point but who does not bring it alive politically and in social terms.
[43] Such as that propounded in Strange (1996).

to external pressures at one time, but despite continuity in institutional structure and even personnel, incapacity at another? What is more, the state-market dichotomy presents a distorted view of business strategies and the process of competition as consisting solely of the deployment of firms' relative capacities in terms of organization, innovation, and capital. Thus *political* resources deployed in governance processes, the ability to shape, through regulatory or other outcomes, the very terms of competition in line with the preferences of private actors, are discounted as an add-on extra which is good if one can have it instead of integral to the very nature of inter-firm competition itself.

So how might we transform the political economy of governance into a true inter-discipline in touch with its classical roots, overcoming the politics versus markets dichotomy and bringing together political scientists and heterodox economists who still remain in a tacit state of mutual negligence and ignorance? A lead is provided by the literature on institutional economics. Douglass North argued that the ways in which markets are structured, the sorts of values embedded in the prevailing regulatory systems, and which actors/organizations are able to develop within the prevailing incentives, makes all the differences to outcomes.[44] In this view, the institutions of the market and the institutions of the governance process are integrated into the notion of what a market is. Markets cannot thrive without the reduction of transaction costs which governance (not to mention hierarchically organized firms) provides. But if these techniques of economics (in this case, the transaction cost approach) are to be imported successfully into political economy theories of governance or vice versa, we must fully recognize the implications of such formulations and think of the market setting as part of a wider process which includes the crucial functions which both states and firms, political authorities and markets, each as contrasting forms of institutions, perform along with other social constituents.

Let us take one recent proposal to replace the dichotomy with a broader concept[45] integrating political and market institutions in the process of governance. Remembering the classical tradition, we can conceive of political authorities and their political conflicts as active constituents of the marketplace, and reciprocally of market actors and their constituencies as participants in the wider process of governance. Rethinking the state-market relationship, we focus upon the process of regulation that is taking place in interactions between firms and other, compound market actors. Governance processes at the (trans)national level are furthermore as much a part of business strategies as the game of investment and marketing. Firms simultaneously deploy their political

---

[44] North (1990, p. 109).

[45] See Underhill (2003).

and competitive resources to achieve the outcome they seek. The preferences of powerful coalitions of market agents are integrated into the policy process. Political authority and markets can be regarded as analytical parts of an integrated ensemble of governance, the *state-market condominium*.

In such a model, change occurs simultaneously through the process of economic competition among firms on the one hand, and the policy and regulatory processes mediated by the institutions of the state on the other. Market agents enhance or protect their position and prosperity by making simultaneous calculations through (a) their business strategies, deploying their competitive resources, and (b) through the deployment of their political resources in the policy processes of the state and in less formal institutional settings. They position themselves politically and institutionally so as to achieve the sort of market and regulatory underpinning which best suits their interests. The model therefore recognizes that different sorts of markets (competition-oriented, oligopolistic, monopolistic) can coexist with a range of different forms of governance (hierarchy, association, networks, etc.) which underpin the basic state-market relationship. It is not a question of hierarchy or associative networks versus competitive markets as patterns of governance. Governance works simultaneously through the forms of regulation and competition which evolve over time. This is clearly visible in corporatist systems in western Europe, where even labor is integrated into both state policy processes and the strategic decision-making of firms, or in the close integration of private firms/associations into the system of bureaucratic management which characterizes the economic development process in Japan and other parts of Asia.[46] The point is less obvious to observers of Anglo-Saxon political economies where the independence of the private sector appears more marked than in other societies. But the considerable evidence of 'regulatory capture' of the agencies of governance in the US economy should indicate the need to avoid the stereotypes developed in the economics literature in particular.

Of course this conceptualization of political authorities and markets appears counter-intuitive in our global era increasingly dominated by private sector market processes. Our contemporary experience of modern capitalism and the prevalence of economic modes of analysis engraves on our intellects the idea of the state-market dichotomy. Yet it is precisely against this sort of orthodoxy that political economy teaches us to react. There is nothing surprising in the idea that a transnational market structure, or indeed any market, should have multiple institutional nodes exercising authority in different ways and even with different functions.

---

[46] See Underhill and Zhang (2005).

The analogy of a federal system or of the European Union is useful here: Different layers of political institutions can fulfill the 'state' function over time, and we should not misconceive the identifiable institutional/organizational structures of the state as a phenomenon external to the dynamics of the market, in whichever form the latter may be found.

The state-market condominium model also facilitates understanding of the role of 'non-state' private interests, integrated into the complex institutional fabric of the state, in driving the process of global integration. As the pattern of material interests in national political economies has become more transnational, so the state has changed. The state has become far more a facilitator of global market processes than a protector of domestic market structures and interests over the past three decades. The pattern of political authority becomes more transnational in symbiosis with the transformation of the market. The state has progressively delegated a number of tasks either to private bodies or to institutions of international cooperation, though it maintains its functions in terms of domestic political legitimacy and all the tensions that entails. In this sense what we have seen is not so much a *retreat* of the state in the face of market forces, but a transformation of the state in symbiosis with the transformation of economic structures. This argument also implies that the state could claw back (at a cost!) its authority, repacking the market into a more national form, should political and market circumstances make this likely. Political agency, depending on the balance of social forces and their organizational and institutional capacities, can be deployed to liberalize or indeed to invoke closure, as has happened many times in history. It should be clear that the form and functions of the state will continue to evolve as indeed they have in the past. The question then is not why is the state in retreat, but how long is the currently emerging transnational form of state-market condominium sustainable in the face of increased volatility on the global markets?

IMPLICATIONS FOR FINANCIAL ARCHITECTURE REFORM

This brings one to a concluding discussion of the practical and policy implications of the state-market condominium model in a situation of increasingly multi-level global financial governance. The model can be directly applied to understanding governance in the financial and monetary domain. While the process of global capital market liberalization appears at first glance as a story of markets freeing themselves from international and domestic forms of governance, it can be better explained using the state-market condominium model than by more traditional approaches based on a state-market dichotomy. The process was far from spontaneous: The creation of global financial markets was a political strategy pursued by a state-market alliance of interests which became transnational in nature. Private preferences were converted, through state policy in the G-10 economies, into the evolving structure of the global market.

If we think of states and markets in terms of dichotomy, then we have difficulty explaining why financial architecture has emerged as it has. There is a rational case for providing at the global level more of the regulatory and supervisory functions normally associated with national financial systems. An approach derived from economic models of governance would expect state authorities to optimize public goods provision with a view to stabilizing the global system and providing at the global level much of what has come to be viewed as essential in terms of preventing market failure at the national level. Yet this has not occurred; global financial architecture has remained minimalist, and despite frequent crises more thorough-going reform has not been undertaken. This situation must please someone or it would not endure, because the costs of such a situation are great for many agents in the global economy. Economic models do not focus on the close relationships between public and private agents or on the way in which the preferences of agents are formed and become shared over time as they interact in the policy process. To fully understand the relationship between market structures (in this case, liberal and transnational) and patterns of financial architecture, we need alternative models which focus on preferences, the institutions of policymaking and who has access to them, and whose interests the present forms of market and governance serve. The state-market condominium model helps us in this task. Several points can be made which help us think more clearly about what should be done:

(i) The state-market condominium model leads us to expect that public-private coalitions will seek to extend changes begun at the domestic level (deregulation and cross-sector liberalization) to the global financial system once the domestic battle has been won. This is because the gains which more liberal domestic policies achieved for the most competitive in crucial financial centers can also be realized through greater cross-border liberalization, especially access to the markets of the less globally competitive firms. One should also expect these liberalizing (and increasingly transnationalizing) condominiums to develop preferences for the sorts of institutions and regulatory framework of governance which support their preferred market structure and terms of competition. In this sense the model helps us to understand why we have the minimalist but global financial architecture which we currently have. A broad G-10 based transnational coalition of increasingly large financial institutions have broken loose from their national settings, opting for market-based forms of regulation and supervision relatively free of the constraints of national politics (of, for example, small banks) and processes of accountability. They have forged alliances with regulators and supervisors participating in transnational processes such as the Basel Committee and the debate over debt restructuring mechanisms. We would expect this alliance to reflect the preferences of the firms which stand behind it, the very firms which benefit most from more liberal global competition and increased cross-border market access. We would also expect a regulatory and supervisory framework which reflects their institutional preferences and their preferences in terms of transaction costs.

The example of the new Basel II capital accord, which extends the cost advantages of its new market-based risk-management approach to supervision to only the most sophisticated and global financial institutions, is instructive here. The first Basel accord had been under critical scrutiny by the private sector in the G-10 countries for some time. The review of Basel I was formally begun by the Group of Thirty, a private think-tank-like body of members drawn from both public/official and private institutions in the financial sector, many of whom had held prestigious appointments in both.[47] The group formed a study group and issued a report on systemic risk in the changing global financial system in 1997.[48] The proposals were also heavily pushed by the Institute of International Finance, a club of the world's largest financial institutions, and also the Basel Committee's almost sole interlocutor in the policy process.[49] In particular, Pillar One of the new accord not surprisingly translates rather directly the policy preferences of the largest financial institutions, indeed those most likely to benefit from the proposed measures in terms of transaction costs, even though there is much evidence that the measures adopted may enhance as opposed to reduce the risks of our global system.[50]

In order to achieve more thorough-going reform which takes a broader range of interests into account, the model tells us to challenge this

---

[47] See Tsingou on the role of the G-30 and OTC derivatives regulation in this volume; also Tsingou (2003).

[48] Group of Thirty (1997). The report includes the names of study group participants (pp. ix–x), and members of the G-30 itself (pp. 47–8).

[49] This can be ascertained from the Basel Committee web site, section on comments on proposals at http://www.bis.org/bcbs/cacomments.htm (comments on second proposal) and http://www.bis.org/bcbs/cp3comments.htm (comments on third consultative document). It is clear that few groups outside the financial industry responded, and that despite responses from national banking industry associations in Europe and elsewhere, the IIF presence was often a dominant one strongly supported by the US and UK in particular; see also Institute of International Finance (1998). On the global influence of national and international financial industry associations, see the article by Porter in this volume.

[50] As argued in Claessens and Underhill (2003).

powerful coalition directly. Institutional design must be altered to facilitate access to the policy process for interests which are currently excluded, those who would benefit from greater financial and monetary stability and debt workout mechanisms, especially developing countries. Such proposals restrict the freedoms and impose relative costs on the dominant financial services firms because they enhance the position of those less able to compete and who do not have the resources to manage risk according to the new Basel proposals.

(ii) In this sense, if we cease thinking about politics and markets as opposing dynamics in permanent tug-of-war with each other, we might put an end to a particularly sterile debate in terms of financial architecture. We would stop expecting, or indeed hoping, that one might triumph over the other, whatever one's preferred outcome. It is not going to happen, because the two go together. We cannot somehow wish politics out of markets, and the behavior of private market constituents is anyway inherently political, whether we choose to recognize it or not.

This both complicates the process of financial governance and liberates it from the constraints of more orthodox approaches to states and markets. The model certainly implies that a variety of solutions are possible. There is no single alternative, but neither the choice nor the politics will be easy. We cannot simply rely on market forces to 'sort it out', and we must devote more time to the question of 'what kind of monetary and financial system, to serve what kind of society?' The nature of the market is inherently contestable, and there is no single equilibrium point which can be rationally determined. Multiple equilibrium models are much the order of the day, but the variables are political and institutional as well as 'economic' as such. This greatly complicates the task of decision-making. We need to confront this world of bewildering choice and imperfection head on, and we need to think carefully about whose interests should best be promoted by political authorities in debates about financial governance: the interests of the dominant firms, or the broader range of interests in the global development process? More inclusive institutions of financial governance at domestic and international levels are likely to enhance the range of interests represented and thus to alter the balance between debtors and creditors in debt workout mechanisms, or to tip the balance in favor of stability despite potentially higher transaction costs for globally active firms. Most important, the financial and monetary system could be made more compatible with a broad range of development goals such as poverty alleviation and environmental considerations, beyond simpler notions of macroeconomic sobriety.

(iii) The model implies that *exclusive* reliance on the concepts of perfect competition, optimality, and general equilibrium inherent in economic theories of governance is likely to yield misleading policy prescriptions and even a misunderstanding of the problem at hand. By understanding that the market operates simultaneously through competitive processes and the policy process, now a policy process which extends across borders, we can much better come to terms with the rent-seeking behavior of both private and public actors. If we do not expect firms or other market agents to behave according to models of perfect competition, we will more easily understand that rent-seeking behavior is not the exception, but the rule. If we all admit that perfect competition is an abstraction from a messy, more prosaic reality of various forms of second-best market-fixing, we can begin to see more clearly the reality of the political economy of governance: If the state does not rig the market, private interests will. It is better that we make clear and well-informed decisions about how and why we want it rigged in particular ways.

We can therefore never disconnect the world of policy choice from the rather tawdry world of self-interest and particularistic advantage. We should be aware that governments sometimes constitute the most private interests of all, and a fully democratic process is there for a reason. We should also understand that there is nothing particularly noble about the interests of business or any other economic agent. Nobility of intent or behavior is bound to be in short supply. Business in a market system, particularly big business, carries huge responsibilities in terms of the realization of public policy objectives. It does not exist in some purely private market domain where it can do nothing but good, or indeed ill to its detractors. None could be more clear on this point than Adam Smith, who advocated market solutions but remained guarded in important ways:

> The interest of the dealers . . . in any particular branch of trade or manufactures, is always in some respects different from, and even opposite to, that of the public. To widen the market and narrow the competition, is always in the interest of the dealers. . . . The proposal of any new law or regulation of commerce which comes from this order, ought always to be listened to with the greatest precaution . . .[51]

Democratic processes should be understood as much for keeping private interests accountable for the public interest functions they perform in our societies, as they are for keeping politicians accountable to the electorate. The rhetoric of the free market makes it all too easy to forget this point. The task is difficult in a situation of globally integrated monetary and financial space, but it does mean that private firms are also accountable in terms of the public good in relation to outcomes, not just to shareholders

[51] Smith ([1776] 1937, p. 250).

or self-indulgent management teams. Public institutions must also ensure that a range of interests consistently and demonstrably benefit from the financial and monetary system. States must overcome the constraints of their close integration with the world of business at the global level and begin to think about how broader economic and social development goals were achieved in the past through state-market combinations which attenuated the competitive dynamics of the market and built governance and economic success on a platform of inclusion.

(iv) If the state-market condominium model helps us to come to terms with the endemic nature of particularistic rent-seeking in the market, we might stop expecting a smooth, equilibrium process to global financial integration. The integration process is not about the rational pursuit of optimality or spontaneous market development, but is driven by particularistic interests. As different constituencies compete to shape the process to their own advantage, the multiple equilibrium idea comes back to mind, and there are good and bad equilibria in various guises. Furthermore, as political and economic competition to control the terms of market integration gains momentum, it becomes apparent that we are not integrating *like* entities. Just as even the most 'rational' of corporate mergers often founder on tensions between contrasting corporate cultures, we should expect local and regional ways of doing things to come together in a dynamic and sometimes difficult tension. Integration is not of like with like, but a linking together of diverse state-market condominiums. It will be a bumpy process, and diversity is bound to persist. Strict convergence to single 'rational' standards is unlikely to be possible or healthy, and there is no single formula which can admit universal application. Many models will work, each infused with different values. The democratic process must ensure that a choice of values and solutions is consistently available, even to the weak and economically deprived. Competitive market-based financial and monetary governance is not the only and may not be the best option in terms of overall welfare maximization. A variety of debt workout mechanisms are far from detrimental to the workings of domestic economies, for example, where beneficial outcomes are engineered through robust legal and regulatory constraints on the freedoms of investors and banks/issuers alike, to resolve collective action problems in default situations.[52] Thus why not a system at the global level for developing countries (perhaps separate from arrangements for developed countries) which distributes the costs of workout more evenly than at present and enshrines long-run development objectives to counter capital scarcity as a fundamental principle of the system? In the long run, few

[52] See Kumar and Miller (2003).

would lose, as has long been historically demonstrated at the domestic level.

(v) If global integration is an imperfect, bumpy process infused with rent-seeking activity and the pursuit of private gain, and a straightforward equilibrium outcome is unlikely, then we should expect and prepare for crisis, particularly financial crisis. The Asian crisis caught everyone napping, bar a few, and we should have been better prepared. But there is a further point: If equilibrium is problematic and crises likely to occur, perhaps we should devote less time to casting aspersions on solutions which appear to 'interfere' with the rationality of the market, such as capital controls. Such policy devices can obviously be wrongly and inappropriately employed. But the model would indicate that the same can also be said of free market solutions. Private greed must not be allowed to plunge the political economy into troubled waters.

(vi) Most importantly, the state-market condominium model allows us to understand how markets are integral to governance and the formal activities of government. The state *is* involved in the market and *should* be involved in the market; the market cannot function as a system without the political and regulatory processes which the state and its international cooperative extensions represent. We should be very wary, echoing Smith, of those who argue that the state should leave market agents alone to get on with the job; there is nothing sacred about them and market agents are more than likely pursuing the sort of narrow private agenda associated above with Basel II. State interference could easily be ill-informed or simply wrong, but the same can be said of the public interest functions delegated to market agents.

CONCLUSIONS

If various possible forms of market are integral to the broader process of governance, and the state is an integral part of the market, then the 'market as governance' is also closely tied to the issue of political legitimacy, particularly in a democratic context. If the functioning of the market does not satisfy enough of the people enough of the time, we have a problem. This might apply as much to 'no growth' or 'slow growth' as it does to *unequal* growth. In this sense, distributional outcomes do matter:[53] Aggregate gains may not always be the crucial variable. If market pressures bring democratically unacceptable results, they must be rethought and redesigned, and they *can* be. If change induced by market forces comes at a politically unacceptable pace, the potential benefits of

[53] In contrast to the arguments presented in Feldstein (1998).

liberal solutions may be lost for lack of political realism. The bottom line is therefore not an economic one, but a political one, and the *outcome* must be perceived as legitimate.

In terms of contemporary financial governance reform, these points mean that the current piecemeal reform process with its emphasis on facilitating market efficiency is likely to prove deeply flawed. We need to move beyond reform proposals based essentially on economic theories of governance. We need in the first place to separate out two discussions: (1) The broad discussion concerning the role and purpose of financial governance and its various national and multilateral instances, such as the IMF, should be separated out from the more technical discussion of (2) the means we design to operationalize the global financial architecture, such as the *specific* functions of individual global institutions and states, the types of financing facilities and appropriate levels for indebted countries; debates concerning crisis management versus crisis prevention, the specific content of public and private sector standards, and the like.

To do this we first need to return to the 'Bretton Woods' question discussed at the outset: the broad relationship between the international imperatives of adjustment and the economic and social development aspirations of individual political communities, usually national states. We need financial architecture which facilitates access to capital markets and adjustment financing, long and short-term, for countries which perform to reasonable macroeconomic standards (not those of the more sober advanced economies, and certainly not the standards of those developed economies which have succumbed wholesale to the temptations of current account and fiscal indebtedness). This financing can be provided through a combination of coordinated regional, multilateral, national, and even bilateral reserves. Different types of financing are appropriate for countries in different sorts of situations. We need to make available not just bail-ins and a greater commitment to private sector burden sharing, but burden sharing in another way: Both deficits *and* surpluses should be looked upon as part of payments disequilibria. This means that the resources of surplus countries should be more systematically available to those with deficits, especially during crises. If this results in long-run improvement in the international development process, it will benefit all many times over.

Secondly, it follows that we need to think of conditionality not just in technical economic terms. Paul Volcker recently stated that when IMF conditionality confronts a poor indebted country, the country gets into line. When IMF conditionality confronts a wealthy member of the IMF board (debtor or not), the Fund gets into line. This point can be taken a stage further. IMF conditionality and international bond holder clubs not only confront the preferred *policies* of indebted countries. They often also confront the preferred outcomes of democratic processes. This is part of the difficulty in Argentina: The government, confronted with the issue of elections after considerable social unrest, faces calls for economic stringency and debt repayment which contradict the aspirations of a democratic political community where social instability could overturn the democratic process itself. We all know that if 'democracy' in a major EU country confronts the budgetary pacts of EMU, or if IMF conditionality confronts electoral preferences in a wealthy, developed economy, it is likely that these transnational rules will give way to national priorities if domestic pressure is strong. This is not very likely in Latin America and definitely not in Africa, and one might include World Bank conditionality as well. If democracy is to be considered integral to international security, and most security threats come from the developing world at the moment, why is this so consistently the case?

Finally, as the global financial system and the markets become increasingly integrated, we should expect pressures for adapting our patterns of governance to the new reality. Why not lead from out front and demonstrate our human capacity for foresight and improvement? There is a clear need to replicate at the international level more of the infrastructure of governance we normally associate with domestic political economies. Nowhere does this apply more urgently than in the realm of debt workout. Standstills and workout mechanisms have long been a feature of domestic financial governance. We know they make the market function better and that they provide vital elements of stability and fairness to weaker parties in the market, compensating for informational deficits and stabilizing expectations. They help compensate for loss and therefore to legitimate the dynamic nature of our political economy. In the international domain, we cannot simply leave countries to sort it out with incoherent clubs of bondholders.

The principal reason this is not done, and why other urgent reforms to global financial and monetary governance are not properly addressed, is because a condominium of state and market agencies dominates the financial and monetary governance process in a self-interested fashion. One final point: We tend to associate financial instability and crisis with development *failures*. If this were consistently the case, then historically speaking the successful developing (now rich) countries could not have experienced financial or monetary turbulence, but they did. For example, the crisis of 1947 was due to the very success of European reconstruction efforts, sucking in imports faster than liquidity could be generated and pushing economies toward insolvency. The Asian crisis was in many ways due to the maturation of successful developing economies struggling with politically difficult reform processes. Much of the turbulence and disequilibria of the monetary and financial system is thus due to success as well as failure. It would be helpful to stop rewarding success with punishment as opposed to long-run support.

REFERENCES

Aglietta, M. (1979), *A Theory of Capitalist Regulation*, London: New Left Books.

Alt, J. and K. Schepsle (1990), *Perspectives on Positive Political Economy*, Cambridge: Cambridge University Press.

Axelrod, Robert (1984), *The Evolution of Co-operation*, New York: Basic Books.

Bernstein, Marver (1955), *Regulating Business by Independent Commission*, Princeton: Princeton University Press.

Bratton, W. and J. McCahery (1966), *International Regulatory Competition and Co-ordination*, Oxford: Oxford University Press.

Cerny, P.G. (1990), *The Changing Architecture of Politics: structure, agency, and the future of the state*, London: Sage.

Cerny, P.G. (ed.) (1993), *Finance and World Politics: markets, regimes, and states in the post-hegemonic era*, Aldershot, UK and Brookfield, US: Edward Elgar.

Claessens, Stijn and Geoffrey R.D. Underhill (2003), 'Basle II Capital requirements and Developing Countries: a political economy approach', paper presented at the workshop *Quantifying the Impact of Rich Countries' Policies on Poor Countries,* Washington, DC, 23–24 October 2003, organized by the OECD Center for Global Development and the Global Development Network.

Coase, Ronald (1937), 'The Nature of the Firm', *Economica*, **4** (15), August, 386–405.

Coase, Ronald (1960), 'The Problem of Social Cost', *Journal of Law and Economics*, 3, 1–44.

Cohen, Benjamin J. (1977), *Organizing the World's Money*, New York: Basic Books.

Coleman, William D. (1996), *Financial Services, Globalization, and Domestic Policy Change*, London: Macmillan.

Cooper, Richard N. (1968), *The Economics of Interdependence*, New York: McGraw-Hill.

Cox, Robert W. (1987), *Production, Power, and World Order*, New York: Columbia University Press.

Cox, Robert W. (1996), *Approaches to World Order*, Cambridge: Cambridge University Press.

Cutler, C., V. Haufler and T. Porter (1999), *Private Authority and International Affairs*, Albany: State University of New York Press.

Evans, P. and J.D. Stephens (1988), 'Studying development since the sixties. The emergence of a new comparative political economy', *Theory and Society*, 17, 713–745.

Feldstein, Martin (1998), 'Income Inequality and Poverty', NBER Working Paper No. W6770.

Gilpin, Robert (1987), *The Political Economy of International Relations*, Princeton: Princeton University Press.

Goodhart, Charles et al. (1998), *Financial Regulation: why, how, and where now?*, London: Routledge.

Gourevitch, Peter (1986), *Politics in Hard Times*, Ithaca: Cornell University Press.

Greenwood, Justin and Henry Jacek (eds) (2000), *Organized Business and the New Global Order*, London: Routledge.

Group of Thirty (1997), *Global Institutions, National Supervision, and Systemic Risk*, Washington, DC: Group of Thirty.

Hall, R.B. and T. Biersteker (eds) (2002), *The Emergence of Private Authority in Global Governance*, Cambridge: Cambridge University Press.

Heilbroner, Robert (ed.) (1986), *The Essential Adam Smith*, Oxford: Oxford University Press.

Higgott, R., G. Underhill and A. Bieler (eds) (2000), *Non-State Actors and Authority in the Global System*, London: Routledge.

Hume, David (1752), 'Of Interest, Of Money and Of the Balance of Trade', in E. Rotwein (ed.) (1970), *David Hume: Writings on Economics*, Madison: University of Wisconsin Press.

Institute of International Finance (IIF) (1998), *Recommendations for Revising the Regulatory Capital Rules for Credit Risk*, Report of the Working Group on Capital Adequacy, Washington, DC: IIF.

Katzenstein, Peter J. (ed.) (1978), *Between Power and Plenty: foreign economic policies of advanced industrial states*, Madison: University of Wisconsin Press.

Keohane, Robert O. (1984), *After Hegemony: co-operation and discord in the world political economy*, Princeton: Princeton University Press.

Keohane, Robert O. and Joseph Nye (1977), *Power and Interdependence: World Politics in Transition*, Boston: Little Brown.

Kindleberger, Charles (1973), *The World in Depression 1929-39*, Berkeley: University of California Press.

Krasner, S. (ed.) (1983), *International Regimes*, Ithaca: Cornell University Press.

Krätke, M. and G. Underhill (2005), 'Political Economy: Revival of an Inter-Discipline', in R. Stubbs and G. Underhill (eds), *Political Economy and the Changing Global Order*, 3rd edition, Oxford: Oxford University Press.

Kumar, Manmohan S. and Marcus Miller (2003), 'Bail-outs, Bail-ins, and Bankruptcy: evolution of the new architecture', in Geoffrey R.D. Underhill and Xiaoke Zhang (eds), *International Financial Governance under Stress*, Cambridge: Cambridge University Press, pp. 343–59.

Landreth, H. (1976), *History of Economic Thought*, Boston: Houghton Mifflin.

Moran, Michael (1984), *The Politics of Banking*, London: Palgrave-Macmillan.

Noël, Alain (1987), 'Accumulation, Regulation, and Social Change: an essay on French political economy', *International Organization*, **41** (2), 303–33.

North, Douglass C. (1990), *Institutions, Institutional Change, and Economic Performance*, Cambridge: Cambridge University Press.

Olson, M. (1982), *The Rise and Decline of Nations*, New Haven: Yale University Press.

Peltzman, Sam (1976), 'Toward a more General Theory of Regulation', *Journal of Law and Economics*, **19** (2), 21–40.

Polanyi, Karl (1944), *The Great Transformation*, Boston: Beacon Press.

Rodrik, Dani (1997), *Has Globalization gone too Far?*, Washington, DC: Institute for International Economics.

Rosenau, James N. (ed.) (1967), *Domestic Sources of Foreign Policy*, New York: Free Press.

Rosenau, J. and E.-O. Czempiel (eds) (1992), *Governance without Government: order and Change in World Politics*, Cambridge: Cambridge University Press.

Shonfield, A., V. Curzon et al. (1976), *Politics and Trade*, Vol. 1 of A. Shonfield (ed.), *International Economic Relations of the Western World 1959-1971*, Oxford: Oxford University Press.

Skinner, Andrew (1970), 'Introduction', in Adam Smith, *The Wealth of Nations*, London: Penguin.

Smith, Adam ([1776] 1937), *An Inquiry into the Nature and Causes of the Wealth of Nations*, New York: The Modern Library.

Stigler, George (1971), 'The Theory of Economic Regulation', *Bell Journal of Economics*, 2, 113–21.

Strange, Susan (2002), *Authority and Markets: Susan Strange's Writings on International Political Economy*, London: Palgrave.

Strange, Susan (1970), 'International Economics and International Relations: a case of mutual neglect', *International Affairs*, **46** (2), 304–15.

Strange, Susan (1976a), *International Monetary Relations*, Vol. 2 of A. Shonfield (ed.), *International Economic Relations of the Western World 1959-1971*, Oxford: Oxford University Press.

Strange, Susan (1976b), 'The Study of Transnational Relations', *International Affairs*, **52** (3), 333–45.

Strange, Susan (1988), *States and Markets*, Oxford: Blackwell.

Strange, Susan (1996), *The Retreat of the State*, Cambridge: Cambridge University Press.

Tsingou, Eleni (2003), 'Transnational Policy Communities and Financial Governance: the role of private actors in derivatives regulation', CSGR Working Paper No. 111/03.

Underhill, Geoffrey R.D. (2003), 'States, Markets, and Governance for Emerging Market Economies', *International Affairs*, **79** (4), 755–81.

Underhill, G. and X. Zhang (2005), 'The Changing State-Market Condominium in East Asia: rethinking the political underpinnings of development', *New Political Economy*, **10** (1), 1–24.

van Kersbergen, K. and F. van Waarden (2004), 'Governance as a Bridge between Disciplines: Cross-disciplinary inspiration regarding shifts in governance and problems of governability, accountability, and legitimacy', *European Journal of Political Research*, **43** (2), 143–71.

Verdun, A. and T. Lawton (eds) (2000), *Strange Power*, Aldershot: Ashgate.

Williamson, Oliver (1975), *Markets and Hierarchies*, New York: Free Press.

Zysman, J. (1983), *Governments, Markets, and Growth*, Ithaca: Cornell University Press.

2. Political Economy Approach to Financial Reform

Susanne Lütz*

1. INTRODUCTION

Regulatory change lies at the core of financial globalization. Deregulation and liberalization have blurred market boundaries and spurred the development of financial innovations which have substantially transformed the character of the finance industry. Market transformations, in turn, have been accompanied by the redefinition of rules, instruments and institutions of prudential regulation.

While normative approaches see financial regulation first and foremost as providing collective goods such as financial stability, transparency or investor protection, regulatory reform in finance is nevertheless a contested terrain in which conflicting interests attempt to influence the design of governance mechanisms. Some actors may not be permitted to contribute to the common good, while others are in a hegemonic position to shape rule-setting processes according to their own preferences or national regulatory traditions. It is exactly the pattern of exclusion and inclusion in processes of regulatory change which lies at the heart of a political economy perspective on financial regulation.

In line with the overall theme of this volume, I present in this article several analytical dimensions for the purpose of studying regulatory change in finance. The argument is that the preferences of and power relationships between government and market actors are key variables in understanding how regulatory problems are tackled, what kinds of regulatory solutions are chosen and how regulatory change comes about. In the second half of the paper, the analytical categories are applied to two cases of regulatory change in Germany. By drawing on the process of transformation in capital market and banking regulation, it is argued

* The author would like to thank Helene Schuberth, Brigitte Unger, Beat Weber and the participants of the workshop 'The Political Economy of International Financial Governance' (Vienna, 26 November 2004) for their helpful comments.

that regulatory reforms were driven by *modernization coalitions* consisting of different constellations of public and private actors. In the case of capital markets, a transnational coalition of institutional investors, regulators and banks spurred the horizontal diffusion of a US model of insider trading regulation. In banking, national regulators and national banks joined forces to minimize the costs of adapting to a new model of risk management negotiated at the global level in the Basel Committee. In both cases, those who – for one reason or another – benefited most from open and integrated financial markets formed the core of these modernization coalitions, while others, mostly regional actors, only participate to a minor extent in rule-making processes but nevertheless have to bear their distributional consequences.

2. ANALYTICAL FRAMEWORK FOR THE STUDY OF REGULATORY CHANGE

In this section, I sketch out three analytical dimensions for the study of regulatory change in finance: the type of regulatory problem, the pattern of regulatory change and the relationship between state and market actors. The main argument is, however, that the power relationship between public and private actors is crucial to understanding what pattern of regulatory change is evolving and why problems of financial regulation are resolved in a certain manner. The analytical perspective presented here is largely based on a power-distributional account of institutional creation and change (Knight 1992). It is assumed that social institutions, or in our case frameworks of financial regulation, reflect power asymmetries in society. Institutions are forged out of political struggles; they change in response either to changes in the balance of power among various social actors or to changes in the preferences or interests of the most powerful actors. As will be shown below, in this case different coalitions of public and private actors were crucial both in defending the existing regulatory setting and in changing it.

2.1 Problem of Regulation

Using normative approaches to regulation, economic regulation is supposed to provide collective goods that are not produced by the market itself. While regulatory regimes in other formerly nationalized industries such as telecommunications, electricity or railways are primarily meant to create and ensure competition, prudential regulation in finance seeks to guarantee financial stability and investor protection.

In banking, the objective is usually to prevent what are called *systemic risks*. Since credit institutions function as a link between debtors and creditors on financial markets, banking failures not only hurt private investors but also cripple other enterprises in their ability to invest and to create new jobs. This systemic character of financial risks is exactly the normative reason why in banking, unlike in other branches of the economy, the management of economic risk has always been an issue which concerns the state. Ultimately, the aim is to prevent situations in which the state and thereby its national central bank are forced to intervene as the lender of last resort, leaving the taxpayer burdened with the losses created by privately undertaken risks (on financial regulation, see Kay and Vickers 1988; Herring and Litan 1995; Goodhart et al. 1998).

Problems in investor protection usually arise from *information asymmetries* between the buyers and sellers of equities in capital markets. Banks or traders of securities usually know more about the quality of financial products than individual investors. Therefore, providers of financial services are likely to exploit their informational advantages in order to raise stock prices and to profit from insider trading.

Why is it useful to distinguish regulatory problems, if the fact that regulatory regimes are meant to serve certain public imperatives does not necessarily tell us whether they actually do so? Regulatory problems can, in fact, have multiple solutions and inhabit different kinds of institutional arrangements which are developed along different historical paths and function differently. In my view, it is helpful nonetheless to ask what kind of problem regulation is supposed to solve, since this allows us to compare normative propositions with reality. Moreover, we may analyze regulatory change from a historical perspective and compare regulatory practices and institutional designs at different points in time. How did countries once tackle a certain regulatory problem, and what are their best practices now? Is there cross-national variation, or can we find functional equivalents to institutional solutions which were once developed in national frameworks at the European or global level? What are the 'policy communities' centered around different regulatory problems – who participates in 'problem-solving' processes, and who are the outsiders?

2.2 Patterns of Regulatory Change

Financial regulation has become an issue of multilevel governance. Rules and standards are defined in global, European and national arenas which are not separated, but increasingly interrelated. But what kind of dynamics evolve in these multilevel decision-making settings? Following Radaelli (2003, p. 40), I distinguish here between *vertical* and *horizontal* mechanisms which arise in multilevel systems of governance. Vertical mechanisms clearly demarcate the global or the EU level, where the respective regulation is defined, and the domestic level, where policy has to be implemented. Although the vertical dimension does not necessarily predict a top-down direction of regulatory change, it is assumed that there is a certain pressure to adopt a specific model of regulation. By contrast, horizontal mechanisms look at regulatory change as a process where there is no clearly specified model to be exported at first, but where change is triggered either by negotiation leading to a harmonized regulatory solution, by the market and the choice of the investor, or by the diffusion of ideas and discourses on the notion of good policy and best practices.

Two forms of vertical dynamics can be distinguished: the uploading and downloading of rules and regulatory models (Dyson and Goetz 2003, pp. 15–16).

States are usually interested in uploading their regulatory model to the European or global level in order to shape further processes of rule definition. Success in uploading domestic preferences to the upper level reduces adaptive pressures from above. Level shifting also allows states to purposely upload constraining effects to other actors, who may adopt them as internal discipline in order to catalyze further reforms. In finance, powerful countries like the United States have always been able to impose their own preferences and models as blueprints for regulation in other countries. The latest example is probably the revision of the Basel Accord and the move toward a more flexible and market-based approach to measuring and managing financial risks, known as 'Basel II'. As will be shown below, Basel II forces countries without a rating tradition (like Germany) to bring their own systems of risk management into line with a rating-based approach, thereby triggering a shift in regulatory paradigm and practice. Why has the US very often been successful in uploading its regulatory preferences to other countries? Borrowing from Susan Strange (1996, 1998) we may refer to its 'structural power', that is, power of resources and power of knowledge. In the case of Basel II, especially the latter power has obviously been of crucial importance – both US investment banks and US regulatory agencies had already gained experience with rating-based methods of measuring and buffering financial risks, so using their informational advantage they sought to upload a new model of regulation to the level of the Basel Committee in order to gain a competitive advantage as well (see Lütz 2002, pp. 264–8).

In the EU framework, uploading can also occur when countries are in a 'first mover position' to influence early phases of agenda-setting and to shape the discourse of potential problem-solving strategies. The challenge is here to win the support of the EU Commission, because if a proposal is compatible with the Commission's views on the issue, the initiator country has a good chance of seeing its national approach become the received view of the issue in the ensuing drafting phase. Research on European environmental policy has shown that pioneer states have been much more successful in uploading their own ideas and concepts to the European level than states who seek to veto policy proposals in later negotiations in the Council of Ministers (Héritier et al. 1996).

Rule-taking or *downloading* regulatory models usually implies some form of coercion. In European politics, the decisions of the European Court of Justice or the European Commission may include elements of hierarchy. In finance, however, member states, regulatory agencies and central bank governors engage in rule-setting negotiations both at the European and the global level in order to define standards which then have to be implemented domestically. Rule-taking implies power asymmetries, either due to the fact that some actors are not able to defend their own national models of regulation in high-level negotiations or because they do not even participate in global rule-making processes, but nevertheless have to implement the outcome. As will be shown below, for countries like Germany, Basel II means a definite break with its own regulatory traditions, while those European countries which are not members of the Basel Committee still have to implement the European banking directives modeled on Basel agreements.

In a *horizontal* perspective, regulatory change also comes about through the cross-border diffusion of rules, standards and practices.

The *deliberate harmonization* of rules involves negotiating standards, for instance in the EU Council of Ministers or the Basel Committee. As mentioned above, countries usually seek to minimize the costs of adaptation to a harmonized solution, either by defending their national models or by trying to impose their own regulatory practices on other countries. Harmonization involves the adoption of an international standard that adjusts the regulatory procedures of two or more countries until they are more or less the same (Slaughter 2004, p. 59). In the EU framework, however, harmonizing prudential regulation usually involves defining a minimum standard (e.g. referring to one's own capital levels or transparency duties) beyond which countries mutually recognize their domestic regulatory settings. Mutual recognition by two countries of each other's regulatory standards and decisions on specific cases can trigger competition between countries for the best regulatory practices.

In finance, regulatory change has very often been triggered by *competition* among states or even subnational units. The deregulation of financial markets and the dismantling of capital controls came about in a snowball-like process in which unilateral deregulation by the US in the 1970s prompted other countries to follow suit for fear of competitive disadvantages (Helleiner 1994). A key step towards deregulation was actually taken on 1 May 1975 ('May Day'), when the New York Stock Exchange announced the end of fixed commissions for securities trading. 'May Day' was the precursor of liberalization elsewhere, including Britain, France and, to a minor extent, Germany. Domestic governments retracted exchange controls, dissolved former price and interest rate cartels, lowered access barriers to banking activities and stock exchange membership for foreigners, and allowed innovative financial instruments to be traded.

(De-)regulatory competition was also the crucial mechanism eroding the system of territorial and functional market barriers which had governed the US banking market since the banking crisis of the 1930s. Territorial market barriers were based on the McFadden Act of 1927 and limited interstate banking as well as interstate branch banking. Functional barriers were upheld by the well-known Glass-Steagall Act of 1933, which introduced a strict separation of commercial and investment banking activities. A process of lowering geographical market barriers towards universalization in banking was set in motion in 1975, when the state of Maine adopted interstate banking legislation; within a decade, virtually all states had passed some form of interstate banking laws, partly in hopes of attracting new investment capital, but also based on reciprocity clauses. Market making through a 'race to the bottom' was not only spurred by a fragmented system of federalism, but also by federal regulators and the courts – as one financial firm gained a regulatory advantage, others would seek a compensatory regulatory change from a different regulator or the courts. Especially the Federal Reserve lowered market barriers in a piecemeal fashion, for instance by allowing commercial banks to begin limited investment banking activities on a case-by-case basis (Deeg and Lütz 2000, pp. 381–93).

Regulatory competition may also lead to 'market shaping' and even trigger a 'race to the top' in terms of risk management and transparency standards. With reference to the spread of insider trading regulation in the 1990s, it will be argued below that stricter regulatory standards may help to enhance the position of financial producers in competition for institutional investors and thereby improve the international competitiveness of a domestic financial marketplace as a whole.

The horizontal diffusion of rules and regulatory practices also comes about through the adoption and imitation of perceived 'best practices'. In finance, '*mimetism*' (DiMaggio and Powell 1991) of regulatory practices is facilitated by networks among regulators which allow the exchange of information and knowledge on 'how to do it'. Both the Basel Committee and IOSCO have issued codes of best practices on how to regulate securities markets, deal with risk management problems and prevent money laundering. In 1997, the Basel Committee released its *Core Principles for Effective Banking Supervision*, distilled from the practices and policies of member states, which provide a comprehensive blueprint for a financial supervisory system. For its part, the US Securities and Exchange Commission hosts major training programs for securities regulators, and by the year 2000 over 1 260 regulators from more than 100 countries had been trained in these programs (Slaughter 2004, pp. 54–7).

2.3 Relationship between State and Market Actors

Rules are defined by government representatives, market actors, experts and international organizations, to name just a few actors. From a political economy perspective, the state-market relationship is crucial in understanding the dynamics of regulatory reforms and the way regulatory problems are resolved. A closer look at the relevant literature reveals at least three competing views at the state-market nexus:

Market actors capture the state

This is basically what the positive theory of regulation has argued by focusing on the relationship between US regulatory agencies and their market constituencies (see Stigler 1971 and Peltzman 1976, among others). Unlike the normative public interest school, the positive school assumes that public regulation follows producers' interests and that regulation is a good sold by politicians and bureaucrats to the regulated firms. In essence, public regulation is seen as a source of *state* instead of market failure. In US banking regulation, capture has always been present; the case of dismantling geographical and functional market barriers on the US market illustrates how market actors put pressure on both regulators and courts to repeal barriers which had previously prevented commercial banks from interstate activities and investment banking.

Authors like Susan Strange see markets winning in the contemporary period of transnational integration, thus yielding a general 'retreat of the state' in the face of market ascendancy (Strange 1996). With financial markets outgrowing the public domain, market actors may use their opportunities to broaden their sphere of activity either in order to circumvent public policies that would impose regulatory costs on them (exit) or to lobby for less regulated environments (voice). European banks, for instance, used their exit options in the early 1970s to avoid creating expansive capital reserves as risk buffers by building credit pyramids in less regulated markets abroad (OECD 1983, p. 109).

States pool sovereignty to bind market actors

A more state-centric perspective sees states as still very much in control of the process of global financial integration. States may have lost control of policy instruments which would impose binding rules on their market constituencies; but if they pool sovereignty and engage in multilateral collaboration at the European or global level, they can restrict the exit options of market players by agreeing on standards of regulation with which their market constituencies have to comply. Multilateralism and the Regime approach (Ruggie 1993; Krasner 1983) assume that self-centered states may engage in collaboration to further both individual and collective interests such as autonomy vis-à-vis their market constituencies. In finance, government representatives work through the cooperative regulatory and supervisory process of the Basel Committee on Banking Supervision, but also through a growing number of other international fora of regulation (e.g. International Organization of Securities Commissions [IOSCO], International Association of Insurance Supervisors [IAIS], Financial Action Task Force [FATF] and the Financial Stability Forum [FSF], among others). Kapstein (1996), for instance, sees the principle of 'home country control' governing the relationship between domestic regulators. Under home country supervision, states look to one another – as opposed to some supranational or multilateral entity – to legislate and enforce agreements which have been reached collectively. In the European Community, this concept is far more expansive, involving the mutual recognition by each member state of the others' home country regulations. As a result, the linkages between states and their national banks have not been broken by globalization; in this way, every international bank is accountable on a consolidated basis to a single, national regulator (Kapstein 1996, p. 9). Slaughter (2004) considers states not as unitary, but as disaggregated actors who form nodes in dense and multilayered webs which allow them to exchange information, to harmonize standards and to learn how to enforce them. According to Slaughter, these government networks, which are basically networks among bureaucrats, form the core of a new and potentially just world order.

States and market actors join forces

A third perspective regards states and market actors as allies in matters of regulation. Underhill (2003 and in this volume) sees the development of both global financial markets and financial market regulation as simultaneously driven by a 'state-market condominium' – prudential banking regulation is not only a device to protect the public interest, but since global risk management standards also contain risks for market participants, they serve to facilitate the process of global market integration itself (Underhill 2003, p. 773). Porter (2004 and in this volume) puts more emphasis on the role of private, non-governmental actors in matters of global financial regulation. Private-sector actors construct private authority either to enhance their own power or to complement or even replace the power of states. The International Accounting Standards Committee (IASC; later renamed IASB), for instance, is a private-sector standards body that has taken the lead in producing a set of financial reporting rules which rival or even surpass the level of detailed specification that characterizes most international laws and other agreements among states. Private regimes such as the IASC, however, operate and institutionalize due to official recognition, either by powerful regulators such as the US Securities and Exchange Commission (SEC), by international organizations such as the World Bank or by international jurisdictions such as the EU. For its part, the EU has refrained altogether from harmonizing accounting standards and instead prefers to seek input into the work of the IASC (Porter 2004, pp. 4–9).

State and market actors not only join forces in order to push the globalization of financial markets and at the same time to adapt the respective regulatory framework, they might as well form protectionist coalitions to buffer adaptation pressures. Protectionism does not necessarily mean upholding market barriers, it may also involve defending existing national standards and models of prudential regulation in order to minimize adaptation costs. State and market actors form status quo coalitions in order to obviate the need to download regulatory models from above. In the US, not only regulatory agencies but also sub-national (i.e. state) representatives have defended the interests of their respective state banks in Congress with regard to banking legislation (Reinicke 1995).

The analytical perspective I present here comes closest to the third approach, which sees states and market actors not as separate, coexisting or even opposed units, but as interrelated and integral to each other in the processes of financial reform. However, I will emphasize the fact that the state is not a unitary actor, nor do market actors constitute a homogeneous group in struggles over financial reform. Financial globalization feeds back into the domestic political economy by disembedding from the domestic terrain those actors which benefit most from market integration, while the champions of national idiosyncrasies are left behind. It is the unevenness of financial market integration, the unequal dynamics and distributional effects of more open financial markets that make financial governance a contested issue characterized by uneven patterns of exclusion and inclusion. Drawing on the cases of regulatory reform in the German capital market and banking sectors, I will argue that different types of modernization coalitions between state and market actors were the driving forces behind the transformation of the domestic regulatory framework. Depending on what these coalitions looked like, different patterns of regulatory change emerged and different institutional solutions were employed to solve problems of financial regulation.

3. THE CASE OF CAPITAL MARKETS – FROM PRIVATE TO PUBLIC REGULATION

Capital market regulation usually has to tackle the problem of how to protect investors against information asymmetries regarding the quality of equities. Traders of securities usually know more about the quality of financial products than individual investors and may exploit their informational advantages in order to raise stock prices and to profit from insider trading. However, a closer historical look reveals that the regulatory setting of stock exchanges and organized capital markets did not provide for transparency or disclosure but privileged the interests of financial service providers. In fact, for a long time regulation was a private matter among stockbrokers, investment houses, banks and the stock exchanges themselves (parts of the following section are adapted from Lütz 1998).

The Old Model

The New York Stock Exchange (NYSE) and the London Stock Exchange (LSE) operated as exclusive clubs of stockbrokers or investment houses, banding together by fixing prices for services rendered to nonmembers and by sophisticated systems of market segmentation (e.g. the division between brokers and jobbers in Britain; for an overview, see Sobel 1994, Moran 1991, and Coleman 1994 and 1996). In Germany, the institutionalization of the stock exchanges was closely linked with the incorporation of the merchant class. Organized markets were mostly implemented by local chambers of commerce and enjoyed the status of public-law bodies. Internally, the exchanges were governed by a number of self-regulating committees which dealt, for example, with admission to listing, fees for equity trading or disciplinary procedures when exchange rules were violated (Insider Commission, Court of Honor, Arbitration Tribunal).

It was mostly the 'producers' of financial services, that is, underwriters of equities, stockbrokers and, in particular, the large universal banks which held the majority of seats in these self-governing committees, while individual investors had no voice at all. In 1896, the

German provincial states assumed responsibility for the legal supervision of their respective stock exchanges and appointed 'State Commissioners' to oversee the implementation of federal and state law. However, the states exercised a limited form of legal supervision over their respective exchanges and basically practiced a policy of non-intervention by granting licenses for self-regulation to private actors. This policy was continued after the Second World War, when eight regional stock exchanges were re-established and the Stock Exchange Legislation became part of Art. 74 of Germany's Basic Law. The regional governments (*Länder*) were granted co-decision rights in stock exchange matters, which allowed them to bargain in the Federal Council (*Bundesrat*) over the approval of new legislation. The federal government (i.e. the Ministry of Finance) only played a minor role in this model of sectoral regulation. The Ministry had to share legislative competences in matters of capital market and especially stock exchange legislation with the *Länder*. The framework of federal law contained no significant provisions regarding the role of the federal government in sectoral supervision or in the regulation of behavior. It should be added that sectoral self-regulation, which was tolerated by the federal government, was accompanied – if not made possible – by cartel-like relations between the eight stock exchanges. Despite obvious power differentials – Frankfurt alone covered almost 75 per cent of all stock market trading in 1990 – one of the circle's 'unwritten rules', for example, was that some of the most attractive shares had to be traded at all exchanges.

Taken together, the German model of sectoral governance resembled self-regulated cartels embedded in the system of German federalism. Stock market actors and regional governments were joined together by a common interest in defending their sphere of influence against intervention by the federal government. For market actors, in particular for German banks, the model of sectoral self-regulation was a very comfortable one, since it required low regulatory effort. As the universal banks controlled the majority of seats in the self-regulating committees of the exchanges, in effect the community of producers of financial services themselves decided on the costs they were willing to take on for the sake of transparency and openness in their market transactions. Not surprisingly, insider trading was not criminalized, nor were disclosure rules established in order to ensure transparency in the issuance, registration and trading of securities.

The New Model

In the mid-1980s, a worldwide process of domestic financial market restructuring was set in motion. Reorganization partly aimed to modernize the infrastructure of stock exchange trading, but it was the regulatory framework of stock markets in particular that underwent profound transformation. Probably the most distinct feature of the financial services revolution was that the liberalization of market activities was accompanied by a tightening of the rules for investor protection (on the general point of freer markets and tighter rules, see S. Vogel 1996). In a large number of industrialized countries, systems of stock exchange governance underwent a process of 'institutionalization, codification and formalization' of rules (Moran 1991), together with the strengthened role of the state. Either regulatory tasks were delegated to newly founded independent agencies such as the Commission des Bourses (COB) in France, or regulatory activities were increasingly embedded in public law as in Britain.

Germany was the definite laggard in this process. In January 1992, Finance Minister Waigel announced a campaign to further promote Germany as a financial center (*Finanzplatz Deutschland*). The need for a new market supervisory body at the federal level was stressed, and further regulations were passed to protect against insider trading and ensure the equal treatment of shareholders. These decisions were basically the outcome of consultation with members of the Commission of Experts for Stock Exchange Matters, a body which advised the Ministry and represented banks, banking associations, politicians and academics in the field. These actors formed the core of a new coalition of globally oriented players which placed the need to meet international standards of regulation in the center of the debate. This 'Frankfurt coalition' was joined by the state government of Hesse, which from the beginning of the *Finanzplatz Deutschland* discussion had voted for a federal solution to the oversight problem modeled on the US Securities and Exchange Commission.

After a long and bitter turf battle with the other German *Länder*, which used their co-decision rights under stock exchange legislation to lobby for the establishment of a common supervisory agency, a new and complex regulatory structure was decided upon which reflects the kind of 'interlocking politics' characteristic of the German model of federalism (Scharpf et al. 1976). The crux of the new model was a supervisory agency for securities trading (*Bundesaufsichtsamt für den Wertpapierhandel*) under the jurisdiction of the Federal Ministry of Finance. The agency's tasks involve the surveillance of large share transactions and rules of conduct in securities trading. Moreover, the agency enforces a strict regime to control insider trading. The *Länder*'s supervisory powers over their regional exchanges were expanded, while the stock exchanges themselves lost power, as formerly self-regulated matters became the subject of federal supervision or were regulated by public law. In recent years, the state's role as regulator has been steadily expanded to include financial analysts and hedge funds in addition to stock exchanges, securities firms, banks and insurance companies. Auditors and listed firms are also likely to be added to these groups. The law on the supervision of financial statements passed in 2004 (*Bilanzkontrollgesetz*) established a system of 'self-regulation in the shadow of hierarchy' for listed firms. In this system, a private body is supposed to control audits and auditing practices. If this form of control fails, the financial regulator may intervene and investigate the books of a company (BMJ 2004; more in Lütz 2005).[1]

For its part, the stock exchange sector underwent a process of centralization as well as marketization driven by the big three universal banks (Deutsche Bank, Dresdner Bank and Commerzbank). In 1991, the large banks founded Deutsche Börse AG, a common joint-stock company which acts as an umbrella organization for the stock exchange sector. In the meantime, the 'Deutsche Börse Group' itself has become a global company that builds and operates trading, clearing and settlement systems; 80 per cent of Deutsche Börse's shares are held by foreign institutional investors. In 2005, 15 years after the crucial reform battles, the Frankfurt Stock Exchange is still the largest of the German exchanges, with a 90 per cent share of total turnover. Besides traditional floor trading, Frankfurt runs XETRA, one of the world's leading electronic trading platforms which is supposed to attract foreign investors by facilitating large share transactions and cross-border trading. The other seven regional exchanges are struggling to survive and compete by specializing in certain types of shares and by offering services for private investors and small to mid-sized regional firms.

Patterns of Reform

In general, the German regulatory framework would not have undergone this restructuring without financial globalization and the integration of the German financial marketplace in the global economy. In fact, large German banks were the drivers of reform on the domestic scene, but they were part of a broader, transnational modernization coalition which included foreign (mostly American) institutional investors, the US Securities and Exchange Commission (SEC), the German Federal Ministry of Finance as well as the state government of Hesse.

Institutional investors have become the major players, first on the American capital market and then on international securities markets. Between 1955 and 1975, pension and investment funds became the

---

[1] These legislative measures have to be seen against the background of the scandals which have occurred in firms like Parmalat or Enron and the proposal of the EU Commission to modernize the Company Law Directive on Statutory Audit.

largest investor group at the New York Stock Exchange (NYSE). With their size and importance steadily increasing since the 1970s, American investors have been able to extend their influence to foreign countries. As for the transformation of the regulatory framework in Germany, investors were joined by the SEC, which is considered to be the world's most reputable watchdog organization in capital markets (at least since the 1980s). The power of the SEC not only rests on the fact that it is the oldest regulatory agency in the securities sector, but also on the fact that the agency pursues a mission of being the 'investor's advocate' by upholding a regulatory model regarded as the most investor-oriented in the world. Given the fact that the American model of regulation imposes the highest costs on its domestic producers in terms of disclosure rules and transparency standards, the SEC had a strong interest in exporting it. Under conditions of increasingly internationalized markets, high regulatory standards could have turned into competitive disadvantages for US investment companies.

First, the SEC began working to intensify collaboration between national regulatory agencies using the instrument of bilateral Memoranda of Understanding (MOUs). The objective of these bilateral agreements is to ensure reciprocal assistance from the foreign regulatory agency in cases of cross-border fraud. This could include conducting investigations at the request of foreign agencies or obtaining documentary evidence from abroad. This kind of reciprocal exchange between two international watchdogs, however, is much easier if both are public authorities with the same competences and the same kind of autonomy from their market constituencies. In 1988, the SEC contacted Germany and requested assistance in the prosecution of two cases of insider trading in which German firms had apparently been involved. Since Germany had no legal procedure for cross-border investigations of this kind, it was unable to fulfill the request for collaboration. Signing an MOU with the SEC more or less imposed direct pressures on the foreign counterpart to bring its domestic system of sectoral supervision into line with US standards. Starting with Switzerland in 1982, the United Kingdom and Japan in 1986, the SEC had signed 20 MOUs worldwide by 1994. In almost all of these countries, MOUs with the SEC either preceded the establishment of new public regulatory agencies or followed shortly thereafter.

Second, the SEC forced foreign investment banks eager to sell their own products on the American markets to accept US standards of transparency. For example, the SEC prohibited the trading of German DAX options in the United States by arguing that they came from a market which operated under lower regulatory standards than those of the US. Although German banks still maintained that their model of self-regulation worked, they realized nonetheless that it had become a major liability in global competition for investors. In order to participate in the global game, it clearly became necessary to prove one's fairness and honesty as a financial firm by operating in a market under close state supervision. The state's new role is to ensure transparency, fairness and access to markets by criminalizing insider trading and by defining legal penalties for non-compliance with rules. This is not to say that public regulation always works or that private actors always follow the rules. Public oversight of the German capital market was meant to signal to foreign investors that they could rely on the soundness of regulation. This is why German banks had an interest in 'bringing the state back in' to the regulatory setting. Especially since 1990, this has become a significant goal.

All in all, regulatory change came about as horizontal, cross-border diffusion driven by regulatory competition and the political and economic power of the US. The dynamics of this process fit into what David Vogel describes as the 'California effect' (D. Vogel 1995): Regulatory competition can promote a 'race to the top' if the country which exports the higher regulatory standards is of considerable size and has a large domestic market. The trading partners are then forced to meet this standard in order to maintain or expand their export markets. In this case, both the market power of institutional investors and the bargaining power of the SEC in matters of regulation were instrumental in changing the preferences of the large German banks with regard to the domestic regulatory framework. It was only later that horizontal change was transformed into vertical pressure to download the more investor-oriented model by embedding it in European directives (Insider Trading [1989] and Investment Services [1993]).

4. THE CASE OF BANKING – FROM PUBLIC TO MIXED REGULATION

In banking, the state had always been part of the regulatory framework. Historically, the development of banks reflected the need to finance public expenditures for war or efforts to spur processes of monetary integration. In one way or another, banks were 'servants of the state'. Since banking failures could harm not only private customers and other firms, but also public finance in general, countries like the US, Great Britain and Germany extended government oversight powers over banks mostly in response to financial crises.

The Old Model

The characteristic feature of German banking regulation was that oversight competences were shared between a federal regulatory agency and peak associations representing the main German banking groups: private commercial banks, public savings banks and private cooperative banks. These three groups attempted to compete with each other in what is known as group competition (*Gruppenwettbewerb*), which refers to the fact that savings and cooperative banks did not compete with each other within their own groups. Instead, these banks are organized in formal associations and use cooperative arrangements within their respective groups to compete against other bank groups.

Associational self-regulation was established long before the federal state entered the regulatory scene. Historically, associations of savings banks and credit cooperatives developed around the mid-19th century, and from very early on they organized cross-subsidies and bailout operations within their group, acted as accountants for their member banks and ran some basic form of deposit insurance organization. In the wake of the banking crisis of the 1930s, the federal government made the first arrangements for federal banking regulation and supervision. The German Banking Act (*Kreditwesengesetz, KWG)* of December 1934 introduced norms of prudential regulation, some of which are still in place today. The law also institutionalized the Central Credit Committee (*Zentraler Kreditausschuss, ZKA*) as a coordination platform of the main banking associations. After the Second World War, the ZKA was re-established on a voluntary basis and became the platform for the different banking associations to agree upon standards of capital adequacy and liquidity before these were discussed with the federal regulatory agency. The ZKA enjoyed the status of a public body, as the German Banking Act (*KWG*) allows the associations be heard when capital adequacy and liquidity standards are to be revised.

In 1957, the central bank (*Bundesbank*) was established with the legal mandate to secure the stability of the currency. Unlike its Anglo-Saxon counterparts, the Bundesbank never perceived the 'lender of last resort' function as part of its mandate. Responsibility for banking supervision was shared by the Bundesbank and a new Federal Banking Supervisory Office (*Bundesaufsichtsamt für das Kreditwesen, BAKred*), a higher federal agency established under the jurisdiction of the Federal Ministry of Finance in 1961. Levels of capital adequacy and liquidity were negotiated in a well-practiced corporatist manner by the *BAKred* and the peak banking associations, while the monitoring and enforcement of these standards were largely delegated to the associations. For its part, the state practiced a legalized and basically off-site style of regulation without any interaction with individual banks in daily regulatory operations. On the other hand, the corporatist model of regulation ensured the equal treatment of all banks and low transaction costs, since the federal agency had no need for its own administrative substructure but was nevertheless able to impose uniform capital adequacy standards on the German banking market of about 3 000 banks (Lütz 2002, p. 128, and Lütz 2004).

The New Model

The German model of corporatist rule-making remained relatively untouched by financial globalization until the 1990s. The move towards a greater formalization of rules accompanying the European banking directives affected neither the structure nor the style of regulation, but only led to several revisions of the German Banking Act (*KWG)*.

However, the development of a multilevel system of rule-making with the EU and the Basel Committee at core decision-making levels in matters of banking regulation strengthened the position of the federal supervisory agency (*BAKred*) vis-à-vis the banking associations. The *BAKred* has turned into a 'gatekeeper' to higher levels of decision-making. The supervisor not only benefited from informational advantages, but was also able to better control the implementation of EU directives at home. From time to time, this has allowed the agency to push for a tighter implementation of EU directives than required (interviews with German banks and the *BAKred*).

However, the core challenge for the German form of corporatist standard-setting is the implementation of a more flexible and market-oriented model to calculate and buffer financial risks. This new model – known as 'Basel II' – is basically the outcome of negotiations in the Basel Committee. The new regulatory approach accords greater significance to highly differentiated instead of uniform regulatory solutions, to risk measurement and management based on internal or external rating assessments, to qualitative regulatory measures and to cooperation between public and private actors in particular. In this way, the approach entails a 'mixed' public-private form of regulation at the level of *individual* banks. Since this requires interactivity and flexibility in daily regulatory operations, it has a greater impact on regulatory culture and puts more pressure on countries to converge on certain 'best practices' in regulation than the former uniform approach. For Germany, 'Basel II' is a break with its national tradition of treating all banks equally through universally applied rules and regulations, a system upheld by corporatist traditions of power sharing between the federal supervisory agency and the three main banking associations, and upheld by a banking supervision system monopolized by lawyers.

Due to its lack of a rating tradition, Germany's banks and banking associations were under pressure to develop a rating scheme to calculate their credit risks. While the larger private banks prefer risk management techniques that are tailored to their individual needs, the associations of savings banks and credit cooperatives are still eager to provide 'club goods' (Buchanan) by setting up internal credit rating schemes for their members. While the regional banks (*Landesbanken*) have set up a collective 'rating provider' to develop internal rating procedures for wholesale business, the savings banks association (DSGV) runs a 'transparency committee' to define standards of risk measurement and to classify its member firms into different risk categories.

For its part, the state is now collaborating more closely with global players and reorganizing the supervisory structure to keep up with modeling and measurement specialists from the banking business. The federal banking regulator created a new department employing statisticians and economists who now collaborate with risk managers at the head offices of the major banks in Germany. The need to build up in-house expertise in risk management by hiring practitioners from the industry has also raised the question of a more flexible remuneration structure. The institutional answer to this problem was to found the *BAFin (Bundesanstalt für Finanzdienstleistungsaufsicht)* as a formal umbrella regulator for banking, capital markets and insurance in 2002. Unlike its British counterpart, the new agency is not independent, but still under the jurisdiction of the Federal Ministry of Finance. The three existing sectoral oversight bodies were not dissolved but became departments of the new regulator, and the division of regulatory tasks among them remains unchanged. Restructuring should allow for more flexible remuneration of the agency's staff, since the supervisor's funding is provided by the banks and no longer by the state (BMF 2001 and 2002).

At present, it remains to be seen what the implementation of Basel II will eventually mean for the large number of small and mid-sized German firms which used to rely on loans, mostly provided by public-sector banks. In general, we might expect Basel II to push banks to increase the differentiation of credit terms in line with the borrowers' creditworthiness. Since German public-sector banks will lose their government guarantees by July 2005 and thus expect to be assigned lower ratings, they are under pressure to cut risk-weighted assets and use capital more efficiently. It is likely that both commercial and public banks will concentrate on particularly lucrative business sectors and give lower priority to possible investments in longer-term credit relationships which represent less profitable lending. Lending terms and conditions will vary increasingly depending on the industrial sector, range of business and most importantly on the borrowers' own capital base (Deutsche Bundesbank 2002, pp. 44–5). The core challenge for small and mid-sized firms is to increase their own funds in order to be able to receive loans at acceptable interest rates (*Frankfurter Allgemeine Zeitung*, 13 October 2003, p. 22; 28 June 2004, p. 18). Against this backdrop, the new debate centers on alternative sources of company financing, such as private equity companies or mezzanine capital (more in Lütz 2005).

Patterns of Reform

Unlike in capital markets, regulatory change in banking came about through negotiation by regulators and central bank governors, who have increased their interaction with global market actors since the mid-1990s. The Basel Committee on Banking Supervision, which comprises central bankers and regulatory agencies from the Group of Ten (G-10) countries,[2] has to be considered the dominant coordinating body in matters of risk regulation. The Basel Committee issues recommendations with the character of 'soft law'. In the European Union, however, this soft law is transformed into statutory rules, since the Committee's recommendations serve as blueprints for core EU directives in prudential banking supervision. It is fair to say that multilateral coordination has a longer and probably more successful history in banking than in the capital market sector.

Coordination efforts have been driven by the failure of international banks and by recurring financial crises with which regulators and central banks have had to cope. Since banks tended to use formerly unknown loopholes in the regulatory safety net in order to circumvent rules which involved higher costs (e.g. the banking failures of Herstatt Bank in 1974; Franklin National Bank in 1975; Banco Ambrosiano in 1982; and Johnson Matthey in 1984), governments had a permanent incentive to deprive banks of any exit options through regulatory coordination. In this way, government representatives sought to pool sovereignty in order to define binding risk management rules with which their constituencies should comply. However, since unilateral reregulation could entail competitive disadvantages for national banks, countries with a highly internationalized domestic banking market (such as the UK) and those with large numbers of international banks (like the US) actively pushed the harmonization of rules forward.

In the mid-1990s, this pattern changed somewhat towards a wider inclusion of market actors in the process of rule definition at the level of the Basel Committee. The 'Group of Thirty' (G-30) and the Institute of International Finance (IIF) became more active in matters of risk management. The G-30 is a study group of high-ranking representatives from the banking business, the IIF a Washington-based association of the

[2] In fact, the G-10 consists of 13 states: Apart from the original members – Belgium, Canada, France, Germany, Italy, Japan, the Netherlands, Sweden, United Kingdom and United States – Switzerland, Luxembourg and Spain have joined the group in recent years.

world's largest banks which now represents 320 banks from 60 countries worldwide. The IIF was established during the debt crisis in the early 1980s to act as a type of early warning system by supplying banks with better information and risk analysis. Both organizations observe the market and agree, with increasing frequency, on desirable, self-imposed restrictions concerning risk management and accounting standards.[3] In September 1999, the IIF founded a 'Steering Committee on Regulatory Capital' representing risk managers of global players in order to comment on the various consultative papers issued by the Basel Committee.[4]

Against this backdrop of increasing institutionalization in private self-help organizations at the global level, it is not surprising that the representatives of these two organizations were also the ones to introduce into the debate the decisive elements of a new, rather qualitative and flexible approach to risk regulation in 1994: Banks themselves should be allowed to calculate capital adequacy ratios for derivative transactions based on their own computer models. The application of bank-specific models would promise to create capital requirements tailored to each bank's own loan portfolio and thereby save overall on capital reserves. It was no accident that this impulse came primarily from American banks such as J.P. Morgan and Chase Manhattan, which have long been active in securities trading and also possess the corresponding expertise with internal systems of risk measurement. Therefore, they expected to enjoy an international competitive edge if such models were quickly introduced to measure market risks (Hartmann 1996, pp. 37–8). Moreover, US regulatory agencies such as the Office of the Comptroller of the Currency (OCC) and the Federal Reserve Bank (Fed) had already experimented with rating-based techniques at the beginning of the 1990s in order to evaluate not only market risks but also credit risks (OCC 1997; Phillips 1996; Lütz 2002, pp. 264–7). Not surprisingly, it was the US regulatory agencies which then proposed to extend the flexible and rating-based risk management approach to all types of credit risk. Assessing and buffering financial risks exclusively on the basis of rating agencies' assessments would have privileged countries with large numbers of rated firms like the US. Countries without a rating tradition like Germany feared that they would run short of credit funds if banks had to hold back higher portions of own capital for loans to unrated firms, as was originally suggested. Between 1999 and 2000, negotiations at the level of the Basel Committee were characterized by struggles, particularly between Germany and the United States, on how to adapt the flexible, risk-based approach of

---

[3] On the role of the Group of Thirty and the IIF in shaping rules in global finance, see Tsingou and Porter in this volume.

[4] Handelsblatt, 13 April 2000, p. 25.

banking regulation to the needs of Continental countries without a rating tradition – a topic also hotly discussed at the annual meeting of the IIF in September 1999.[5] Against this background, it was seen as a success of the German negotiators that the Committee finally decided to allow banks to calculate risks and capital cushions based on their own internal ratings

Table 2.1 Reform Patterns in Germany

	Capital Market	**Banking**
Regulatory problem	Asymmetric information	Systemic risk
Old model of regulation	Private (federalist) self-regulation	Public regulation
New model of regulation	Public regulation	Mixed / public-private regulation
Function	Ensure transparency	Coping with complexity of financial risks
Reform coalition	US SEC /institutional investors / investment banks /German federal government	States /global banks
Convergence by	Regulatory competition ('California effect')	Harmonization /download of negotiated model

instead of only external ones. Germany did not have an internal rating tradition, but the large banks as well as the associations of savings banks and of credit cooperatives were maintaining 'credit records' to indicate the soundness of their clients. Based on these data, it was not particularly difficult for the associations to develop internal rating schemes and to classify clients into different risk categories. The case illustrates how national regulators and their domestic constituencies have allied either to shape the rule-setting process by shifting their own regulatory model to the global level (as in the case of the US) or to minimize the costs of rule-taking by adapting the global model to their own regulatory tradition (as in the case of Germany).

[5] Handelsblatt, 28 September 1999, p. 34; 29 September 1999, p. 39; FAZ, 28 September 1999, p. 33–4.

5. CONCLUSION

One lesson we can draw from these two case studies is that we cannot predict how regulatory problems will be tackled, what kinds of institutional frameworks or regulatory instruments will be chosen to deal with information or risk management problems, or how effective the chosen instruments will be. What we can do using the political economy approach to financial reform, however, is explain how institutional frameworks of regulation have evolved and which forces make them change.

Domestic frameworks of capital market and banking regulation reflect certain historical legacies to deal with regulatory problems, but it is probably more important that institutional equilibria also correspond to power relationships between state and market actors. Both public and private actors are in charge of sustaining, reproducing and restructuring systems of financial regulation.

Financial globalization has transformed the coalitions behind these domestic frameworks of regulation basically by changing the preferences of those market actors who benefit most from open and integrated financial markets (e.g. institutional investors and global banks). German banks which had defended the model of private capital market regulation for decades changed their mind when they realized that it would turn into a liability in global competition for institutional investors, thus they opted to 'bring the federal government in' to the system of sectoral oversight. In banking, sophisticated models of risk management and rating-based methods of measuring and buffering financial risks were not welcomed, but accepted by German large banks, as they had to economize on their own capital reserves in order to be able to compete head-to-head with their US counterparts.

In both cases, global banks joined forces with the government to modernize the regulatory setting. Federal regulators, central bank representatives as well as the Federal Ministry of Finance have to be considered the winners in regulatory restructuring – the regulatory bureaucracy has not only extended their oversight competences but also acts as a 'linking pin' to higher levels of regulatory decision-making which may occasionally create room for strategic maneuvering. In our two case studies, it was the federal state in particular that shaped and moderated the process of adapting to the global rules of the game, thereby 'internalizing globalization' pressures (Soederberg et al. 2005) in domestic reforms.

Regional actors such as the German *Länder* governments, regional stock exchanges, as well as small and mid-sized banks and companies either sought to slow down the process of regulatory reform substantially or did not participate in regulatory struggles at all. Nevertheless, the small and mid-sized firm segment has to bear the distributional consequences of adapting to global standards – regional stock exchanges are struggling to retain a market position which allows them to survive; the associations of savings banks and of credit cooperatives are eager to smooth adaptation pressures for their member banks by standardizing their internal rating schemes; and the extent to which Basel II will weaken the lending conditions of the German *Mittelstand* (mid-sized companies) remains to be seen. After all, financial globalization and the corresponding pattern of regulatory reform are highly selective and uneven processes.

REFERENCES

BMF (German Federal Ministry of Finance) (2001), *Gesetz über die integrierte Finanzdienstleistungsaufsicht (FINDAG) (Finanzdienstleistungsaufsichts-gesetz). Entwurf und Begründung.* Drucksache 14/7033, Berlin: BMF.

BMF (German Federal Ministry of Finance) (2002), *Grünes Licht für neue integrierte Finanzdienstleistungsaufsicht*, press release, 22 March, Berlin: BMF.

BMJ (German Federal Ministry of Justice) (2004), *Bilanzrechtsreform und Bilanzkontrolle stärken Unternehmensintegrität und Anlegerschutz*, press release, 21 April, Berlin: BMJ.

Coleman, William D. (1994), 'Keeping the Shotgun behind the Door. Governing the Securities Industry in Canada, the United Kingdom and the United States', in J. Rogers Hollingsworth, Philippe C. Schmitter and Wolfgang Streeck (eds), *Governing Capitalist Economies. Performance and Control of Economic Sectors*, New York and Oxford: Oxford University Press, pp. 244–69.

Coleman, William D. (1996), *Financial Services, Globalization and Domestic Policy Change: A Comparison of North America and the European Union.* London: Macmillan.

Deeg, Richard and Susanne Lütz (2000), 'Internationalization and Financial Federalism. The United States and Germany at the Crossroads?', *Comparative Political Studies*, **33** (3), 374–405.

Deutsche Bundesbank (2002), 'The development of bank lending to the private sector', *Monthly Report*, October, Frankfurt: Deutsche Bundesbank, 31–46.

DiMaggio, Paul J. and Walter W. Powell (1991), 'The Iron Cage Revisited: Institutional Isomorphism and Collective Rationality in Organizational Fields', in Walter W. Powell and Paul J. DiMaggio (eds), *The New Institutionalism in Organizational Analysis*, Chicago and London: University of Chicago Press, pp. 63–82.

Dyson, Kenneth and Klaus H. Goetz (2003), 'Living with Europe: Power, Constraint and Contestation', in Kenneth Dyson and Klaus H. Goetz (eds), *Germany, Europe and the Politics of Constraint*, Oxford and New York: Oxford University Press, pp. 3–35.

Goodhart, Charles et al. (1998), *Financial Regulation. Why, how and where now?* London: Routledge.

Hartmann, Philipp (1996), 'A Brief History of Value-at-Risk', *The Financial Regulator*, **1** (3), 37–40.

Helleiner, Eric (1994), *States and the Reemergence of Global Finance. From Bretton Woods to the 1990s,* Ithaca: Cornell University Press.

Héritier, Adrienne, Christoph Knill and Susanne Mingers (1996), *Ringing the Changes in Europe. Regulatory Competition and the Transformation of the State*, Berlin: de Gruyter.

Herring, Richard, J. and Robert E. Litan (1995), *Financial Regulation in the Global Economy*, Washington, DC: The Brookings Institution.

Kapstein, Ethan B. (1996), *Governing the Global Economy. International Finance and the State*, 2nd edition, Cambridge and London: Harvard University Press.

Kay, John and John Vickers (1988), 'Regulatory Reform in Britain', *Economic Policy,* **7** (8), 285–351.

Knight, Jack (1992), *Institutions and Social Conflict*, New York: Cambridge University Press.

Krasner, Stephen D. (ed.) (1983), *International Regimes*, Ithaca: Cornell University Press.

Lütz, Susanne (1998), 'The revival of the nation-state? Stock exchange regulation in an era of globalized financial markets', *Journal of European Public Policy*, **5** (1), 153–68.

Lütz, Susanne (2002), *Der Staat und die Globalisierung von Finanzmärkten. Regulative Politik in Deutschland, Großbritannien und den USA*, Frankfurt am Main: Campus.

Lütz, Susanne (2004), 'Convergence Within National Diversity: The Regulatory State in Finance', *Journal of Public Policy*, **24** (2), 169–97.

Lütz, Susanne (2005), 'The Finance Sector in Transition: A Motor for Economic Reform?', in Kenneth Dyson and Stephen Padgett (eds), *The Politics of Economic Reform in Germany: Global, Rhineland or Hybrid Capitalism?*, Special Issue of *German Politics*, 14 (2), 140–56.

Moran, Michael (1991), *The Politics of the Financial Services Revolution. The USA, UK and Japan*, New York: St. Martin's Press.

Office of the Comptroller of the Currency (OCC) (1997), *Strategic Plan 1997–2002*, Washington, DC: OCC.

Organisation for Economic Cooperation and Development (OECD) (1983), *The Internalisation of Banking*, Paris: OECD.

Peltzman, Sam (1976), 'Toward a More General Theory of Regulation', *Journal of Law and Economics,* **19** (2), 211–40.

Phillips, Susan (1996), 'The Federal Reserve's Approach to Risk Management', *Journal of Lending and Credit Risk Management*, 6, 30–6.

Porter, Tony (2004), *Private Authority, Technical Authority, and the Globalization of Accounting Standards*, paper presented at the ARCCGOR workshop on 17–18 December 2004, Vrije Universiteit Amsterdam.

Radaelli, Claudio M. (2003), 'The Europeanization of Public Policy', in Kevin Featherstone and Claudio M. Radaelli (eds), *The Politics of Europeanization*, Oxford: Oxford University Press, pp. 27–56.

Reinicke, Wolfgang H. (1995), *Banking, Politics and Global Finance. American Commercial Banks and Regulatory Change 1980–1990*, Aldershot, UK and Brookfield, US: Edward Elgar.

Ruggie, John G. (ed.) (1993), *Multilateralism Matters: The Theory and Praxis of an Institutional Form*, New York: Columbia University Press.

Scharpf, Fritz W., Bernd Reissert and Fritz Schnabel (1976), *Politikverflechtung*, Königstein am Taunus: Athenäum.
Slaughter, Anne-Marie (2004), *A New World Order*, Princeton and Oxford: Princeton University Press.
Sobel, Andrew C. (1994), *Domestic Choices, International Markets. Dismantling National Barriers and Liberalizing Securities Markets*, Ann Arbor: University of Michigan Press.
Soederberg, Susanne, Georg Menz and Philip G. Cerny (eds) (2005), *Internalizing Globalization: The Rise of Neoliberalism and the Erosion of National Models of Capitalism*, London: Palgrave (forthcoming).
Stigler, George J. (1971), 'The Theory of Economic Regulation', *Bell Journal of Economics and Management Science*, 2, 1–21.
Strange, Susan (1996), *The Retreat of the State. The Diffusion of Power in the World Economy*, Cambridge: Cambridge University Press.
Strange, Susan (1998), *Mad Money. When Markets Outgrow Governments*, Ann Arbor: University of Michigan Press.
Underhill, Geoffrey R.D. (2003), 'States, markets and governance for emerging market economies: private interests, the public good and the legitimacy of the development process', *International Affairs*, **79** (4), 755–81.
Vogel, David (1995), *Trading Up. Consumer and Environmental Regulation in a Global Economy*, Cambridge: Harvard University Press.
Vogel, Stephen K. (1996), *Freer Markets, More Rules: Regulatory Reform in Advanced Industrial Countries*, Ithaca: Cornell University Press.

3. Who Governs? Economic Governance Mechanisms and Financial Market Regulation

Brigitte Unger

Who governs financial markets and financial market reforms? Which mechanisms are involved? And who plans or can be held responsible for the outcomes which ultimately not only affect the financial sector itself but also the real sector in the form of altered income distribution or changes in unemployment, to name but two examples? Outcomes that include or exclude the interests of different parts of society and increase or decrease the incomes and opportunities of various groups or individuals.

The financial governance debate stemming from international relations (IR) and international political economy (IPE) has addressed these issues (for a survey, see Underhill in this volume). One advantage of this debate is that it analyzes the complexity of global financial aspects as well as the overlapping structures of multi-level and global financial governance. It analyzes regulatory reforms in specific financial sub-sectors and stresses the democracy deficits that might accompany the new forms of governance at the global level.

However, the debate also has some deficiencies. In the following, three major weaknesses of the governance debate in general and of financial governance in particular will be addressed. First of all, the concept of governance is still vague. Section 1 thus gives a short overview of concepts of governance and shows that financial governance definitions have converged, but this has also reduced the richness of the original concept of economic governance. Today, every international agreement seems to have to do with some kind of network governance or private-sector governance. And every governance mechanism is supposed to be able to provide all kinds of positive outcomes for good governance.

Second, the economic governance literature originally drew a clear distinction between different types of governance and identified their pros and cons, the interests they included and excluded, the stability they provided, etc. In today's financial governance literature there are either only two types of governance, the market and the state, or public and private authorities, or several types of governance in a strange combination. The types of economic governance have become blurred. Since the question of who determines the outcome and whose interests are being pursued was central to the original economic governance debate in comparative political science, which clearly distinguished between labor and capital interests, it seems worthwhile to bring back to mind the origins of this debate. Combining IR and IPE literature with the original thoughts from the economic governance debate in comparative political science therefore appears to be a promising way to bring important elements back into the debate. Section 2 shows how the original types of economic governance, the market, communities, networks, associations and the state are reduced in today's financial governance literature. A major deficiency of this development is the fact that power relations (i.e. the question of who governs) are no longer addressed adequately.

This brings us to the third deficiency of financial governance literature, which will be explored in Section 3. Who governs financial markets and financial regulatory reforms? In the financial governance literature, it looks as if it were nobody. A few actors from the private and the public sector negotiate issues, and this somehow has to be acceptable to the public. Some argue that the state has withdrawn and that it is the private sector which governs, but who do they mean? Others maintain that the state negotiates with the private sector and that the negotiations lead to some joint outcome. But who, then, determines policy? Unfortunately, Section 4 cannot give a definite answer to this question, but it will elucidate seven approaches which might be useful in the future for exploring who governs financial markets.

1. GOVERNANCE – IS THERE ANY CONVERGENCE OF CONCEPTS? AT WHAT COST?

Today, the term 'governance' is used with different connotations in a wide variety of fields and disciplines. Underhill (in this volume) gives a survey of the historical development of governance concepts in economics (focusing mainly on the regulation theory that started with Arrow and Stigler, and the classical political economy theories of Smith and Marx) and in contemporary political science (focusing mainly on rational choice approaches and international political economy as pursued by Coase and Olson, as well as international relations approaches, including his own). In a survey that focuses less on historical development than on the use and meaning of the term in different disciplines and sub-disciplines, Hirst (2000) distinguishes five versions of 'governance', and Kersbergen and van Waarden (2004) extend this approach to find even nine different meanings of the term.

From the latter work, one can extract three major meanings of governance: good governance, governing without government and economic governance.

1.1 Good Governance

Recently the international relations term 'good governance' has been used increasingly in the field of development, where the World Bank and other international organizations are stressing sound or good governance. Bad governance, such as wasteful public spending, is being increasingly regarded as one of the root causes of all evil within our societies. Major donors and international financial institutions are increasingly basing their aid and loans on the condition that reforms are undertaken to ensure 'good governance'. Good governance has eight main characteristics: It is participatory, consensus-oriented, accountable, transparent, responsive, effective and efficient, equitable and inclusive, and it follows the rule of law. It assures that corruption is minimized, that the views of minorities are taken into account and that the voices of the most vulnerable ones in society are heard in decision-making (adapted from UNESCAP 2004).

Kersbergen and van Waarden (2004, p. 147) define corporate governance as 'good governance in the private sector'. The concept of 'corporate governance', which originally dealt with the enterprise, its internal structure and its transactions with its environment (see Unger 1997, Chapter 5; Lütz 2003, p. 5) deals with the accountability of management (Hirst 2000, p. 17). Corporate governance issues in the financial sector include, for example, whether managers have strong incentives to act in the shareholders' interest (fiduciary duty), the channels through which shareholders monitor and influence managers, the type of elections for the board of directors, the number of external directors, etc. (see, for example, Amable 2004, p. 24). While corporate governance brought good governance practices to the business sector, 'good governance in the public sector' can be found in new public management literature, which tries to introduce good governance into public organizations.

1.2 Governance without government

This concept also stems from international relations and refers to the possibility of governing without a government. International politics is perceived as cooperation between independent states without a hierarchy. 'The international system is characterized by an anarchy of competing interdependent states that acknowledge no authority other than their own' (Kersbergen and van Waarden 2004, p. 145).

Another kind of governance without government is the self-organization of societies and communities. In her book *Governing the Commons*, Elinor Ostrom (1990) gives an impressive empirical overview of how different societies in different parts of the world have organized themselves in order to deal with the tragedy of the commons problem.

1.3 Economic Governance

The idea of economic governance is that markets are not spontaneous social orders but have to be created and maintained by institutions. Societies have produced a variety of institutions to govern economic transactions. Developed in the field of comparative political science, economic governance literature distinguishes different mechanisms of governance and analyzes their advantages and disadvantages for the economic performance of a country.

Since the seminal paper of Streeck and Schmitter (1985), 'economic governance' has become a popular term not only in political science but also in sociology and economics. It has branched off into many other fields in addition to labor relations and corporate relations, where it was originally developed. Sectoral governance, regional governance, supranational and global governance concepts eventually appeared as well.

Globalization has challenged the rather closed 'economy and politics' approach of economic governance. How do national actors and institutions react to global challenges? With globalization and the extension of the economic governance debate to IR and IPE literature, some major changes and modifications vis-à-vis the original economic governance debate have arisen.

With globalization, the problem of accountability also emerged. At the nation-state level, when the state delegates tasks to private authority, this is normally backed up by a rescindable mandate from the state. Thus, if citizens are affected negatively by the actions of private authorities, governments can hold these authorities accountable (Coleman and Porter 2000, p. 382). However, at the global level there is no such government.

The term '*multi-level governance*' was introduced in order to point out the co-existence of supranational (e.g. European), national and sub-national (regional) levels in a complex web of permanent interaction (Grossman 2005, p. 130).

1.4 Convergence in the Definitions of Governance?

Though the controversy surrounding the concept rumbles on, there seems to be some agreement nowadays that governance refers to the institutions, mechanisms or processes backed by political power and/or authority which allow an activity or set of activities to be controlled, influenced or directed in the collective interest (Commission on Global Governance 1995; Baker, Hudson and Woodward 2005, p. 5).

Kersbergen and van Waarden (2004, p. 151) also find some common characteristics in all the definitions mentioned above: First of all, the approach is pluricentric rather than multicentric (based on the market) or unicentric (based on the state). Governance deals with different forms and mechanisms of governance. Second, networks play an important role. Lately, the term '*network governance*' has even appeared in the EU (see Eising and Kohler-Koch 1999). Third, one can identify a clear emphasis on the processes of governing or functions as opposed to the structures of government. These processes are relatively similar in the public and private sectors and relate to negotiations, accommodation, concertation, cooperation and alliance formation rather than the traditional processes of coercion, command and control.

There seems to be some convergence in the definitions of governance. However, this convergence has had its costs. In the economic governance literature, there was originally a clear distinction between different types of governance, their pros and cons, the interests they included and excluded, the stability they provided, etc. Over time, these clear distinctions have become blurred. Today, every international agreement seems to have to do with some kind of network governance. And every governance mechanism is supposed to be able to provide all kinds of positive outcomes for good governance.

From an economic governance perspective, it makes a difference whether associations govern finance or networks of bankers, and the preconditions for good governance seem more like a child's Christmas wish list than a feasible concept. Good governance does not seem to be aware of the trade-offs between different institutions. A governance mechanism which provides consensus, most prominently associational governance in some neocorporatist setting, will not be transparent and participatory. A governance mechanism which is efficient and inclusive, such as the market, will not be very equitable.

It therefore seems worthwhile to remember the types of governance that have been mentioned in Streeck and Schmitter's seminal paper on economic governance and to describe their advantages and disadvantages.

2. ECONOMIC GOVERNANCE AND WHAT IT HAS LOST IN TODAY'S FINANCIAL GOVERNANCE DEBATE

2.1 The Original Economic Governance Debate in Comparative Political Science

A key feature of the 'economic governance' debate, initiated by Streeck and Schmitter (1985, 1985a) and extended by Hollingsworth, Schmitter and Streeck (1994), Powell (1996), and Boyer and Hollingsworth (1997), is that it regards the distinction between the state and the market or between the public sector and the private sector as insufficient for understanding who and what determines which economic and political activities take place in a society. In order to understand public policy, the antinomy of the state versus the market has to be augmented by a variety of 'governance mechanisms' between the market and the state (Streeck and Schmitter 1985). The debate originally stemmed from labor relations and systems of capitalist production, hence from real sector issues.

Building on typologies created earlier by Williamson (1975), Ouchi (1980), Streeck and Schmitter (1985) as well as Hollingsworth, Schmitter and Streeck (1994), we can distinguish the following governance mechanisms in an economy:

- the market;
- communities or clans, that is, informal groups which are based on primary relations such as the family and in which 'trust' is an important lubricant;
- networks, which can be formal and informal;
- associations, a more formal and goal-oriented form of social cooperation as compared to communities;
- the state.

This list of governance mechanisms can be extended to include firms (see, for example, Lütz 2003) and courts (van Waarden 2004).

Common to all these governance mechanisms is the fact that they are forms of organized cooperation. However, they differ in a number of dimensions, and these differences can be important for their performance and their capacity to change and initiate reforms. For example, some are better able to make fast decisions, while others are more apt to reduce uncertainty and create stability. They also differ with regard to the groups and interests they include and exclude in the decision-making process.

Table 3.1 lists the main differences between the five types of economic governance. Except for the state, all governance mechanisms –

associations, networks, communities and the market – are 'private' and consist of self-governing bodies. However, the state often delegates tasks to associations and sometimes also to networks, thus making them some kind of semi-public entities. Given the quite different ways in which governance mechanisms function, it is important to keep their special features distinct from each other. Classifying them all as 'private' without pointing out their different capacities, for example to negotiate and implement reforms, would lead to a loss of important information.

The approach was originally designed for a closed economy and for analyzing how governance mechanisms change in a country when it is challenged from abroad, for example due to increased internationalization. When economic governance is applied at an international or global level, the category 'state' should become a supranational state, which still retains all the features described for a state but can also turn into a confederation of nation-states or a group of intergovernmental negotiators. It is the latter which poses problems for analysis. Is it indeed governance without government, since there is no supranational authority to steer, and since every state can back out at will in order to retain its national authority (see, for example, the IPE literature of Susan Strange)? Or is it a network of state agents who meet and negotiate as private agents do, with the state taking a new function as negotiator in the state-market condominium (see, for example, Underhill in this volume)? Or is it a new form of hybrid supranational state (Coleman and Porter 2000)?

Depending on the perspective taken in analysis, the issue of whose interests are represented and whose are left out will differ, as will the governance mechanism studied.

The table below distinguishes five economic governance mechanisms on the basis of sixteen criteria. All of these five mechanisms are somehow involved in financial governance, but to different degrees.

In order to analyze financial deregulation and re-regulatory reforms, especially those which aim for prudential finance (as opposed to reforms aiming to liberalize finance; see Coleman and Porter 2000), it seems important to highlight those characteristics which are significant for creating stability and trust, to highlight which governance mechanisms are more able to provide long-term stability, and to correct and prevent market failures related to long-term inefficiencies in the market (see Traxler and Unger 1994).

The *state* (Table 3.1, Column 2) is characterized by hierarchical control; it can give orders and acts through bureaucratic agencies. In addition to other functions, the state can use coercion in order to implement its policies. At the national level, central banks are an important institution representing the state in financial governance. When several states or central banks have to reach an intergovernmental agreement or sign a treaty, they still have the power of coercion at the national level, but a global authority is still necessary for the hierarchical control of cross-border transactions. Since such an authority is often lacking in international relations, the literature on the international political economy was inclined to assume a withdrawal of the state (see Strange 1996). However, as Underhill convincingly shows in this volume, a more refined picture of the changed role of the state has to be drawn instead of leaving the state out of the analysis.

The state can delegate tasks to *interest associations* (Table 3.1, Column 3), which represent the interests of their members. Business associations represent firms and are often grouped by economic sector, while trade unions represent workers and employees. Groups with usually conflicting interests have to find compromises. Concertation is the dominant coordination principle. Interest associations are usually more familiar with specific complex issues than state agents, and they can also help to increase the acceptance of unpopular reforms among their members by developing convincing arguments. It is expertise and the mutual recognition of interests that make interest associations a powerful semi-public governance mechanism which often relieves the state of unpopular tasks (see Porter in this volume for a description of the role of associations in financial governance).

Networks can take many different forms, such as firms pooling their resources for joint research and innovation, supplier chains for production, or elite groups contacting each other occasionally. In global finance, such groups include networks of central bankers, for example. A common feature of all networks is that the dominant principle of coordination is reciprocity. The other participants have some resources (such as tacit knowledge) or intangible goods (such as connections) which make cooperation worthwhile (see Table 3.1, Column 4). Viewed from an actor-centered perspective, intergovernmental groups with supranational authority such as the G-20, which consists of finance ministers and central bankers from various countries, now also operate in the form of a network. These are networks of public policy organizations. Networks of private organizations (such as banking networks) and networks of public and private organizations are even more common today. The state now delegates tasks not only to associations but also to networks.

Communities such as families, tribes and clans are based on spontaneous solidarity as the coordination principle. Esteem and honor form the medium of exchange (see Table 3.1, Column 5). In particular, a lot of underground banking is governed by transnational networks. Eventually, these networks, which are unregulated and unchecked, were (and still are) used as a channel for money laundering and terrorist financing (see Unger et al. 2005).

A new form of community with increasing importance in a global world is that of epistemic communities (see van Waarden and Drahos 2002). An epistemic community is defined as a network of professionals with recognized expertise and competence in a particular domain and an authoritative claim to policy-relevant knowledge within that domain or issue area (Haas 1992, p. 3, quoted in van Waarden and Drahos 2002). But epistemic communities are more than just networks. They share the same culture, the same norms and values, and the same symbols – the characteristics typical of a community. Epistemic communities consist of specialists and experts trained at the same universities and schools who share a common understanding of 'technical' matters to be resolved. They share a common world view (episteme) made up of the following:

1. a shared set of normative beliefs;
2. shared causal beliefs with regard to the linkage between policy actions and desired outcomes;
3. a consensual knowledge base built on shared notions of validity, that is, clear criteria for validating knowledge in their field;
4. a common set of practices associated with a set of problems to which their professional competence is directed (Haas 1992, p. 3, quoted in van Waarden and Drahos 2002).

The increasing complexity of fields such as finance amplifies the need for such specialists. This community functions as a channel of information exchange, learning and imitation, and as an important channel for the convergence of ideas.

The *market* (consisting of firms and buyers) or the political market (consisting of parties and voters) works through competition and uses money or votes as a medium of exchange (see Table 3.1, Column 6). Examples in global finance include international banks or the stock market.

The 'lubricant' which allows these five governance mechanisms to work is the predominant resource which they have and which distinguishes them from each other. While the state has legitimate control over the means of coercion, associations are institutionalized and recognized forms of representation of interests. In order for networks to function, it is the complementarity of resources that makes the other partners indispensable. Communities are based on trust and inherited status, whereas the market is based on calculative rationality.

For prudential financial reforms, an important factor is that these five governance mechanisms differ in their capacity to create regulations that reduce uncertainty. Van Waarden (2004) composes an ordinal scale of the capacity to reduce uncertainty in economic governance mechanisms;

the scale consists of the three organizational components listed under B in Table 3.1.

As one moves further from right to left in Table 3.1, that is, from the market toward the state, the governance mechanisms have a greater capacity for creating and maintaining more specific rules and regulations to reduce risk and uncertainty. This progression can be seen as an ordinal ranking from a weaker to a stronger capacity for reducing uncertainty (van Waarden 2004, p. 12).

With regard to the type of goods produced, only the market produces private goods, whereas all other economic governance mechanisms can produce some kind of collective (public) or club (semi-public) goods. The danger with networks (and depending on the type, also with associations) is that they might produce club goods only for their members and not produce (or possibly under-produce) public goods where one cannot exclude non-members from consumption. Financial stability is typically a public good where no one can be excluded from consumption. Therefore, it is important that the network members' benefits from the public good of prudential financial regulation are so large that they are willing to bear the costs of regulation on their own.

The advantages and disadvantages provided by each economic governance mechanism differ (see Table 3.1). Each governance mechanism excludes specific groups and people, and thus does not represent their interests. The state excludes people outside its territory. Associations very often tend to exclude the interests of non-members, in particular those of consumers. Financial associations deal with the interests of financial institutions, but not with those of the financial consumer (see Porter in this volume). Networks tend to forget about taxpayers, consumers and voters. The market allows everyone to participate, except those with no money.

The boundaries of who is in and who is out are clear for the state, the market and associations, but less so for networks and communities.

As a result, it should make a difference whether associations, networks or communities govern global finance. The public-private/state-market distinctions abstract too much from the differentiation of various private economic governance principles, which differ in communities, associations, networks and corporate hierarchies. And these differences have consequences for the interests served by policy and regulations. Governance mechanisms affect whether there is a symmetry (an egalitarian, public interest which serves all), or a particular bias in policy, in regulation, and in the rules that regulate international financial markets.

Table 3.1 Properties of different governance mechanisms

Criteria	State	Association	Network	Community/ Clan	Market
A. Coordination					
Dominant principle of coordination	Hierarchical control, orders	Inter- and intra-organizational concertation	Reciprocity	Spontaneous solidarity	Competition
Predominant collective actor	Bureaucratic agencies	Interest associations	Firms, elite groups	Families, tribes, etc.	Firms/ parties
Dominant medium of exchange	Coercion	Mutual recognition	Tacit knowledge, intangible goods	Esteem	Money/ votes
Predominant resources	Legitimate control over the means of coercion	Institutionalized forms of representation	Complementary resources (knowledge, know-how, goods)	Trust, inherited status	Calculative rationality
B. Organization					
Form of organization	Formal	Formal	Informal or formal	Informal	Informal
Form of organization	Vertical	Horizontal	Horizontal or vertical	Horizontal	Horizontal
Type of organization	Public	Private	Private	Private	Private

Table 3.1 (cont.)

Criteria	State	Association	Network	Community/ Clan	Market
C. Function					
Capacity to reduce uncertainty	Very high	High	Medium	Low	Very low
Type of goods	Collective goods	Club goods or collective goods	Club goods or collective goods	Collective goods	Private goods
Advantages	External security, equitable and predictable treatment	Less class exploitation, social peace, symmetric distribution of benefits, expertise	Flexibility, learning process possible, expertise	Mutual affection, collective identity	Material prosperity, efficient allocation, low transaction costs
Disadvantages	Government failure, bureaucracy, oligarchy of political leaders	Oligarchy of the peak of the association, exclusion of non-members, lack of transparency	Exclusion, tendency to form cartels	Inefficiency, nepotism	Market failures such as externalities, under-provision of collective goods
D. Inclusion/Exclusion					
Principal line of cleavage	Rulers vs. ruled	Members vs. association leaders	Club members vs. non-members	Natives vs. foreigners	Sellers vs. buyers
Groups excluded	People outside the state territory	Consumers	Taxpayers, consumers, voters	Foreigners, people not born within the community	Those without money. For the rest, individual property rights make participation possible.
Degree of inclusion	Very high	High	Low	Low	Very high
Clarity of boundaries	Clear	Clear	Vague	Vague	Clear

Source: Streeck and Schmitter (1985, pp. 5 and 9), Unger (1997, Chapter 5), Lütz (2003, p. 12) and van Waarden (2004, p. 12).

2.2 Blurred Distinction between Economic Governance Mechanisms

It therefore seems worthwhile to look at the debate on financial governance and to try to link it to the original economic governance literature. With regard to financial governance mechanisms, five categories of 'authorities' were identified in the literature (see Baker et al. 2005, p. 8):

- the nation-state;
- international multilateral institutions (IMF, World Bank, G-7, G-20, etc.) whose membership consists of states;
- trans-governmental regulatory networks (Basel Committee on Banking Supervision, International Organization of Securities Commissions) which are composed of national regulatory agencies working in a given specialist area of financial governance;
- regional regulatory cooperation (linked to regional financial spaces, EU);
- private authority, including but not reducible to 'the market' (private banks, industry associations such as the International Council of Securities Associations formed in 1988, which now constitutes a framework of rules governing global securities transactions).

These five 'authorities' have the (perceived) *right* to act and can exercise 'structural power' if they also have *the capacity* to act (Baker et al. 2005, p. 8).

If we compare these five mechanisms to the ones in the original economic governance debate, only the nation-state seems to have survived, but with declining importance.

Many financial governance approaches underline the weakening of the state through globalization (for an overview, see Grossman 2005, p. 130; Eising and Kohler-Koch 1994; Marks et al. 1996). Furthermore, they proclaim the structural power of finance, its hegemonic position within societal decision-making structures, and as a consequence the predominance of neo-liberalism.

The governance mechanisms of networks and communities have been diluted in various kinds of multilateral, trans-governmental and regional regulatory networks. In addition, by including not only firms but also associations, the governance mechanism of the market has been enlarged to the category of private authority.

Governance *of* finance, that is, the governance of the financial sector, and governance *by* finance due to the predominant role of the financial sector in society (Hudson 2005, pp. 69f) both seem to display the characteristics of market governance or of network governance. The governance mechanisms of 'private authority' and 'networks' dominate the web of permanent interaction in multi-level governance.

Ironically, many of the multi-level governance approaches deal solely with formal public structures of authority. 'The study of multi-level governance has been hijacked by state centered approaches that have habitually conflated multi-level governance with multi-level government' (Baker et al. 2005, p. 15).

What has been lost in the financial governance debate is a clear distinction between types of governance. It has to be expected that the private authority of a 'bank' will behave differently from the private authority of an 'international association', and that the two will behave differently when they sit together in some form of network in order to negotiate securities matters. The distinction between the original types of governance is important for the speed and stability of reforms as well as for accountability, among other things. To give an example: an informal network will be more likely to carry out fast and radical reforms than an association. The latter is a formal organization which has to follow all kinds of procedures and is accountable to its members, whereas a network can form and dissolve easily and is only accountable to itself.

3. THE FINANCIAL GOVERNANCE DEBATE FROM AN ECONOMIC GOVERNANCE PERSPECTIVE

3.1 Governance in a 'State-Market Relationship'

In international relations approaches, there are basically only two opposing or concerting actors: the state and the private sector or the state and the market.

It is either argued that the state-market relationship has changed, that states have been rendered powerless by international capital flows, and that governance through market mechanisms dominates financial matters; or that the market has been missing in previous multi-level governance approaches, and that it was only about governance through governments (Baker et al. 2005).

Finally, the market seems to have dominated the debate on financial governance. The state has delegated a number of tasks to private bodies, which finally took over and led to a retreat of the state, as argued by Strange (1996). In the end, the state was once again lost in the debate.

Therefore, in a courageous attempt to bring the state back into the financial governance debate, Underhill created the concept of the state-market condominium. He argues against the dichotomy of state versus market. 'The relationship (between market and state) is typically portrayed as one of interdependent antagonism, where public, political logic pulls one way and private, market-driven logic pulls the other. Such an image is rooted in the 19th century divorce between economics and the other social sciences' (Underhill and Zhang 2005, p. 6). Instead, 'the concept of the state-market condominium is proposed as an alternative approach, . . . states and markets are viewed as an integrated ensemble of governance . . . the central claim is that the state-market condominium is greater than its state-market parts and that the outcomes in terms of governance are significantly different from the preferences of either as identifiable agents' (Underhill and Zhang 2005, pp. 1f).

With this, Underhill also wants to stop the eternal debate on whether the market dominates the state or the state dominates the market, that is, whether there is a primacy of policy or not.

Underhill does so by making politics an endogenous variable. 'Different layers of political institutions can fulfill the "state" function over time, and we should not misconceive the identifiable institutional/organizational structures of the state as a phenomenon external to the dynamics of the market, in whichever form the latter may be found' (Underhill in this volume, p. 22).

Conceptually, in an actor-centered approach political agents and economic agents (i.e. individuals) meet in a condominium. Depending on their individual skills and power, one day the political agent may get a larger piece of the pie, or a larger 'bedroom in the condominium', and on another day the economic agent might get the larger bedroom. The political and the economic agents have become equal partners in the condominium negotiating game. One reacts to the other, they are interdependent, and they each have to pay part of the rent.

The great advantage of such an approach is that it demonstrates that politics reacts to economics and vice versa. It is a dynamic approach which shows that politics reacts to changes in the economy and vice versa, which again leads to changes in politics itself. However – and this seems to be the problem with this kind of approach – what then is the exogenous variable? It does not seem to be economics, and it no longer seems to be politics. But then who or what governs?

The actor-centered approach is reminiscent of economics, where utility-maximizing and profit-maximizing individuals meet at the marketplace to buy and sell. Friedrich von Hayek's old question of how they could know the market clearing price prior to their transaction, and how the market price could already include all information before the transaction has taken place, was resolved by simply assuming a simultaneous world. The question of whether the market price determines the quantities bought and sold or whether the quantities bought and sold determine the market price, hence the question of which is the exogenous variable, went on for a while in economics and was answered in a pragmatic manner. Walras' model, which considers the price exogenous, eventually prevailed, but Menger's supply and demand schedule (*das Mengersche Kreuz*), which considers the price endogenous, is still the graph used to explain Walras' results. This is not only done to confuse students and to challenge the smart ones, but also because with the assumption of simultaneity it does not matter which variable comes first.

Who is the Walrasian auctioneer in IR or in IPE? If politics and economics are determined simultaneously, it does not matter which one comes first. It does not matter whether political interests or economic interests come first, nor does it make a difference which actor in the private sector has a say, whether it is a representative of firms, a representative of associations, or an actor in networks. They are all individuals engaging in some kind of interdependent financial negotiation game. Which actor has a say might only affect the outcome of the game, since some actors have more power than others and might negotiate a larger share of the condominium, but it does not affect the game itself. The condominium itself is exogenous, it is given, as are the preferences of the actors in the state-market bargaining condominium. The 'power' of the actors is reduced to the weight of their voices in the negotiation game.

Changes occur when power relations change or when preferences change. 'In such a model, change occurs simultaneously through the process of economic competition among firms on the one hand, and the policy and regulatory processes mediated by the institutions of the state on the other' (Underhill in this volume, p. 21).

But where is the Leviathan, the designer of the condominium, the one who shapes political preferences, and where is policy in this approach? The state-market condominium is a model that nests many different power constellations of markets and policy in financial governance. But it is indecisive in the crucial question of whether politics takes precedence over economics or vice versa. Hence, it does not help to explain the driving forces behind regulatory change.

3.2 The State as a Bargaining State

Globalization leads to an increase in the importance of 'technical' private authorities. The growth of technical and private authority has traditionally been legitimized by claims that these matters are not political and therefore do not need to be integrated into democratic processes. Hence, legal procedures are devised to safeguard the public interest, providing recourse for citizens who are the victims of technical errors. These procedures also seek to segregate technical or scientific matters from political questions. But this division between private and technical matters and public policy concerns is becoming increasingly ambiguous (Coleman and Porter 2000, p. 387).

New supranational authorities are emerging. However, they are not focused on policy, but on technical matters. This technical character and the emphasis on procedures is typical of financial governance. With regard to prudential regulation, that is, rules that aim to limit the likelihood of financial firms' failure and to prevent financial crisis, the Basel Committee on Banking Supervision (BCBS) and similar committees based in the Bank for International Settlements (BIS) provide a flow of high-quality technical reports. Their analysis has clarified the nature of international financial risk. Their work has also contributed to developing recognized best practices for regulators responding to these risks (Coleman and Porter 2000, p. 391).

In 1999, the G-7 set up a BIS-based Financial Stability Forum consisting of 21 G-7 national representatives and 14 representatives from international public institutions concerned with regulation. This was followed by the creation of the G-20, which included finance ministers and central bank governors from key emerging markets. In this way, supranational authority at the global level has strengthened significantly in the area of prudential regulation in the last three decades (Coleman and Porter 2000, p. 392).

The perception of what a state can do has changed quite substantially (see also Weber in this volume, who describes the transition from the old interventionist state to the regulatory and then the competition state in finance).

According to March and Olsen (1989), the state can act and be modeled in four ways:

1. as a bargaining state, with emphasis on the state actors that negotiate;
2. as an institutional state, with emphasis on the courts and legal processes;
3. as a supermarket state which provides the most efficient services;
4. as a sovereign state which sets the political agenda.

In today's financial deregulation and reform analyses, the model of the state comes closest to the corporate-bargaining state, which has a stable, institutionalized political process and is characterized by a reduced role assigned to legislators, ideological parties and the public. Delegating authority to a network of boards and committees in which bureaucrats and organized interest groups are the main participants, focusing the political agenda on technical issues rather than ideological ones, ensuring a low level of conflict and placing emphasis on compromise are also typical (March and Olsen 1989, p. 113).

The advantage of this technical determinism is that political and economic institutions have time to adjust without losing time and resources in disputes over new goals and instruments. The disadvantage is that existing, perhaps superior, options are not even discussed. Policy, the element of design, and debate on political outcomes are lost.

The task of the sovereign state is to shape preferences, plans and visions of a 'good' society. Political discourse in such a state is more controversial and ideological, though common values are agreed upon. This means that economic policymaking options are also discussed in more detail. The disadvantage is that the implementation of new goals and instruments is more difficult due to more controversy than in a corporate-bargaining state.

The idea of a sovereign state is absent in global financial governance. Models either perceive a reduced role of the sovereign state, for example due to state competition (Weber in this volume) or the transition from a sovereign state to a bargaining state (Underhill in this volume). This poses the serious question of who then shapes preferences and governs ideas.

3.3 The Role of Networks and Associations is Unclear

The literature on IR and IPE does not differentiate systematically between networks and associations. While the former is more flexible, can be an informal relationship between several actors and is based on reciprocity, the latter is a formal institution based on representativity. On the one hand, almost everything seems to be some kind of network, on the other hand it does not matter whether this 'network' consists of state agents, of banks or of associations. This muddling of categories defines away the fact that state agents, bankers and associations face different organizational structures, different constraints, and that they have different goals and are accountable to a different degree and to different groups.

3.4 Need for More Precise Analysis of How Governance Mechanisms Function

What is lacking in all these approaches is a systematic separation of different types of governance and the search for the predominant governance mechanism. Is it the state, markets, networks, associations, or communities which govern global finance? Moreover, which typical patterns emerge? As long as the outcomes are a complex description of a complex reality, one cannot draw more general theoretical conclusions than the fact that patterns change. Many of the approaches are descriptive rather than analytical and focus on the process rather than the content.

If the typology of private authorities' governance mechanisms is more precisely distinguished in IR and IPE, one may also find effects of regulatory financial reforms which van Waarden (2004) called 'communicating vessels'. Using various examples, he shows that in many cases it was not deregulatory reforms that brought about the governance mechanism of the market, but some other, unintentional kind of economic governance. Similarly, the deregulation of finance has led to prudential financial regulatory reforms. It would be important to analyze the underlying governance mechanisms in more detail, in particular the role of informal networks. For an example, see Lütz in this volume.

4. ASSESSING POLITICAL POWER

Mainstream international relations theory displays a deficiency in assessing the political power of the actors. In fact, global governance approaches, as some of the youngest theoretical approaches in international relations and the ones most open to attributing prominent political roles to non-state actors, have faced fervent criticism for initially assuming conflicts of power away (Fuchs, 2005, p. 1).

When the analysis concentrates on the way in which state actors negotiate with market actors in order to reach a joint outcome, some of the essence of power relations is lost. Following Lukes (1974), Fuchs (2005) argues that there are three faces of political power.

The first face of political power is instrumental power. Which influence do specific groups or actors have on political/policy output? In traditional power theories of international relations, the literature on lobbying, interest group politics and the use of power by states in pursuit of national interests deals with this kind of power. But this instrumentalist perspective fails to capture the potential influence that the dependence of the political elite on private-sector profitability has on political agendas and policy options.

Therefore, a second face – the structuralist perspective on power – has to be added. Why are some issues never on the agenda and some proposals never made? Who has the agenda-setting power? And who has the rule-setting power? In international political economy, it is frequently argued that multi-national corporations (MNCs) held increasing structural power due to their ability to punish or reward countries for their policy choices (Fuchs 2005, p. 5). This kind of power is difficult to assess empirically, since the threat to move funds away in the case of unfavorable policy does not even have to be voiced.

The acquisition of rule-setting power by non-state actors has become a focal point in the discussion of global (financial) governance and new forms of governance through 'private authorities'. The relative bargaining power of state and market actors depends on the specific distribution of assets and capabilities (see, for example, Underhill in this volume). But why are some proposals never made?

Even an analysis of both the instrumental and the structural facets of an actor's power still lacks the third face of power, the discursive perspective, the systemic conditions of power. In this perspective, power is exercised through norms and ideas. It is reflected in discourse, communication practices, and cultural values and institutions. 'Actors strategically use discourse to shape norms and ideas, for instance, by employing symbols and story-lines, and by the strategic linking of issues and actors to established norms and values. Discursive power precedes the formation and articulation of interests in the political process, due to its role in the constituting and framing of policies, actors, norms and ideas. An analysis of discursive power would consider the socialization of politicians and the public into accepting "truths" about desirable policies' (Fuchs 2005, p. 6). The role of media and public relations as well as the role of epistemic communities would have to be studied. But this third face of power is the most difficult to recognize and measure. It relies on persuasion, the perception of legitimacy, and voluntary compliance rather than coercion and hierarchies. It will often not even be perceived as an exercise of power and therefore not be questioned.

4.1 Is There Any Actor Who Governs?

An issue that also seems to have been lost in recent governance literature, including that on financial governance, is whether someone, some actor, individual or organization, actually governs, and if so, who that is. Who has the power in the end, and whose interests are being served (best)?

It is not surprising that this question has been lost in modern governance literature. The change in emphasis from 'government' (an identifiable actor) to 'governance' (a process), and from national policymaking (a level with identifiable actors) to 'multi-level governance' has made it unclear who is actually making policies, regulating and setting standards. And that is not unproblematic, because if we do not know who wields power, we also do not know who to hold accountable.

Many past theories have linked *policy and regulation* to *power* positions, and those in turn to *interests*. It has often been assumed that those in power will use that power to serve their own particularistic interests in the policies they pursue and the regulations they enact. Power and interests were thus closely linked to one another.

Economists have always started from the assumption of a close link between action/choice and self-interest. Thus the 'economic theory of regulation' (for a survey, see Underhill in this volume) argued that public policy output (i.e. regulation) was influenced by powerful lobbies, and that regulations thus served the particularistic interests of some at the cost of others, on the whole reducing economic efficiency and prosperity. Mancur Olson (1965) provided a logical argument as to why associational governance also does so: Small groups (e.g. concentrated industries such as the financial industry) find it easier to form strong associations than larger groups (e.g. consumers of financial services), and as the former have more powerful associations that lobby governments, they also succeed in obtaining regulation which is biased in their interest. If there is an asymmetry in the distribution of costs and benefits of regulation, it is likely that this regulation will be biased. Groups in which costs or benefits are concentrated (e.g. a concentrated steel industry that profits from protectionism) have a stronger incentive to lobby governments to serve their interests than those groups over which the consequential costs or benefits are diffused. Therefore, the banking industry profits greatly from vague financial product information requirements, while the costs (i.e. misinformation) are spread over a large group of consumers of financial services, for whom this is a relatively minor concern. This means that they have less of an incentive to organize and mobilize against such regulation. All such economic theories of regulation assume that most regulation will be influenced by the more powerful actors and will therefore be biased toward their interests (see also Rothschild 1971).

In political science, we can see a similar concern. From the 1950s to the early 1980s, political scientists were concerned with the question of 'who governs' (see, for example, the famous title of the classic work by political scientist Robert Dahl [1961]). Dissatisfied with the formal institutionalism of the 1920s and 1930s – which located political power where the formal institutions laid it: with ministers, judges and members of parliament – the political scientists of the 1950s tried to identify who 'really wields power' (for an early example, see Lynd and Lynd 1937). Thus a whole series of studies on local political communities tried to identify the real power holders in those communities through a variety of empirical techniques: not the mayor, but the big industrialist or the head of the local church (e.g. Lasswell and Kaplan 1950, Polsby 1963, Lundberg 1937, Schattschneider 1960; international: Kolko 1962). This was followed in the 1970s by a series of studies focusing on economic power, including studies which tried to identify indirect and underlying political power: the power to set political agendas, to prevent issues from being placed on the agenda or, conversely, to place them on the agenda (Bachrach and Baratz 1970).

All these studies in economics and political science from the 1950s to the 1980s share a concern with the issue of 'who governs', who has power, and subsequently whose interests are served by government measures. This knowledge-guiding interest seems to have disappeared with the change in discourse from 'government' to 'governance'. It would be a good idea to put it back on the research agenda.

4.2 Bringing Power Back

Tsingou (2005) argues that the policies that make up global financial governance are accepted as legitimate primarily due to the high level of expertise involved in the policy process. But, as she also states, this does not automatically legitimize the policy priorities chosen. The answer to the question of who governs must include not only a description of who serves on which committees, but also an analysis of who governs and why specific political priorities are set and followed.

In most countries, finance remains an 'esoteric' topic with few or no publicly debated issues (Grossman 2005, p. 131, quoting Coleman 1996, pp. 9–10). The question of who governs is addressed to a lesser extent. This article is merely an attempt to put the issue back on the research agenda. I cannot answer it yet, but I can outline some literature and some theoretical approaches which claim to have some answers to this question.

Coincidence: Is it coincidence – that is, the unintentional outcome of some actors negotiating with each other – which governs, and, depending on their individual skills of diplomacy and negotiation as well as their relative power, which makes one outcome more likely once and another outcome more likely the next time?

March (1994), when analyzing 'How Decisions Happen', stresses the role of accident. Many decisions are unplanned. In his 'garbage can' model of decision-making, he shows that the logic in decisions has a temporal order: Who was at the right place at the right time when decisions were taken, and under which contingencies (external threats, emergencies or incidents) were these decisions made?

It seems quite convincing that policy is the outcome of some muddling or interdependence between the economic and the political sectors, or of the coincidental skill of some convincing negotiator or strategist, etc. However, if this is the case – if policy is only an incidental outcome of negotiations – how is it possible that neo-liberal politics have been predominant and unanimously proclaimed almost everywhere since the mid-1980s? Newspapers, politicians and even academics have become neo-liberal.

Optimality: Neoclassical economics would interpret the worldwide convergence toward market-friendly policies as the growing insight into reason: Neo-liberal policies are considered optimal approaches to fostering economic prosperity, so any other policies are either not feasible or lead to inferior outcomes. The failures of neo-liberal policies in practice are attributed to faulty implementation, not concepts.

Structural forces: Structuralist approaches in a Marxist tradition interpret the switch from Keynesianism to Neo-liberalism and the growing role of finance in politics and economics as a result of the changing needs of capital, induced by changes in the forces of production. In this account, politics is seen as by and large determined by economic developments (Duménil and Lévy 2004). This is typically rejected in political science, which insists on the existence of a specificity of the political domain.

Conspiracy approaches assume that there is some secret, centrally directed strategic action to serve the interests of a small group of powerful people. In finance, popular literature on the Bilderberger organization (Fosar and Bludorf 2005), for example, sees this group consisting of nobility, bankers, politicians and businessmen as 'the high priests of globalization' and as the political career makers since World War II. According to this literature, this group planned the liberalization of trade and capital and strives to establish a single World Central Bank. The existence of secrecy and conspiracy is impossible to evaluate using scientific methods.

Recent articles in academic literature include that of Fuchs (2005), who gives some empirical evidence that MNCs strategically plan to shape ideas, to capture politics and to be present in the media. In international finance, Harmes (1998) argues that institutional investors deliberately worked to reproduce neo-liberalism by threatening governments, the threat being to withdraw money.

Hegemony, a concept which goes back to the Italian communist leader Antonio Gramsci, also believes in some kind of conspiracy, but it does not necessarily assume coordinated strategic action to serve the interests of the powerful. There is some leadership or dominance of one group over others. The more powerful class has the ability to persuade other classes to see the world in terms favorable to its own ascendancy. Hegemony is a ruling class's domination of subordinate classes through the elaboration and penetration of ideology in their common sense and everyday practice. It is the systematic, albeit not necessarily deliberate, engineering of mass consent to the established order (see www.caledonia.org.uk/hegemony.htm). Epistemic communities can be an important tool for financial hegemony, which does not govern through coercion but through ideology (cf. Gill 1998).

Epistemic community governance does not assume coordinated strategic action, but actors make similar choices on the basis of belonging to the same community, defined by a body of knowledge (episteme). This body of knowledge can be derived from an academic discipline and joint socialization in it (law, engineering, scientific medicine, economics, or sub-disciplines like mainstream neo-classical economics), or from joint socialization in a belief system (Catholicism, Islam, esoterics); or it can be derived from shared task contingencies such as air traffic controllers' need to ensure the safety of airplanes. In finance the shared task could be to safeguard the value of money and keep inflation low. This usually shows up in shared (though not explicitly coordinated) perceptions of problems and shared perceptions of acceptable and appropriate solutions (cf. Markussen 2000).

In finance, it is argued that the influence of elite groups, bankers, the lobbies of leading financial firms and the Wall Street Treasury complex in pursuit of their own interests has increased (Soederberg 2005). 'The regime for prudential regulation has been developed by central bankers from different states. These actors commonly share a world view based on established central banking practices such as secrecy, an aversion to political interference, and a commitment to the primacy of economic and technical knowledge in decision making' (Coleman and Porter 2000, p. 392).

Bankers form an epistemic community; they have the same education and similar working conditions, thus they perceive similar problems that have to be solved and are important. As they attended similar schools and universities, they also share similar ideas of how to solve those problems. They share the same symbols, such as dressing in similar ways and driving similar cars. They exchange information informally in golf clubs, while hunting, etc. All this adds to the development of common ideas and world visions. Furthermore, there are numerous networks of the political elite, such as the World Economic Forum or Bilderberger, a group formed around J.D. Rockefeller in 1954. These networks also add to the shaping of joint values and ideas.

Networks of the elite play an important role in global financial governance. In particular, this is because they have a relatively homogenous political perception of how the global financial world should be.

In this way, they exclude specific interest groups such as consumers or African countries, which do not appear on the maps of the international financial community but are considered the suppliers of raw materials and the recipients of foreign aid. These groups do not have the same opportunities to form networks or epistemic communities. They receive their world vision from the newspapers and television, which corresponds to the view of the experts. As Fuchs (2005) states, there is an increased number of private businessmen figuring as experts on economic issues and spreading neo-liberal ideas in television and the media.

Imitating theory: Following fashions, jumping on the bandwagon, or behaving like lemmings might also explain the bias toward neo-liberalism. If one actor imitates another, and if efficiency and the lean state become fashionable ideas, herd behavior might explain the outcome. The rise of herd behavior among institutional investors, their tendency to ignore economic fundamentals (relying instead on technical analysis and newspapers, and therefore buying and selling on the basis of asset prices only) and to follow the behavior of others, can be mentioned here (Harmes 1998, p. 102). Also, deregulation itself can become a fashion where one public sector, country or community copies another.

It is most likely that some combination of the above-mentioned factors determines who governs. Finance does share the same values, partly because it belongs to the same epistemic community. But it can also organize much better at the international level than consumers or workers. Labor and consumers have not (or only barely) managed to organize at the transnational level. The world vision is transported by the press and by television, which convey the neo-liberal ideas of technical experts from epistemic communities. It may be coincidence, or maybe these groups are better organized and know what their interests are. And, even without communicating it, this has been able to make neo-liberal ideas so popular today. In addition, internationally mobile finance can exert powerful economic pressure on politics, which can foster its success in attaining the policies most suitable to its interests.

Finally, the question emerges whether finance automatically has to be neo-liberal. Could it be that in the long run an excessive redistribution between the financial and the real sector will hollow out the income of finance itself? A balance between the interests of the financial and real sector seems necessary for the long-term survival of both parts.

REFERENCES

Amable, Bruno (2004), ‘An Overview of Financial Systems’ Diversity’, in Peter Mooslechner and Ernest Gnan (eds), *Workshop on The Transformation of the European Financial System. Where Do We Go? Where Should We Go?*, Proceedings of OeNB Workshops No. 1, 20 June 2003, Vienna: Oesterreichische Nationalbank, pp. 23–53.

Bachrach, P. and M.S. Baratz (1970), *Power and Poverty: Theory and Practice,* New York: Oxford University Press.

Baker, Andrew, David Hudson and Richard Woodward (eds) (2005), *Governing Financial Globalisation: International political economy and multi-level governance*, RIPE studies in Global Political Economy, London and New York: Routledge.

Boyer, Robert and Rogers J. Hollingsworth (1997), ‘The Variety of Institutional Arrangements and Their Complementarity in Modern Economics’, in: Hollingsworth, J.Rogers and Robert Boyer (ed.) *Contemporary capitalism.*

The embeddedness of institutions'. Cambridge: Cambridge University Press, 49-54..

Coleman, William D. and Tony Porter (2000), 'International Institutions, Globalization and Democracy: Assessing the Challenges', *Global Society*, **14** (3), 377–98.

Commission on Global Governance (1995), *Our Global Neighbourhood: The Report of the Commission on Global Governance*, Oxford: Oxford University Press.

Dahl, Robert A. (1961), *Who Governs?* New Haven: Yale University Press.

Domhoff, G. William (1967), *Who rules America?*, Englewood Cliffs: Prentice Hall.

Duménil, Gerard and Dominique Lévy (2004), *Capital Resurgent: Roots of the Neoliberal Revolution*, Cambridge, MA: Harvard University Press.

Eising, Rainer and Beate Kohler-Koch (1994), 'Inflation und Zerfaserung: Trends der Interessensvermittlung in der Europäischen Gemeinschaft', *Politische Vierteljahreszeitschrift*, 25, 175–206.

Eising, Rainer and Beate Kohler-Koch (1999), 'Network Governance in the European Union', in Rainer Eising and Beate Kohler-Koch (eds), *The Transformation of Governance in the European Union*, London: Routledge, pp. 3–13.

Fosar, Grazyna and Franz Bludorf (2005), 'Die Bilderberger, Hinter den Kulissen der Macht', available at http://www.fosar-bludorf.com/bilderberger/.

Fuchs, Doris (2005), 'Commanding Heights? The Strength and Fragility of Business Power in Global Politics', Leipzig Graduate School of Management and Wittenberg Center of Global Ethics mimeo, paper presented at the Conference of the European Consortium for Political Research in Granada, 14–19 April 2005.

Gill, Stephen (1998), 'European Governance and New Constitutionalism: Economic and Monetary Union and Alternatives to Disciplinary Neoliberalism in Europe', *New Political Economy*, **3** (1), 5–26.

Grossman, Emiliano (2005), 'European banking policy between European governance and Europeanization', in Andrew Baker, David Hudson, and Richard Woodward (op. cit.), pp. 130–46.

Haas, Peter (1992), 'Introduction: Epistemic Communities and International Policy Coordination', *International Organization*, **46** (1), 1–35.

Harmes, Adam (1998), 'Institutional Investors and the Reproduction of Neoliberalism', *Review of International Political Economy*, **5** (1), Spring 1998, 92–121.

Hirst, Paul (2000), 'Democracy and governance', in J. Pierre (ed.), *Debating governance: Authority, steering and democracy*, Oxford: Oxford University Press.

Hollingsworth, J. Rogers, Philippe C. Schmitter and Wolfgang Streeck (eds) ([1994] 2004), *Governing Capitalist Economies: Performance and Control of Economic Sectors*, New York: Oxford University Press.

Hudson, David (2005), 'Locating and understanding the marketplace in financial governance: IPE, interdisciplinarity and multi-level governance', in Andrew Baker, David Hudson and Richard Woodward (op. cit.), pp. 64–82.

Kersbergen, Kees van and Frans van Waarden (2004), 'Politics and the Transformation of Governance: Issues of Legitimacy, Accountability, and Governance in Political Science', *European Journal of Political Research*, 43, 143–71.

Kolko, Gabriel (1962), *Wealth and Power in America. An Analysis of Social Class and Income Distribution*, New York: Preager.

Langley, Paul (2005), 'The everyday life of global finance: a neglected "level" of governance', in Andrew Baker, David Hudson and Richard Woodward (op. cit.), pp. 85–101.

Lasswell, H.D. and A. Kaplan (1950), *Power and Society. A Framework for Political Inquiry*, New Haven: Yale University Press.

Lukes, Steven (1974), *Power, a Radical View*, London: Macmillan.

Lundberg, F. (1937), *America's 60 Families*, New York: Vanguard Press.

Lütz, Susanne (2003), 'Governance in der politischen Ökonomie', Max Planck Institut für Gesellschaftsforschung Discussion Paper 03/5, Cologne, May 2003.

Lynd, R.S. and H.M. Lynd (1937), *Middletown in Transition*, New York: Harcourt.

March, James G. (1994), *A Primer on Decision Making: How Decisions Happen*, New York: The Free Press.

March, James G. and Johan Olsen (1989), *Rediscovering Institutions, The* Organizational *Basis of Politics*, London: Macmillan.

Marks, Gary, Fritz W. Scharpf, Philippe C. Schmitter and Wolfgang Streeck (1996), *Governance in the European Union*, London: Sage.

Markussen, Martin (2000), *Ideas and Elites: The Social Construction of Economic and Monetary Union*, Ålborg: Ålborg Universitetsforlag.

Olson, Mancur (1965), *The Logic of Collective Action: Public Goods and the Theory of Groups*. Cambridge: Harvard University Press.

Ostrom, Elinor (1990), *Governing the Commons*, Cambridge: Cambridge University Press.

Ouchi, William (1980), 'Markets, Bureaucracies, and Clans', *Administrative Science Quarterly*, 25, 129–41.

Polsby, N.W. (1963), *Community Power and Political Theory*, New Haven: Yale University Press.

Powell, Walter W. (1996), 'Weder Markt noch Hierarchie: Netzwerkartige Organisationsformen', in Patrick Kenis and Volker Schneider (op. cit.), pp. 213–73.

Rothschild, Kurt W. (ed.) (1971), *Power in Economics*, Harmondsworth: Penguin Books.

Schattschneider, E.E. (1960), *The Semi-Sovereign People*, New York: Holt, Rinehart and Winston.

Soederberg, Susanne (2005), 'The New International Financial Architecture (NIFA): an emerging multi-level structure of neo-liberal discipline', in Andrew Baker, David Hudson and Richard Woodward (op. cit.), pp. 189–209.

Strange, Susan (1996), *The Retreat of the State: The Diffusion of Power in the World Economy*, Cambridge: Cambridge University Press.

Streeck, Wolfgang and Philippe C. Schmitter (1985), 'Gemeinschaft, Markt und Staat – und die Verbände? Der mögliche Beitrag von Interessenregierungen zur sozialen Ordnung', *Journal für Sozialforschung*, **25** (2), 133–59.

Streeck, Wolfgang and Philippe C. Schmitter (eds) (1985a), *Private Interest Government: Beyond the Market and the State*, London: Sage.

Traxler, Franz and Brigitte Unger (1994), 'A Cross-National Comparison of Governance: Its Determinants and Economic Consequences in the Dairy Sector', in: J. Rogers Hollingsworth, Philippe C. Schmitter and Wolfgang Streeck (op. cit.), pp. 183–214.

Tsingou, Eleni (2005), 'Transnational Private Governance and the Basel Process: Banking Regulation and Supervision, Private Interests and Basel II', paper prepared for the Joint Sessions of the European Consortium for Political Research, Granada, 14–19 April 2005.

Underhill, Geoffrey R.D. and Xiaoke Zhang (2005), 'The Changing State-Market Condominium in East Asia: Rethinking the Political Underpinnings of Development', *New Political Economy*, **10** (1), March 2005, 1–24.

UNESCAP – United Nations Economic and Social Commission for Asia and the Pacific (2004), 'What is Good Governance?', available at http://www.unescap.org/huset/gg/governance.htm.

Unger, Brigitte (1997), *Room for Manoeuvre of Economic Policy Making*, post-doctoral research project (*Habilitation*) at the Vienna University of Economics and Business Administration, Vienna, Austria.

Unger, Brigitte, Melissa Siegel, Joras Ferwerda, Wouter de Kruijf, Madalina Busuioc and Kristen Wokke (2005), 'The Amounts and the Effects of Money Laundering', Report for the Ministry of Finance, The Hague, Netherlands.

van Waarden, Frans (2004), 'Market Institutions as Communicating Vessels: Unintended Effects of Deregulation', in J. Rogers Hollingsworth, Karl H. Mueller, and Ellen Jane Hollingsworth (eds), *Advancing Socio-Economics. An Institutionalist Perspective*, Lanham, Boulder, New York and Oxford: Rowman and Littlefield, pp. 171–212.

van Waarden, Frans and Michaela Drahos (2002), 'Courts and (Epistemic) Communities in the Convergence of Competition Policies', *Journal of European Public Policy*, **9** (6), 913–34.

Williamson, Oliver E. (1975), *Markets and Hierarchies: Analysis and Antitrust Implications*, New York: The Free Press.

PART II

CASE STUDIES

4. The Significance of Changes in Private-Sector Associational Activity in Global Finance for the Problem of Inclusion and Exclusion

Tony Porter*

A defining feature of the past quarter century has been the globalization of finance. This has brought a widely recognized expansion of the role played in international and domestic affairs by private-sector actors and markets. There has been a great deal of debate about whether these changes are good or bad, and about the question of precisely how extensive they have been. Most of the debates have focused on the relationship between states and markets, and have asked questions such as 'Have states been rendered powerless by cross-border capital flows?' or 'Should states strengthen their regulation of global capital markets?' While such debates are important, they tend to ignore a different set of questions that must be addressed if we are to understand the significance of the change in the role of the private sector that has accompanied the globalization of finance. These are questions about how private-sector financial actors are organized. This chapter addresses those questions.

Understanding how private-sector financial actors are organized is important not just for understanding how global markets function and the influence of market actors relative to states, but also what this changing private-sector role means for the problem of inclusion and exclusion. When people get anxious or excited about the globalization of finance, it

* Revised version of a paper prepared for Workshop on the Political Economy of International Financial Governance, 26 November 2004, at the Oesterreichische Nationalbank in Vienna, Austria. The paper draws on a database of associations managed by Heather McKeen-Edwards and developed with research assistance from Diana Cucuz and Sarah Eaton. Research funding from the Social Sciences and Humanities Research Council of Canada and from the Schulich School of Business National Research Program in Financial Services and Public Policy is gratefully acknowledged, as is the commentary on the earlier draft from discussant Geoffrey Underhill and other workshop participants, including the editors of this volume.

usually has to do with this problem. The problem can be expressed in many different ways, such as the idea that the world is increasingly controlled by a powerful and exclusive financial elite, that wealthy speculators have taken advantage of the inability of the average citizen to understand global financial transactions, or, on the other side, that since global finance has been freed from the heavy hand of the state it has vastly expanded the available opportunities for accumulating wealth or controlling risk, drawing new actors into a world that used to be the preserve of a wealthy few on Wall Street and in the City of London. However to go beyond inchoate fears and celebratory clichés it is important to examine the concrete way in which private-sector actors are organized, and to carefully assess the implications of this organization for the problem of inclusion and exclusion.

The chapter looks first at prevailing perceptions of the effects of the changing role of private-sector actors on inclusion and exclusion. It then carefully examines the organization of private-sector financial actors. The final section considers the implications of this organization for the problem of inclusion and exclusion. Two key findings and a suggestion for further research will be highlighted. The first finding is the wide variety of relatively disconnected forms that private-sector organization takes in global finance, a picture that is at odds with the common tendency to see financial globalization as a homogenizing and integrating force, and also with the idea that a cohesive financial elite controls the system. The second finding is that while the globalization of finance has alleviated the problem of exclusion to some extent, and old barriers have been broken down, new ones have been constructed, and some of these new ones have serious implications for inclusion. The organization of global finance is a work in progress, and whether exclusionary tendencies can be alleviated will be determined by the ongoing activities of those who see themselves as central to it and by the attitude of policymakers toward those at its periphery who have little control over the daily and systemic risks to which they are exposed. The suggestion for further research is to explore more fully the relative weights of different associations in key policy and regulatory processes as well as the relationships between influential member firms and individuals that may link or cut across various associations.

INCLUSION, EXCLUSION, AND PREVAILING PERCEPTIONS OF THE ROLE OF PRIVATE-SECTOR ACTORS

The central role played by finance in political and economic systems, the secrecy in which many financial decisions are made, the arcane character of the technical language that those in finance speak, and the close connection between power and wealth have all contributed to an enduring popular concern with the relationship between finance on the one hand and the problem of inclusion and exclusion on the other.

Broadly speaking, two main perspectives that are diametrically opposed to one another can be distinguished in analytical discussions of the problem of inclusion and exclusion in global finance. In the first perspective are approaches that are critical of globalization and capitalism, and that see finance as a powerful force that increasingly shapes all aspects of contemporary life, undermining the ability of citizens to control their own political and economic destinies. In the second perspective are liberal approaches that see finance as the leading edge of the liberating phenomenon of economic globalization more generally. I look briefly at each of these in turn.

The Critical View: Finance as Exclusion

Two main overlapping themes have been developed in the literatures that are critical of the role of private-sector actors in the globalization of finance. The first emphasizes the deliberate efforts of a financial elite to exercise control over states and markets. This includes identifying the involvement of financial elites in high-level international venues where policy issues are discussed, such as the Trilateral Commission (Gill 1990); tracing the linkages between corporate board members from the financial sector (Carroll and Carson 2003); examining the lobbying efforts and campaign contributions of leading financial firms (Roberts et al. 2003, p. 443); looking at the 'Wall Street-Treasury complex' (Bhagwati 1998); and examining the influence that bankers wield over industrial firms (Mintz and Schwartz 1985), the micro-social connections between participants in global finance markets (Cetina and Bruegger 2002), or the role of the US and other governments in opening foreign financial markets in a way that is seen to serve the particular interests of financial firms headquartered in their jurisdictions (Soederberg 2003).

A second theme has emphasized the structural factors that promote the dominance of finance over other aspects of contemporary life. These include the idea that capital markets and financial firms are putting undesirable levels of pressure on governments to pursue their favored policies as a result of the threats of capital outflows that come with increased cross-border capital mobility (Andrews 1989; Gill and Law 1989); the use of assessments of government performance by financially-oriented bond rating methodologies (Sinclair 1994); the promotion of a popular financially oriented 'investment culture' by the growth of mutual funds (Harmes 2001, 2002); the use of auditing techniques in government as a generalized mechanism of accountability and control (Power 1994); and a generalized process of 'financialization'– the prevalence of financial techniques and values seen as an expression of a broader process where non-market values and relationships become commodified (Froud et al. 2002). Often the US government is seen as consistently and enduringly acting to promote the interests of US financial actors and markets, as with Gowan's (1999) analysis of the 'Dollar Wall Street Regime'.

These critical approaches are consistent with the popular intuition that finance is exercising more control over contemporary life today than it has in the past, and taken as a whole they suggest that the forces that are bringing about this control are ubiquitous and cohesive. Not surprisingly, given the scale and elite or deeply structural character of the phenomena they are studying, these literatures do not provide direct evidence of this ubiquity and cohesion. Instead they tend either to provide careful institutional analysis of particular examples of financial control which are then taken to be emblematic of financial control more generally, or to link together many instances of the growing prominence of finance and explain these with reference to the initiatives of a cohesive elite or the effects of deep structures.

The Supportive View: Finance as Inclusion

While supporters of financial globalization have primarily stressed its economic benefits, they have also often explicitly or implicitly seen it as breaking down traditional patterns of exclusion. Some of these arguments are similar to those for free trade more generally in suggesting that access to international markets will provide more opportunities for impoverished countries and social groups, as when a developing country government uses the proceeds from an international bond issue to create needed infrastructure, or when jobs provided by foreign direct investments allow women to escape oppressive traditional relationships in villages. Other types of barriers that are undermined are more distinctively financial, such as the breaking apart of the traditional club-like character of financial elites with the entry of more aggressively competitive US banks in the City of London in the 1970s (Moran 1984); the 'Big Bangs' and demutualization that have replaced fixed commissions and informal ties among stockbrokers in London, New York, and elsewhere by more competitive or corporate relationships (Karmel 2002); the feeling among offshore centers in the Caribbean and elsewhere that their focus on financial services has been a successful development strategy;[1] and the argument made by multilateral institutions such as the World Bank or OECD that the privatization of pensions allows ordinary workers to share in the wider investment opportunities that come with financial globalization.[2]

The logic that underlies the idea that financial globalization promotes greater inclusiveness is based on three arguments about markets. The first has to do with the competitive aspect of markets, which, it is suggested, will inevitably undermine exclusionary arrangements, such as cartels or bureaucratic regulatory mechanisms, because of the dynamism, efficiency, and fluidity that competition brings. The second has to do with equalizing pressures that come with markets: convergence to a single price, including for labor, and the deployment of financial and other resources to uses where they are relatively scarcer, will equalize incomes and opportunities over time. The third has to do with individual property rights, which are seen as inseparable from markets, and as a precondition for meaningful participation in contemporary societies.

There are some serious deficiencies in these arguments. Markets may not have the equalizing and barrier-reducing effects set out above, either because of problems inherent to markets themselves, or because the expansion of global finance involves not just the expansion of markets, but also the growing influence of powerful financial firms that act to create new non-market exclusions. On a related note, this perspective on the problem of inclusion and exclusion is mainly economic, quite narrow, and tends to obscure the negative impacts of financial globalization that critical approaches have identified.

---

[1] For instance, in July 2000 St. Kitts/Nevis Attorney General Delano Bart condemned efforts of industrialized countries to crack down on offshore centers as a 'careful and determined effort by the Group of 7 countries to curtail the efforts of small jurisdictions to develop a financial services centre'. A report on the anger felt by the CARICOM Heads of Government at being excluded from decisions related to the crackdown noted that they 'remained convinced that international rules and practices must evolve from genuine consultative processes and in international forums in which all interests are represented. They affirmed that international rules must be made and applied democratically based on accepted principles and norms'. See 'Offshore Financial Sector: BVI Attends Special Meeting on G-7 Initiatives', *Island Sun*, July 2000, at www.islandsun.com/2000-july/200700/local1-v4i14.html.

[2] As an OECD report notes in speaking about the reasons to expand a 'third pillar' of private savings relative to a traditional government-funded first pillar in countries in transition: 'A partial switch would allow workers to diversify risks better . . . The third pillar serves the needs of those who wish to retire earlier or have living standards in retirement that exceed those likely to occur from required social security contributions . . . Introduction of multi-pillar pension systems is likely to increase the workers' sense of individual responsibility about their future retirement' (Lindeman et al. 2000). The idea is captured in the title of an essay by José Piñera (2001), who was responsible for privatizing Chilean pensions: 'Liberating Workers: The World Pension Revolution'.

There are a number of reasons that financial markets may not have the equalizing and barrier-reducing effects that supporters claim. First, as in other high-technology industries, the cost of learning to get to the industry's rapidly changing technological frontier is so high that a few leading firms can continually produce new products that maintain the distance between them and other firms that might wish to compete with them. Second, in continually producing these innovations the leading firms are not just increasing their lead as their employees accumulate tacit knowledge about how to produce further innovations, but also setting new product standards to which competitors must adjust. Third, products are not just complex, but interdependent, so that, for instance, one derivative can create a risk which a new derivative can be designed to offset, privileging existing leading firms that can offer new products to their clients on an ongoing basis. Fourth, the property rights created in financial markets are often created primarily by self-enforcing private contracts that may not be subject to the political, legal and ethical constraints that limit the unfairness that may be associated with the inherently exclusionary character of property rights in all markets. In short, financial markets may continually reinforce the dominance and exclusionary effects of the market activities of a few leading firms.

Aside from underestimating the potential exclusionary effects of financial markets, supporters of the globalization of finance have tended to greatly underestimate the non-market exclusionary activities that financial globalization can produce. When applying political economy approaches, supporters of the globalization of finance have generally focused on the self-interested political initiatives of domestic economic actors seeking protectionist measures, or of public-sector regulators seeking to enhance their own power and wealth – in other words, the non-market exclusionary activities of those actors who have sought to use political measures to slow down or control globalization (Harms et al. 2003, Hartwell 2001, Macey 2003). Similarly, insider trading is seen as a non-market exclusionary activity that is best solved by further expanding market forces, such as mandating greater reliance on markets for the distribution of information. However, supporters of the globalization of finance have remained remarkably silent about the possibility that the expansion of transnational financial markets could empower actors who exacerbate patterns of exclusion, a silence that would affirm for critics the ideological character of the supporters' arguments. There are many possible ways in which organized international private-sector financial sector actors could create exclusionary arrangements in their own interest. For instance, they could obtain privileged access to regulators and skew global rules in their favor, a relationship labeled 'capture' in the public policy literature. This could provide them with a competitive advantage over other firms, or it could allow them to extract resources from, or shift costs onto, the public sector. A few leading firms or an international industry association could work to exclude other firms from markets or to otherwise suppress competition, initiatives that in some forms would be the traditional target of anti-trust policies.[3] They could also take organized initiatives that remain below the radar of regulators and public opinion but that may have serious consequences for citizens, or the public interest more generally. All these types of exclusionary activities are ones that would benefit from the type of political economy approaches that supporters of globalization have applied so far only to actors that have resisted financial globalization.

The narrowness of the types of economic inclusion that supporters of financial globalization highlight is also a problem. Much of the openness that comes with the growth of financial markets provides new opportunities for some globally-oriented financial actors at the expense of other actors that are more locally oriented. The counterposing of words like 'openness' against 'protection' or 'barriers', or the elimination of 'financial repression' implies that this process always reduces exclusion. However, aside from the possibility that that this merely involves a shift in opportunities from one financial actor to another instead of a growth in opportunities as a whole, it tends to obscure the possibility that the impact of financial globalization on non-financial inclusiveness is not always positive. For instance, post-communist Russian integration into global financial markets brought such severe corruption and political manipulation that the credibility among its citizens of its shift toward democracy was severely damaged. Similarly the cutting of social safety nets in order to assure the ability of heavily indebted countries to repay global financial actors is a widely criticized link between the globalization of finance and social exclusion. Cross-national analysis shows a correlation between financial openness on the one hand and democracy and social spending on the other (Dailami 1999). However critics would argue that this is a correlation that would likely disappear in an analysis of change over time, as industrialized countries scoring high on all three variables as a result of the legacy of the post-World War II decades are finding social spending and the scope of democratic policy options to be increasingly constrained by the ability of wealthy individuals and financial actors to achieve their policy preferences for low social spending through enhanced opportunities for exit and voice.[4]

---

[3] For an analysis of these issues in connection with NASDAQ, see Kaplan (2002).

[4] For a useful discussion of the similar methodological problems that may account for the failure of cross-sectional correlations between the adoption of market-oriented 'Washington Consensus' reforms and growth to predict the negative correlation between these two variables over time, see Easterly (2001).

THE IMPORTANCE OF EXAMINING THE WAYS IN WHICH PRIVATE-SECTOR ACTORS ARE ORGANIZED IN GLOBAL FINANCE

Both of the above perspectives on the role of private-sector actors in global finance remain deficient in important respects. While the critics make a useful contribution in highlighting the systemic dangers associated with the organized power of financial actors and markets, and provide insightful illustrations of the ways that this power can be developed, exercised, and abused, they do not provide convincing evidence that the association between the globalization of finance and exclusion is as uniform and relentless as they suggest. While the supporters make an effective contribution in highlighting the way in which the globalization of finance can enhance inclusion, their neglect of the potentially exclusionary activities of globally oriented financial actors is a problem. The above two perspectives also differ in the scale of the units they see as relevant to their analysis. The critics tend to put more emphasis on very large macro-social institutions, while the supporters tend to emphasize the micro-level activities of rational individual actors, with each underestimating the relevance of the other's units of analysis.

Looking at the meso-level world of private-sector associations provides an opportunity to address these deficiencies. Associations allow their members to exercise more control than they would individually, whether this is directed at market actors through self-regulatory initiatives, or in the efforts of private-sector actors to obtain public policies and regulations that they favor. One can assume that if private-sector actors are acting in a manner that promotes exclusion, they will need to do so by engaging in associational activities to obtain and exercise their power to enforce and reproduce the patterns of exclusion. In an industry as large, varied, complex, and competitive as finance, it is unlikely that dominant actors would be able to exercise sufficient control to exclude others from markets or from rule-making processes by relying on hidden informal relationships, even if in some cases there is a strong incentive to do so in order to avoid anti-trust charges, and it is possible that hidden informal relationships supplement formal ones – a point to which I return in the conclusion. There are approximately 180 private-sector associations that play a significant role in global finance. Examining the roles they play should make a useful contribution to assessing the conflicting claims of critics and supporters of financial globalization.[5]

---

[5] The database of globally-oriented financial services associations on which this chapter's analysis draws was constructed through an extensive search of a variety of sources,

Our purpose here in examining private sector associations in global finance is not to provide an encyclopaedic description, but rather to find evidence relevant to the issue of inclusion and exclusion. It is useful to specify three contrasting propositions. The first, consistent with the critics' view, is that we should expect to find that associations are powerful, integrated with one another, dominated by the largest firms, aggressively proactive compared to states in setting key rules in the governance of global finance, and characterized by low levels of participation, transparency and due process. The second, consistent with the supporters' view, is that we should expect to find that the associations exhibit the minimal capacity needed to support competitive markets, with this capacity varying across industry sectors and issues in an unintegrated and decentralized fashion, and with measures designed to foster transparency and participation by as many relevant actors as possible. A third proposition, consistent with the approach of this chapter, is that there will be variation across associations, with some displaying high levels of inclusiveness and others having an exclusive character, a variation that should be related to the initiatives of policymakers and key private-sector participants rather than to macro-structural or market-related factors more generally.

In analyzing private-sector associations it is best to rely primarily on qualitative rather than quantitative analysis for three reasons. First, the importance of associations varies enormously, and it is not possible to find a numerical indicator of this variation. One association, such as the Association for Investment Management and Research (renamed the CFA Institute in 2004) may have a very large membership and formal structure but focus on a particular and relatively technical aspect of global finance, while another, such as the Financial Leaders Group, may be an informal small grouping of CEOs from the largest banks and wield a lot of influence with policymakers. Second, as will become clear, the functions of associations vary greatly, not just according to their financial sector (banking, securities, insurance, accounting, etc.) but also by type of activity (clearing house, lobby group, professional licensing, etc.), and the number of associations involved in each category is too small to be well suited to quantitative analysis. Third, judgment is needed to assess

---

including Google searches, websites of public-sector and private-sector bodies, trade journals, the *Yearbook of International Organizations*, and electronic databases such as LexisNexis and Proquest. A report on the project at an earlier stage, including a list of associations identified at that point, is available at www.paif.ca. Analysis of some of these associations also appears in Porter 2004 and 2005. Nationally focused associations with some influence on global finance are not included in the figures cited in this chapter. Extensive description and analysis of the database as a whole will appear at a later date in a book-length manuscript by Heather McKeen-Edwards and the present author.

the degree to which each organization is oriented toward the global aspects of finance.

Taken together, these three methodological challenges require the analyst to take great care in determining which relationships and associations are really important and which are less so, both with respect to their influence *in general*, and with respect to their significance for *inclusion and exclusion*.

Assessing the influence of relationships and associations *in general* is complicated because they are embedded in a larger set of relationships and social structures that may allow some small informal associations to wield great influence, while other associations that appear more robust on paper may be powerless in practice. These larger relationships and social structures include relatively concentrated industry structures, where small groups of CEOs of a few leading firms may wield tremendous influence in policy debates because of the importance of the organizational or financial resources they control. They also include the vast disparities between associations operating in financial centers, such as London or New York, and those operating in Africa or other parts of the developing world.

Assessing the significance of relationships and associations for *inclusion and exclusion* is complicated by several factors. Participation, transparency, and due process are all important in fostering inclusion rather than exclusion. In democracy and governance more generally, these inclusive values are weighed against other values, such as the need for expertise and stability and the difficulty of making effective decisions with excessively large numbers of participants. In general some compromise between these values is struck, in part for reasons of fairness and efficiency, and in part due to an equilibrium that may arise at the end of an unprincipled struggle for power. A well-recognized principle expressive of this type of compromise is the idea that it is those affected by rules that should have some say in their formulation, either directly or through some form of representation. Another such principle is the idea that more fundamental constitutional decision processes should be held to a higher standard, such as super-majority voting, than more technical decisions.

In addressing these issues with regard to private-sector financial associations it is useful to make two related distinctions. The first distinction is between those associations that are more technically oriented and those that are more politically oriented. The second distinction is between those associations that primarily affect their own members, and those whose work has broader and more fundamental impacts, for instance by working through markets to affect citizens in such roles as consumers, savers, borrowers, retirees, or workers, or by altering the structure of the financial system. As with governance and democracy more generally, greater emphasis should be put on associations with very broad, political and structural significance as compared to ones focused on narrow technical matters only affecting their members.

Despite these analytical challenges, aggregate data on industry associations can be a useful starting point for more qualitative analysis. Aggregate data can be useful because it is an indication of the range in activity and location of associations. For instance, the existence of globally-oriented associations in Africa, even if they are not as influential as associations in London, is important both as an indicator of their practical consequences in Africa and of the general degree of centralization or decentralization in global finance. The inclusion of relatively technical associations such as clearing houses when studying associations is important both because such associations can have significance for inclusion and exclusion if, for instance, they create barriers to entry, and because their relatively technical activities may be an indicator that financial actors are not as consistently oriented toward reinforcing the dominance of elites as is sometimes imagined. Aggregate data will always be limited by variation in the willingness of associations to divulge information about their budgets and staffs, and their tendencies to overstate or conceal their influence.

Any analysis such as this chapter's will inevitably be limited by the various difficulties set out above, but given the importance of associational activity it is best, while acknowledging these limits, to proceed nevertheless, combining aggregate data with qualitative analysis to begin to provide answers to the questions posed above. The next section examines the associations active in global finance, and in the chapter's concluding section we return to the question of what the limitations of our existing knowledge about these associations imply for future research.

A SURVEY OF GLOBALLY-ORIENTED FINANCIAL ASSOCIATIONS

This section seeks to assess the relative merits of the above three propositions by examining private-sector associations active in global finance in two steps. In the first step, I examine the question of whether they are centralized and integrated or decentralized and fragmented, an important component of their tendency to promote exclusion or inclusion. In the second step, I focus on their behavior with regard to transparency, participation and due process.

Centralization and Integration in Private-Sector Associational Activity in Global Finance

Three types of differences immediately become apparent when we look closely at the universe of associations active in global finance: differences in territorial domain, sector, and function.

With regard to territorial domain, of the 182 associations that we examined, 45 per cent were active across regions, and therefore were primarily global in their activities, while the majority (55 per cent) were focused on a particular region. This suggests a significant degree of regional differentiation that is contrary to what the critical perspectives might lead us to expect. When looking at the distribution of regional activity, the 55 per cent breaks down as follows: Europe, 17 percent; Latin America, Pan American and the Caribbean, 10.4 percent; Asia 11.5 percent; Sub-Saharan Africa, 9.9 percent, and the Arab and Islamic world, 6.6 percent. Europe's large share relative to the other regions is consistent with asymmetries in North-South capacities in finance and more generally, but these figures deviate from the expectations of the critical perspectives in two respects.

First, the number of associations (70) that are located in regions other than North America or Europe, the traditional centers of global finance, is greater than one might expect based on the critical perspective. They are not generally subsidiaries of global associations, but, with the partial exception of accounting, instead focus on concerns that are distinctive to their region. In the case of regional accounting associations there is a strong commitment to global standards, which can be explained by the desire of local accountants to inspire trust in foreign investors, or in local investors likely to see international standards as more reliable than local ones (Saudagaran and Diga 1997). In the case of Africa, one main focus is capacity building, while in Asia and Latin America financial associations are also focused on financial activities associated with regional economic activities and display linguistic differences with other regions, such as the use of Spanish. On the basis of the critical perspective, one might expect associations in Asia to be focused on Japan given its financial strength, but this is not the case: Only two of 18 associations have their headquarters in Japan, with the rest spread across eleven other Asian cities.

The second deviation from critical expectations is the surprising absence of North American associations. In part this is due to the smaller number of countries in North America relative to other regions, which reduces the number of different cross-border relations that might give rise to international associational activity. However given the enormous weight of US financial markets relative to all others, one would expect that US financial actors would take care of their own backyard even before extending their activities elsewhere. Instead, as analyzed in detail in McKeen-Edwards, Porter and Roberge (2004), the North American region remains remarkably unintegrated financially with regard to both markets and governance.

With regard to sectoral differentiation, 33 per cent of the globally oriented associations are focused on securities markets, 17 per cent on banking, 12 per cent on insurance, ten per cent on accounting, and 27 per cent on more than one sector. The regionally focused associations showed a similar pattern, although securities associations in Europe constitute a much larger share of all associations (45 percent) than in other regions (e.g. Africa: 11 percent). Insurance constitutes a higher proportion of associations in Africa (33 percent) and Latin/Pan America (29 percent) than in Europe (7 percent), and the share of banking associations of the total is lower in Europe than in all other regions. This regional variation is likely mostly due to the slower pace at which securities markets have developed in the global south relative to banking and insurance, since the latter two are better suited to riskier economies with weaknesses in the types of legal and technical infrastructure that are needed to sustain robust securities markets.

The sectoral distribution of associations deviates from the expectations of critical approaches in two ways. First, the strikingly high proportion of globally-oriented associations that are focused on securities markets suggests that the associations are more oriented toward providing the types of information, infrastructure, and guidelines needed to sustain the competitive arm's length markets that characterize the securities industry than on the type of consolidation of dominance over global finance that one might associate with the more directed character of banking; however, one possibility to be explored in future research is that there are informal relationships across these associations that involve more integration than this numerical analysis might suggest. Moreover it is possible that the relative newness of global securities markets as compared to international banking accounts for the (perhaps temporarily) greater number and diversity of associations in the former.

There are some important examples of coordination among leading banks, and while these have some policy implications, many tend more toward the provision of market infrastructure, much like most of the associations in securities markets.[6] One example is the Clearing House Inter-Bank Payments System (CHIPS), which processes 95 per cent of the world's inter-bank cross-border US dollar transactions through its New York-based electronic network. Run by its member banks and backed up by New York law, its rules and technology contribute to

[6] For a more detailed discussion of some of these associations, see Porter (2004 and 2005).

systemic stability and the expansion of global finance. Similarly, the Emerging Markets Traders Association, established to facilitate the trading of LDC loans and bonds in response to the debt crisis of the 1980s, set up some rules to provide order in the market after being pressured to do so by E. Gerald Corrigan in his capacity as head of the New York Fed and the Basel Committee on Banking Supervision (Buckley 2000). The Asian Pacific Loan Market Association (APLMA) was established in 1998 by 14 major international banks and has worked to establish settlement procedures, standardized loan documentation, and web-based technology for setting up loan syndicates in order to promote primary and secondary banking markets in East Asia.[7] The London-based Loan Market Association plays a similar role and in 2000 also lobbied the UK Financial Services Authority to have tradable loans treated like securities in the revisions of the Basel Capital Adequacy Accord.[8] In 1999, following the nearly catastrophic collapse of the massive Long Term Capital Management hedge fund, the Counterparty Risk Management Policy Group (CRMPG) was formed as an ad hoc committee by about ten of the world's largest banks. The committee was chaired by Corrigan, who had by then taken up a senior post at Goldman Sachs, and it managed to forestall serious public-sector regulation of hedge funds by instead providing a written set of voluntary best practices for the industry.

These collaborative arrangements among banks raise some important concerns about participation, transparency and due process, to which I return in the next section of this chapter. However, with regard to sectoral differentiation, despite the impressive organizational capacity of banks relative to other financial firms and the role they have been suspected of playing in organizing finance or capitalism as a whole, the above associations that they set up tend to focus on infrastructural problems more specific to banking than to global finance more generally. The exception is the CRMPG, where banks used the control conferred on them by their role in lending to hedge funds to substitute their own governance for that of public-sector regulators in an issue area of concern for global finance as a whole.[9]

---

[7] For information on the APLMA, see www.aplma.com, Keenan (1999), Goad (1998), and Jenkins (2001). The Wolfsberg Group is another example of leading international banks coming together to provide rules for a specific problem – in this case money laundering. See Pieth and Aiolfi (n.d.).

[8] 'LMA Knocking Down Barriers', *Euroweek*, 4 August 2000, p. L10.

[9] For these and the other associations discussed in this paper, the author has made a qualitative judgment about their relative importance based on a reading of publications and statements about the associations by the associations themselves, other financial actors or scholars, and this judgment could reasonably be challenged. More precise measures of influence are not presented both because doing so would exceed the scope of this chapter and because there are elements of influence, such as confidential lobbying, that will always

In addition to the technical focus of associations, the second and related way in which sectoral differentiation deviates from the expectations of critical approaches is that it remains far more pronounced than one would expect if finance was as integrated and centralized as the critical approaches suggest. Consistent with the points made above about associations created by banks, it is interesting to note that only 27 per cent of all associations active in global finance focus on more than one sector, and most of these are ones that provide services of use to more than one sector, such as risk analysis, rather than seeking to integrate or coordinate the initiatives of major private-sector financial actors as a whole.

The Institute of International Finance, which notes on its website that it is 'the world's only global association of financial institutions' with '320 members headquartered in more than 60 countries' comes closest to an association that might claim to speak for global financial actors in general. It is also the association that takes the lead in interacting with the most important international public-sector institutions involved in rule-making for global finance, the Basel Committee on Banking Supervision and the International Monetary Fund. Originally, when it was formed to respond to the developing country debt crisis in 1983, the IIF was exclusively an association of commercial banks devoted to sharing information about sovereign debt exposures and risks. Now it has expanded greatly the range of issues it addresses, including the general state of global finance, corporate governance reform, and the question of private-sector burden sharing in financial crises. Nevertheless all of its working groups on financial regulation are focused on banking issues, leaving securities and insurance regulation to others, and the vast majority of its members continue to be banks.

The Financial Leaders Group (FLG), consisting of CEOs from leading financial firms, is also an association that has spoken on behalf of global financial firms as a whole. It was formed during the Uruguay Round of trade negotiations in order to provide a private-sector interlocutor for the trade negotiators working on the Financial Services Agreement (FSA). Following the establishment of the FSA, the group continued to work on trade issues, monitoring the work of officials at the World Trade Organization and seeking to facilitate effective responses to perceived violations of the FSA by WTO member states. While it speaks to issues of concern to more than one financial sector, it maintains a focus on the

---

be impossible to measure accurately. In beginning to study a set of actors such as these financial services associations for the first time, it is inevitable that our knowledge will have to be refined to some degree by challenges and confirmations in future publications by other scholars or by individuals active in the industry.

WTO and does not aspire to a leadership role in global finance more generally.

The Group of Thirty (G-30) is another association that has played a leadership role in policy matters affecting more than one financial sector (Tsingou 2001 and her chapter in this book). Its website notes that it 'aims to deepen understanding of international economic and financial issues . . . and to examine the choices available to market practitioners and policymakers'. The G-30 consists of thirty individuals prominent in global finance, including ones from the public sector, the private sector, and academia. For instance, in 2004 its members included the heads of the central banks of England, Spain, Poland, Mexico, and the European Central Bank. It also included E. Gerald Corrigan, Managing Director at Goldman Sachs & Co. and former head of the New York Federal Reserve and the Basel Committee on Banking Supervision, as well as Andrew D. Crockett, President of JP Morgan Chase International and former General Manager of the Bank for International Settlements, and the chair of the Financial Stability Forum, two key public-sector bodies in the governance of global finance. The group also included Lawrence Summers, President of Harvard University, former Secretary of the US Treasury and Chief Economist at the World Bank, and Stanley Fischer, President of Citigroup International, who previously had been First Deputy Managing Director of the International Monetary Fund (1994–2001), Chief Economist at the World Bank, head of the Department of Economics at MIT, as well as playing important consulting roles in the US Treasury and State Departments.

The G-30 displays a remarkable integration of public-sector and private-sector interests both in the degree to which it draws members from each, and in the degree to which particular members have moved between top posts in key public-sector bodies and top posts in leading financial firms. Tsingou's chapter in this book provides further evidence of the way in which the G-30 exercises its authority. As she shows, the G-30, together with two other associations, the Derivatives Policy Group and the International Swaps and Derivatives Association, played a key role in the adoption by regulators and policymakers of an approach to derivatives that was favored by financial firms engaged in derivatives trading, despite some externalities and systemic risks in derivatives markets that one might have expected to prompt stricter regulation. The G-30's key contribution was to shape the policy debate through its claim of providing high quality non-political expert policy advice. Its membership epitomizes exclusiveness, and the high-level connections between the public and private sectors raise troubling questions about the types of non-transparent and unaccountable forms of influence that could be associated with such connections.

Overall, then, associations active in global finance display significant degrees of sectoral and regional differentiation rather than the integration and centralization that the critical perspective described above would lead us to expect. At the same time, groups like the CRMPG, the IIF, the FLG and the G-30 indicate that associations have some capacity to coordinate on policy matters. All four involve efforts to speak for global financial actors as a whole, or to address problems that affect global finance as whole, and in line with the critical perspective top international banks set up the first two and played a prominent role in the second two. It is therefore important to turn to the question of participation, transparency and due process in order to get a fuller picture of the significance of the world of associations in global finance for patterns of inclusion and exclusion.

Participation, Transparency and Due Process in Private-Sector Associational Activity in Global Finance

The previous section, while showing that there was more regional and sectoral differentiation than critical perspectives would lead us to expect, also provided some examples of initiatives to coordinate global finance as a whole and referred to some close linkages between private-sector firms and public-sector officials that may be of concern with regard to the problem of inclusion and exclusion. In addition, it is certainly possible that uncoordinated and dispersed but globally active financial sector associations could promote exclusion, a possibility that is generally neglected by both critics and supporters of the globalization of finance. It is therefore important to examine the character of the initiatives taken by private-sector associations with regard to participation, transparency, and due process.

In surveying associations active in global finance it is apparent that there is wide variation in the degree and significance of the exclusivity they display. I look at three aspects of the activities of associations in turn.

One aspect of globally-oriented financial associations that is mixed with regard to inclusion and exclusion is their frequent tendency to seek new members and to foster communication among existing ones. With globalization there has been a tendency for associations to shift from having the character of a local club to becoming more like a firm selling services to a dispersed client base. An especially clear example is the ongoing process of demutualization of stock exchanges, where the exchanges are transformed from cooperatives into corporations with publicly traded shares (Karmel 2002). One of the services that most associations sell in one form or another is the provision of opportunities for members to communicate with one another, such as annual conferences, websites, and newsletters. The hefty fees for these activities may exclude the general public and smaller firms, and to the degree to which the process involves the privatization of public discursive space they are problematic. For instance, when the data needed to analyze the public policy implications of the industry is sold at prohibitively high prices through members-only websites instead of being provided freely though public-sector statistical agencies, then the process is exclusionary. Moreover, more traditional backroom networking will continue to accompany more open associational activities. On the other hand, the interest of most associations in publicizing their own activities and in disseminating positive but trustworthy information about the industry to policymakers and the public can promote inclusion, as can their eagerness to enhance their revenues and stature by recruiting new members.

A second aspect of globally oriented financial associations that is mixed with regard to inclusion and exclusion is the reputational and licensing functions that many carry out. From a transaction costs perspective, one of the reasons that associations emerge is that they can more cost-effectively assure customers, financial counterparties, and governments that their members are trustworthy than their members could individually. Part of this is due to the economies of scale that associations enjoy in the production of information needed for an outsider to monitor a member firm's performance, and the distance between an association and its member firms can also create a perception of greater objectivity. Associations may also deliberately create mechanisms for excluding firms or individuals that fail to meet standards, ranging from those that make the observance of a vague code of conduct a condition of membership to those that offer a rigorous process of professional certification. In so far as this type of exclusion promotes high standards of conduct, it is positive. On the other hand, there is always the potential for such exclusionary activities to be used to enhance excessively the incomes of members by creating unnecessary barriers to entry, or to prevent proper public scrutiny of members by using its standards and codes to portray a degree of integrity that does not exist, as has sometimes been the case with associations of accountants and financial analysts.

The third and most important aspect of globally-oriented financial associations that is mixed with regard to inclusion and exclusion is the increased involvement of associations in global public policy and regulatory networks. At the national level, financial associations have a long history of involvement in policy networks. A difference at the global level is that global public policy initiatives and efforts at cross-border regulatory collaboration rely more heavily on informal networks than is the case in domestic settings,[10] which is evident, for instance, in the various committees concerned with aspects of international financial regulation located at the Bank for International Settlements in Basel. For some scholars (e.g. Bohman 1999) this informal and relatively dispersed networking provides new opportunities for participation and inclusion, especially in issue areas in which civil society actors can operate as norm entrepreneurs (Finnemore and Sikkink 1998, Khagram et al. 2002). For others, however, the greater distance between these networks and citizens or formal mechanisms of accountability such as review by legislative committees is problematic, as is their highly technical language and the relative obscurity in which most of them operate (Porter and Wood 2002).

The roles of the Institute of International Finance in the revisions of the Basel Capital Adequacy Accord and of the Financial Leaders Group in the Financial Services Agreement at the World Trade Organization provide useful examples with which we can assess these contrary views of the significance of the role of associations in global policy and regulatory networks. These have been the most important global negotiating processes for private-sector financial actors in the past decade, thus it is not coincidental that two of the associations identified above as being among a very few that can claim to speak for global private-sector financial actors were heavily involved. While a full discussion of these processes goes beyond the scope of the present chapter, it is useful to examine each one briefly in turn.

The original Basel Capital Adequacy Accord, agreed at the Basel Committee on Banking Supervision in 1988, is widely seen as the most developed and successful case of international regulatory collaboration in global finance. The accord halted a previous troubling tendency among international banks to reduce their capital relative to their loans and other assets. Capital, while relatively expensive, is important in cushioning firms from insolvency, and the lack of agreed capital standards in a highly competitive international banking environment had led banks to greatly expand their lending relative to capital, without regard to systemic consequences. The accord was originally agreed by the Basel Committee's twelve member states, but subsequently it was observed by almost all internationally significant banks and banking jurisdictions. Nevertheless, by the end of the 1990s the original accord was seen as too primitive and in need of updating, and a reform labeled Basel II was launched.[11]

---

[10] On global policy networks, see Cerny (2002), Reinicke and Deng (2000), and Slaughter (2001).
[11] On Basel II, see Porter (2005) and Wood (2005).

The contrast between the first and second negotiating processes provides a useful indication of the changing role played by associations in such global policy and regulatory networks. The 1988 accord was negotiated in relative secrecy by regulators, with some input from individual firms or from industry associations at the national level. By contrast the Basel II negotiations involved intense direct interaction between the Basel Committee and the private sector. Hundreds of pages of comments from private sector and public sector actors were posted on the Basel Committee's website along with the Basel Committee's own detailed reports, and the Basel Committee involved banks in a large-scale test of a prototype of part of the revised accord. The IIF played the leading role on the private-sector side, devoting substantial resources and attention to the development of the private-sector response to the reform – in contrast to the earlier accord, which the IIF only began discussing seriously several years after it was agreed.

Was this intensified interaction between the Basel Committee and the IIF a sign of inclusion or exclusion? On the one hand, the process in general was much more open and consultative than the negotiation of the 1988 accord, with Basel II going through an extensive series of revisions in response to feedback from non-members before it was finally agreed. Furthermore, the extraordinarily complicated new accord, which had looked like it might fail due to criticism of the regulatory burden it involved, was approved with some new requirements for firms, especially provisions for regulating operational risk, that suggest that the process was not captured by the IIF and other private-sector actors. On the other hand, Basel II was criticized for conferring an unfair competitive advantage on top international banks by allowing them to use their own internal risk models. Although the data and operational requirements that they had to satisfy before being allowed to do so were strict and costly, their final cost of capital would be significantly lower.[12] Justifying this as a fair incentive needed to encourage them to move to a more efficient way of managing risk than the simpler standards provided for smaller banks is not convincing, both because the large banks were already pushing to be allowed to use these models which are useful for their own purposes, and because it is not clear why the largest international banks should not cover a *larger* share of the cost of regulation aimed at preserving the systemic stability of global finance given their greater contribution to the risks associated with it. Thus while the process was not captured, it was skewed in favor of the largest banks relative to other banks, indicating that there were problematic exclusionary elements in the process.

---

[12] For a more detailed analysis of Basel II that reaches similar conclusions, see Claessens, Underhill and Zhang (2004).

The Financial Services Agreement at the World Trade Organization is consistent with the push to open foreign financial markets that was a priority for leading international banks and their governments, especially for the US. Accordingly, one would expect the Financial Leaders' Group, the main private-sector association involved in this process, to have aggressively taken the lead from the start. In fact, however, it was formed in response to initiatives taken by public-sector negotiators who wanted to have a convenient private-sector interlocutor. As one account notes, a deal on financial services clearly was in the interest of the financial services industry, especially from the US and the EU. Aware of that corporate interest, the US Government, the EU Commission and the WTO Secretariat actively sought the support of US and EU financial services industry leaders to break the deadlock in the negotiations. In the Spring of 1996, the Financial Leaders Group, exclusively consisting of chief executive officers and chairmen, and a lower-level Financial Leaders Working Group, started operating (Wesselius 2003).

Following the agreement, the support for the FLG from the Bank of England and the City of London (through International Financial Services London) is a further indication of the important role played by the public sector in supporting the FLG. [13] Nevertheless, the other important source of support for the FLG was the Coalition of Services Industries in the US,[14] and once constituted, the FLG operated like other lobbying groups in pressing for the interests of the financial services industry.

The relationship between the FLG, IFSL, and the public sector has been criticized as too close. For instance, in an article entitled 'Revolving Doors: Former Trade Commissioner Now Lobbies for Services Industry', the *Corporate Europe Observer* (CEO) notes that former EU Trade Commissioner Leon Brittan became Vice-Chairman of UBS Warburg and then Chairman of the LOTIS Committee of International Financial Services London, the London counterpart to the FLG. Brittan succeeded Andrew Buxton, who as Chair of Barclay's Bank had lobbied Brittan for the FLG during the trade negotiations (CEO 2001). Concern has been expressed that financial services liberalization did not take into account the public interest in social services as fully as might have been the case

---

[13] The IFSL website notes that 'BI (British Invisibles, the IFSL's predecessor) was involved in setting up the FLG and IFSL now plays a leading part in the operations and policy recommendations made by its lower tier body, the Financial Leaders Working Group', at www.ifsl.org.uk/tradepolicy/whatwedo.cfm.

[14] Wesselius (2003) notes 'The US Coalition of Service Industries (USCSI) is undoubtedly the most influential services lobby group in the world. Its origins date back to the mid-1970s, when US financial services companies American International Group (AIG), American Express and Citicorp wanted to improve their access to heavily regulated markets outside the US, especially in South-East Asia'.

if the process had not been so heavily influenced by the presence of representatives of financial firms.[15] Similar criticisms of corporate influence have been made regarding the European Services Forum, which grew out of the FLG experience.

CONCLUSION

The above examination of sectoral and regional differentiation and of participation, transparency and due process in private-sector associational activity in global finance supports this chapter's argument that while there are inclusive impulses in this activity, contrary to the critical approaches that see financial control as entirely centralized and uniform, there are also serious exclusionary impulses, contrary to the supportive approaches that ignore the exclusionary potential of globally oriented private-sector actors. The world of financial associations is fragmented, and much of it is concerned with the provision of infrastructure for market actors rather than with the coordination of global finance as a whole, or with the promotion of private interests at the expense of the public interest. Certainly even a relatively narrowly focused provision of infrastructure can have policy and structural effects, since it can lock in particular policy choices by creating new interests and routines that come to be taken for granted, that reinforce particular ways of carrying out international financial activities, and that are resistant to alternative policy choices. Nevertheless, it is important to be alert to varying mixes of inclusionary and exclusionary effects in the technical work of associations. In some important respects, this work promotes inclusion, such as the capacity-building efforts of associations in geographical areas not traditionally central to global finance, or in the transparent aspects of the policy-relevant technical discussions among private and public-sector actors on the Basel Committee's website. At the same time, there are troubling examples of exclusionary aspects in associational activity, such as the benefits that the largest banks obtained in Basel II with the IIF's assistance, or the way in which financial firms working through the FLG and its associated groups obtained their market-opening goals. This important policy-related activity of financial services associations at the global level is relatively new, but is likely to grow in the years to come.

---

[15] For an interesting critical analysis of the role of business in financial services liberalization based on minutes of meetings apparently inadvertently posted on the IFSL website, see Wesselius (n.d.), which states 'privileged co-operative relationships between business and government as embodied in IFSL/LOTIS do not belong in a truly democratic policy-making process'.

As noted earlier in this chapter, it is a challenge to fully assess the importance of private sector associations relative to one another as well as the importance of firms and individuals that may establish links among associations and between these associations and policy processes. In addition, there are undoubtedly exclusionary activities that take place without involving associations. For instance, in October 2004 New York Attorney General Eliot Spitzer obtained guilty pleas on charges related to bid-rigging involving insurance giant AIG, the world's largest insurance broker Marsh McLennan, and insurer Ace Limited. Different members of the Greenberg family headed all three firms. A *Business Week* cover story (Vickers 2004) commented on 'The Secret World of Marsh Mac . . . where conflicts of interest abound', and more generally questions were raised regarding the practice throughout the industry of non-transparent payments from insurance companies to ostensibly independent brokers in exchange for steering business to the former. Large firms can facilitate inter-firm collaboration. Similarly a 1996 *Asiamoney* story commented, 'The web of ex-Citibankers spreads far and wide. The networks are like an octopi [sic], with tentacles in every country. There is no branch of finance where Citibank alumni are absent. Their diversity and power of contacts, the capacity of the total web, is awesome'.[16] The article also noted that heads of the ASEAN Bankers Association and the Asian Bankers Association previously had been Citibankers. Examples such as these point to the potential for collusive activities that may have their roots in relationships that occur outside associations. This reinforces this chapter's criticism of supporters of financial globalization for not paying sufficient attention to the potential of globally-oriented firms for exclusionary activity. Without taking the more organized institutional form of an association, these informal or firm-specific connections are likely only to affect particular aspects of global finance and not to have a far-reaching effect on the governance of global finance as a whole. This is consistent with this chapter's suggestion that critical approaches to the problem of inclusion and exclusion in global finance have overstated the degree to which the control of leading private-sector elites is centralized, uniform and ubiquitous. Nevertheless, when combined with the above examples of linkages between key individuals across associations and policy processes, these types of connections should inspire further research that could further address the degree to which variation and fragmentation in the world of associations in global finance can obscure exclusionary patterns that operate across and around their formal organizational aspects. On a related note, it would be important to know more about the way in which policymakers and regulators choose to

[16] 'The Alumni Octopi', *Asiamoney*, **7** (4), May 1996, p. 30.

listen to some associations and not others, and thereby create and reinforce exclusionary patterns. From a practical point of view, it is also important for further research to identify concrete and specific measures to ensure that associational activity strikes the optimal balance between inclusion and exclusion. These measures are likely to need to include public policy and regulatory initiatives. Left on their own, some associations will work to unfairly enhance the interests of their members at the expense of other actors, thus damaging the functioning and legitimacy of global finance in the process.

REFERENCES

Andrews, David M. (1989), 'Capital Mobility and State Autonomy: Toward a Structural Theory of International Monetary Relations', *International Studies Quarterly,* 83, 193–218.

Bhagwati, Jagdish (1998), 'The Capital Myth', *Foreign Affairs*, 12, May/June.

Bohman, James (1999), 'International Regimes and Democratic Governance: Political Equality and Influence in Global Institutions', *International Affairs*, **75** (3), 499–513.

Buckley, Ross P. (2000), 'The Role and Potential of Self-Regulatory Organizations: The Emerging Markets Traders Association from 1990 to 2000', *Stanford Journal of Law, Business and Finance*, Fall, **6** (1), 135.

Carroll, William K. and Colin Carson (2003), 'Forging a New Hegemony? The Role of Transnational Policy Groups in the Network and Discourses of Global Corporate Governance', *Journal of World-Systems Research*, **9** (1), Winter, 67–102.

Cerny, Philip G. (2002), 'Webs of Governance and the Privatization of Transnational Regulation', in David M. Andrews, C. Randall Henning and Louis W. Pauly (eds), *Governing the World's Money*, Ithaca: Cornell University Press, pp. 194–215.

Cetina, Karin Knorr and Urs Bruegger (2002), 'Global Microstructures: The Virtual Societies of Financial Markets', *American Journal of Sociology*, **107** (2), 905–50.

Claessens, Stijn, Geoffrey R.D. Underhill and Xiaoke Zhang (2004), 'Basle II Capital Requirements and Developing Countries: A Political Economy Perspective on the Costs for Poor Countries of Rich Country Policies', paper prepared for presentation at the 5th Pan-European Conference of the ECPR Standing Group on International Relations, The Hague, Netherlands, 9–11 September.

Corporate Europe Observer (2001), 'Revolving Doors: Former Trade Commissioner Now Lobbies for Services Industry', *Corporate Europe Observer*, 8, available at www.corporateeurope.org/observer8/brittan.html.

Dailami, Mansoor (1999), 'Financial Openness, Democracy and Redistributive Policy', World Bank Policy Research Working Paper No. 2372, 30 November, available at papers.ssrn.com.

Easterly, William (2001), 'The Lost Decades: Developing Countries' Stagnation in Spite of Policy Reform 1980–1998', *Journal of Economic Growth*, 6, 135–57.

Finnemore, Martha and Kathryn Sikkink (1998), 'International Norm Dynamics and Political Change', *International Organization*, **52** (4), 888–917.

Froud, Julie, Johal Sukhdev and Karel Williams, (2002), 'Financialisation and the Coupon Pool', *Capital and Class*, Vol. 78, 119–39.

Gill, Stephen (1990), *American Hegemony and the Trilateral Commission*, Cambridge: Cambridge University Press.

Gill, Stephen and David Law (1989), 'Global Hegemony and the Structural Power of Capital', *International Studies Quarterly*, 33, 475–99.

Goad, G. Pierre (1998), 'Rules Sought in Trading Asian Loans', *Wall Street Journal* (Eastern Edition), 26 June, p. 1.

Gowan, Peter (1999), *The Global Gamble: Washington's Faustian Bid for World Dominance*, London: Verso (version also available at www.gre.ac.uk/~fa03/iwgvt/files/9-gowan.rtf).

Harmes, Adam (2001), 'Mass Investment Culture', *New Left Review*, 9, 103–24.

Harmes, Adam (2002), 'The Trouble with Hedge Funds', *Review of Policy Research*, **19** (1), 156–76.

Harms, Philipp, Aaditya Mattoo and Ludger Schuknecht (2003), 'Explaining Liberalization Commitments in Financial Services Trade', World Bank Policy Research Working Paper 2999, available at econ.worldbank.org/files/24878_wps2999.pdf.

Hartwell, Christopher A. (2001), 'The Case Against Capital Controls, Financial Flows, Crises, and the Flip Side of the Free-Trade Argument', *Cato Policy Analysis*, 403, 14 June, 1–20.

Jenkins, Huy (2001), 'Hong Kong: Standardization is the Key in the Internet Age', *Euromoney*, October, p. 12.

Kaplan, Arthur M. (2002), 'Anti-Trust as a Public-Private Partnership: A Case Study of the NASDAQ Litigation', *Case Western Law Review*, **52** (1), 111–32.

Karmel, Roberta S. (2002), 'Turning Seats into Shares: Causes and Implications of Demutualization of Stock and Future Exchanges', *Hastings Law Journal*, 53, 367–430.

Khagram, Sanjeev, James V. Riker and Kathryn Sikkink (eds) (2002), *Restructuring World Politics: Transnational Movements, Networks and Norms*, Minneapolis: University of Minnesota Press.

Keenan, Faith (1999), 'Loans On-Line', *Far Eastern Economic Review*, 22 April, p. 70.

Lindeman, David, Michal Rutkowski and Oleksiy Sluchynskyy (2000), 'The Evolution of Pension Systems in Eastern Europe and Central Asia: Opportunities, Constraints, Dilemmas and Emerging Practices', Paris: OECD, available at www.oecd.org/dataoecd/62/10/1816307.doc.

Macey, Jonathan R. (2003), 'Regulatory Globalization as a Response to Regulatory Competition', *Emory Law Journal*, 52, 1353–79.

McKeen-Edwards, Heather, Tony Porter and Ian Roberge (2004), 'Politics or Markets? The Determinants of Cross-Border Financial Integration in the NAFTA and the EU', *New Political Economy*, **9** (3), 325–40.

Mintz, Beth and Michael Schwartz (1985), *The Power Structure of American Business*, Chicago and London: University of Chicago Press.

Moran, Michael (1984), *The Politics of Banking: The Strange Case of Competition and Credit Control*, London: Macmillan.

Pieth, Mark and Gemma Aiolfi (n.d.), 'The Private Sector Becomes Active: The Wolfsberg Process', available at www.wolfsberg-principles.com/pdf/wolfsbergprocess.pdf.

Piñera, José (2001), 'Liberating Workers: The World Pension Revolution', in *Cato's Letter #15*, Washington: Cato Institute.

Porter, Tony (2004), 'The Role of International Private Financial Services Institutions', in Christopher Waddell (ed.), *Financial Services and Public Policy*, Kingston: McGill-Queen's University Press.

Porter, Tony (2005), *Globalization and Finance*, Cambridge: Polity Press.

Porter, Tony and Duncan Wood (2002), 'Reform Without Representation? The International and Transnational Dialogue on the Global Financial Architecture', in Leslie Elliott Armijo (ed.), *Debating the Global Financial Architecture*, Albany: State University of New York Press, pp. 236–56.

Power, Michael (1994), 'The Audit Society', in Anthony G. Hopwood and Peter Miller (eds), *Accounting as Social and Institutional Practice*, Cambridge: Cambridge University Press, pp. 299–316.

Reinicke, Wolfgang and Francis Deng (2000), *Critical Choices: The United Nations, Networks, and the Future of Global Governance*, Ottawa: IRDC.

Roberts, Robin W., Peggy D. Dwyer and John T. Sweeney (2003), 'Political Strategies used by the US Public Accounting Profession During Auditor Liability Reform: The Case of the Private Securities Litigation Reform Act of 1995', *Journal of Accounting and Public Policy*, 22, 433–57.

Saudagaran, Shahrokh and Joselito G. Diga (1997), 'Accounting Regulation in ASEAN: A Choice Between the Global and Regional Paradigms of Harmonization', *Journal of International Financial Management and Accounting*, **8** (1), 1–32.

Sinclair, Timothy J. (1994), 'Passing Judgement: Credit Rating Processes as Regulatory Mechanisms of Governance in the Emerging World Order', *Review of International Political Economy*, **1** (1), 133–59.

Slaughter, Anne-Marie (2001), 'Symposium: Globalization, Accountability, and the Future of Administrative Law: The Accountability of Government Networks', *Indiana Journal of Global Legal Studies*, 8, 347–67.

Soederberg, Susanne (2003), 'The Promotion of "Anglo-American" corporate governance in the South: Who benefits from the new international standard?', *Third World Quarterly*, **24** (1), 7–27.

Tsingou, Eleni (2001), 'Governance in the Financial Markets – Understanding Self-Regulation', paper presented to the ISA International Convention, Panel S 1-4, 'The Politics of Banking', Hong Kong, 28 July, available at www.isanet.org/archive/tsingou.html.

Vickers, Marcia (2004), 'The Secret World of Marsh Mac', *Business Week*, 1 November, online edition.

Wesselius, Erik (2003), 'Driving the GATS Juggernaut', *Red Pepper*, January, available at www.globalpolicy.org/socecon/bwi-wto/wto/2003/01gats.htm.

Wesselius, Erik (n.d.), 'Liberalisation of Trade in Services: Corporate Power at Work', available at www.gatswatch.org/lotis/lotis.html.

Wood, Duncan (2005), *Governing Global Banking: The Basel Committee and the Politics of Financial Globalization*, Aldershot: Ashgate.

5. The Construction of the Single Market in Financial Services and the Politics of Inclusion and Exclusion

Beat Weber*

1. INTRODUCTION

Efforts to build a single financial market in the EU gained momentum around the turn of the millennium. In 1997, the Council approved the Risk Capital Action Plan. In 1999, the European Council took an even broader step with the Financial Services Action Plan (FSAP). In 2001 it approved the report of a Wise Men's Committee under Chairman Alexandre Lamfalussy calling for a streamlined procedure for legislation in the securities area. One year later, this 'Lamfalussy Procedure' was envisaged to be extended to the areas of banking and insurance.

When one considers that financial markets are widely held to be the embodiment of globality, fluidity and borderlessness, it might seem surprising at first sight that so much political effort is considered necessary to bring about integration. Why did market forces not bring about the single market by themselves? Apart from other integration barriers like language and broader policy regimes, financial markets rest on complicated governance arrangements which are still predominantly national and therefore do not encourage transnational transactions in most market segments. While some parts of the markets are heavily internationalized, many areas of the financial sector are geographically segmented (Verdier 2002). In important aspects such as the organization of supervision, there is no universally accepted model or ideal type of financial governance arrangement, so convergence pressure from market forces is not very strong. If the single market is to become reality and function properly, it must be constructed by deliberate effort (Piccioto

* I want to thank Florian Zinnöcker for research assistance, and Reinhard Petschnigg, Vanessa Redak, Stefan W. Schmitz, Helene Schuberth, Martin Schürz and Geoffrey Underhill for comments on an earlier draft of this paper. The views expressed in the paper are those of the author and do not necessarily represent those of the OeNB.

and Haines 1999, Smith 2001). This approach has obviously informed European policymakers to a growing extent in the last few years.

If the single market is something which has to be constructed, the question of choice over its governance architecture comes into focus. We define financial governance as the processes and arrangements that underpin and structure market processes. It comprises state and non-state actors, formal and informal institutions and generates formal as well as informal rules. In analyzing governance arrangements, we are interested in questions such as: Who takes part in the construction and who does not, which rules are chosen and which are not? These questions will be touched upon in this paper.

We investigate the phenomena of inclusion and exclusion occurring in the three dimensions of governance – policy (the content dimension), politics (the processes of shaping policy), and polity (who takes part in decision making and who does not).

2. POLICY: THE AGENDA OF THE FINANCIAL SERVICES ACTION PLAN

In this chapter we look at the EU's recent policy agenda in financial services, give a brief sketch of its possible consequences and assess whether the implementation of the agenda has brought about any traceable results yet. Finally, we briefly consider the approaches excluded from the agenda – blind spots, omissions and roads not taken.

While for a long time financial services legislation did not amount to much text or figure prominently on the EU's agenda, this changed at the turn of the millennium. The first sign was the adoption of the 'Risk Capital Action Plan' in 1997, which was an effort to catch up with the buoyant US venture capital industry of the New Economy years, then widely considered to be a key to investment in innovation. Two years later, the integration of the securities market, up to then the least tackled area of financial services in EU policymaking, became subject to another 'Action Plan' which set the policy agenda in this field for the years to come.

The Financial Services Action Plan (FSAP) was tabled by the European Commission in May 1999. It contained three 'strategic objectives': The first was to develop a 'single EU wholesale market', comprising a common legal framework for integrated securities and derivatives markets, harmonizing the requirements for financial statements for listed companies, measures against systemic risk in securities settlement, measures to facilitate cross-border takeovers of firms as well as the sale of financial products like investment and pension funds across borders. The second objective was to promote 'open and secure retail markets', which implies measures to enable providers to sell financial services like insurance to customers in other member states. The third objective concerned 'state-of-the-art prudential rules and supervision' for financial service providers (European Commission 1999).

The Lisbon European Council in March 2000 endorsed the Plan and made financial integration one of the pillars of its ambitious economic and social reform agenda for the EU, aiming to become 'the most competitive and dynamic knowledge-based economy in the world' by 2010 (European Council 2000). In order to accelerate progress in realizing the plan, a deadline of 2005 was set for its completion. With the institutional innovation of being subject to an 'action plan', financial market reform was now placed on the 'integration track'.

Whereas the FSAP does define the goal of integration while leaving the details, i.e. the specific path toward integration, subject to negotiations, it is not neutral regarding the choice of a specific integration path. 'To deliver the full prospective benefits to European business and the EU economy, to compete in the global market for goods and services and to help European business to compete in the global market for goods and services, EU capital markets need to be dynamic, competitive and innovative' (ECOFIN 2000).

This can be expected to result in the following changes in the European financial sector:

1. Emergence of a European market for corporate control and greater mobility of capital;
2. Increased cross-border consolidation of financial service providers, with the likely result of market concentration and the emergence of larger financial conglomerates on a European scale;
3. Enhanced options for diversifying investment for funds (e.g. pension funds), thus laying the groundwork for the privatization of private pensions.

These changes are consistent with a global trend toward a more competitive approach to the financial sector (Underhill 2002), and toward transferring former domains of social policy (such as old age provision) to the financial market.

The envisaged transformation of the European financial services landscape has important implications which go far beyond the financial sector itself:

1. The increased mobility of capital, enhanced contestability of corporate control and emergence of larger financial service providers will probably increase the bargaining power of investors vis-à-vis

other stakeholders (labor, trade unions, locations, economic policymakers). With the mobilization and dispersal of corporate control, territorially based compromises and bargains will become more difficult (Underhill 2002).

2. The enhancement of competition and restructuring as well as the promotion of disintermediation in the financial sector increase the probability of crises, which can imply huge costs for taxpayers (Coleman 1999, Porter 2001). Financial market integration provides opportunities for better diversification, but also incentives for higher risk-taking, increasing the level of systemic risk and vulnerability to contagion (EEAG 2003, p. 102)

3. The opening up of retail markets probably will increase the possibility and the pressure for the privatization of social security, above all pensions, with important implications for the distribution of risk and for corporate governance, among other issues. Competition in the pension fund industry will increase, which will lead to more pressing demands from industry toward political promotion of private pensions in order to exploit these markets. The consequence of privatized pension arrangements is the individualization of risk formerly socialized in public pension schemes (Gottwald 2003, Heilmann 2003).

The consolidation and de-segmentation of financial markets will most likely also result in orientation toward profitable customers and neglect of financially weaker groups, leading to phenomena of financial exclusion (Leyshon and Thrift 1997).

The FSAP does aim to transform the European financial landscape into a lever for wider economic reform processes (Almunia 2005). Finance-led restructuring will have effects which transcend the financial sector.

After near completion of the FSAP, the effects and results of the legislative program are surprisingly hard to pin down – at least up to now. Despite the centrality accorded to lawmaking in order to enable integration, the extent to which law matters in financial services integration remains unclear (Freixas et al. 2004).

There are signs of the persisting segmentation of markets: Integration should show up in increased cross-border mergers, increased cross-border sales of financial products and converging prices for financial services. But apart from a few wholesale markets, the financial sector in the EU still remains nationally segmented: The interbank money markets are fully unified, exhibiting narrowed interest differentials. Moreover, the government and corporate bond markets have also seen substantial yield convergence and are subject to increasing cross-border investments. The latter is also observed to some degree in equity markets, with the traditional 'home bias' of investments diminishing. However cross-border activity in retail markets is still low (Freixas et al. 2004). Differences in non-financial law (e.g. consumer protection), language barriers, economic and cultural factors have been cited as reasons for the lack of cross-border movement. Business strategies certainly also play a role in this respect (Gardener et al. 2003). Whether the remaining segmentation can be labeled as inefficient or whether there are sound economic reasons that justify, for instance, the domestic control of large regional banks, remains controversial (Barros et al. 2005, p. 32).

On the other hand, the financial services sector has been caught up in a process of continuing restructuring in recent years. There are also signs that growing cross-border flows of capital do have an impact on corporate behavior. Whether this can be attributed mainly to business initiative, national reforms or EU policy is nearly impossible to say. It is clear that initiatives and developments from various sources interact to produce changes currently going on in the financial sector and beyond. Their common denominator is a pro-competitive outlook toward financial services reform. Public policy in financial services regulation largely conforms to what has been called the 'competition state' (Cerny 2005).

What is in danger of being neglected by these forces are considerations of financial stability, consumer protection, taxation as well as engagements between financial resource allocation and democratic processes. The possibility that more competition and European integration in financial services might collide with other policy objectives is only partially acknowledged in EU policy agendas and outcomes. The emerging conventional wisdom seems to favor 'market-friendly regulation', negating even the traditional insight that regulation is needed precisely because of market failure, which is widely held to be pervasive in financial markets.

The Europeanization of supervision faces resistance from national supervisors. While there has been some effort in recent years toward the coordination of tax policy on capital, progress has been minimal. Policy proposals such as the Tobin Tax, raised to the agenda by public pressure from time to time, have been repeatedly dismissed. An attempt to harmonize European laws on the protection of consumers when taking up debt was tabled by the Directorate for Consumer Protection in the European Commission in 2002, but it was rejected twice after severe objections from the banking industry (*Handelsblatt*, 6 May 2005). National rules of consumer protection and the political links of banks have been subject to criticism, being accused of protectionism and interference with market forces.[1]

In the sections that follow, we address possible causes of these asymmetries in the politics of constructing the EU agenda regarding financial services and the polity engaged in it.

3. POLITICS: THE LAMFALUSSY PROCESS – BEFORE AND AFTER

In this section, we trace the political economy of EU financial services integration over the last decade. Starting from the assumption that political actors are decisive in shaping markets and that market participants compete with other groups in civil society for influence on policies, changes in the composition and strategies of the resulting 'state-market condominium' (see Underhill in this volume) arise from the interaction of existing institutions with changing market circumstances, struggles over the hegemony of ideas and political power struggles in a contingent way. These factors are examined in the context of the issue at hand, and its effects on EU decisions, the reform of the decision-making process as well as the implications for the ability of various actors to participate are tackled with an emphasis on processes of inclusion and exclusion.

While efforts by policymakers to create a single market in the financial services area have been stepped up since the 1980s, the policy process only became intense in the late 1990s. Several developments contributed to the shakeup of the status quo, triggering changes in preferences, positions and circumstances.

In the 1990s, the US financial services industry (especially in the fields of securities and investment banking) made efforts to expand abroad, and not only increased its market presence in Europe, thereby contributing to enhanced competition, but also demanded that EU policymakers adapt the regulatory framework to facilitate market access for outsiders.

Internationalization was accompanied by crises in the late 1990s. After the financial crises in Asia and Russia broke out, representatives of leading industrial countries responded with discussions of a New International Financial Architecture. In the wake of these discussions, standards for financial market regulation and supervision were issued for

[1] Major issues in this respect have recently been the discussions about non-profit German banks with ties to German *Länder* (see Smith 2001), and the policy line of the Italian Central Bank toward takeovers of Italian banks by investors from abroad (McCreevy 2005).

worldwide adoption, highlighting the perception of a need to adapt existing regulatory frameworks to new, more global realities in some segments of the financial sector and to the increased possibility of crisis. With the heightened prevalence of global standards, EU policy elites became eager to develop a coherent voice and approach on these matters in order to influence international debates, and eventually to be able to export their own standards (Ferran 2004, Döpke and Lapp 2004).

The dominant approach to the institutional design of the policy process in financial sector governance follows the idea that while financial regulation cannot be completely left to markets themselves, due to the superior knowledge of market participants it has to rely on their expertise and must follow the idea of not disturbing business, just trying to dampen its self-destructive properties and support its self-regulating capacities. The regulatory state in finance is more of a service provider for the financial sector than the old interventionist state, which had some features designed to 'master finance'. Meanwhile, the model seems to have become the 'competition state' (Cerny 2005).

While the pro-competitive approach to financial services legislation had dominated thinking in the US and UK for a considerable time, until recently finance in continental Europe was part of slightly different configurations and institutional setups, partly due to different sector mixes, different business models and different state strategies. In the 1990s there was some movement in the financial sectors in Europe. The internationalization of business (financial and non-financial) was accompanied by a reorientation of the policy preferences and strategies of important actors. Large firms in the financial and business sector in Germany and France, the main European financial centers, were adopting an international outlook and promoting features of a 'shareholder value' oriented strategy. They became important voices for reform within their own countries, joining forces with policymakers and business advocates promoting 'finance-led restructuring' in Europe (Bieling 2003, Gardener et al. 2003, Kleiner 2003, Lütz in this volume, Smith 2001).

The economic environment contributed to this: During the boom of the securities markets in the late 1990s, the benefits and promises of a more market-oriented model of finance in Europe became a prominent topic in economic policy debates, with the bull market providing support and encouragement for reformers.

The introduction of the euro in 1999 provided a further push for the integration of financial markets and competition between financial centers. While some expected the common currency to push financial sector integration forward by itself, reform-minded policymakers argued that legislative hurdles were still inhibiting market forces and policy action was necessary in order to contribute to a 'level playing field'. And an integrated capital market was considered vital in order to fully capture the benefits of the euro as a means of competing with the US to attract global capital flows (Ferran 2004).

In this climate, which can almost be labeled 'change euphoria', the UK – home of the most mature financial services industry in Europe – took over the presidency of the EU at the beginning of 1998. The presidency provided power over the agenda of the EU Council. The UK Treasury seized this opportunity to push financial market liberalization to the top of the agenda, hoping to promote the interests of the UK financial services industry (Davies 2004). The market events provided good arguments against liberalization skeptics. Against some resistance from other member states over the extent of the mandate for the Commission, which was negotiated over several months in the Economic and Financial Committee, the presidency finally managed to gain approval for an initiative to further integrate financial markets. At the Cardiff Council in June 1998, the Commission was asked to draft an action plan on financial services. In the UK's view, the action plan's aim should have been to eliminate the barriers to cross-border competition and to set a strict time table to move things forward.

The Lisbon Council in March 2000 endorsed the plan and made financial integration one of the pillars of its ambitious economic and social reform agenda for the EU, aiming to become 'the most competitive and dynamic knowledge-based economy in the world' by 2010 (European Council 2000). In order to accelerate progress in realizing the plan, a deadline of 2005 was set for its completion. Timing was considered crucial, because according to the Commission, 'there will never be a better chance to create such a market. Economic conditions are exceptionally favourable. EU enlargement will make decision finding more difficult' (Schaub 2002). The Lisbon Council had been preceded by a tug-of-war between market liberals and proponents of a more socially oriented integration model. The argument had finally been settled by a kind of 'mutual recognition' compromise: Competitiveness was broadly defined, and the market liberalization ('structural reform') plans were complemented by a 'pillar' of social aims (reduction of poverty, environmental protection, etc.), leaving eventual contradictions between the two unmentioned, but allowing approval for liberalization plans like the FSAP.

While the ranks of those in favor of reform were growing and the 'mood of the time' was on their side, finally resulting in the approval of the FSAP, the problem of competitive concerns, mainly among the three largest member states in terms of financial sector size (France, Germany and the UK), promised to make fulfillment of the agenda difficult. What theories of Europeanization have termed the problem of 'uploading' or 'downloading' is central here (see Lütz in this volume): Financial sector regulation in the EU is still characterized by significant national differences. Therefore financial service providers and regulators which have adapted their daily routines to the prevailing national environment have a huge interest in shaping EU legislation according to their own model. In this way, they can avoid costs arising from implementation and adaptation, and they can hope to gain competitive advantages over their rivals in other countries. The expected result of financial integration in the EU is consolidation and concentration, therefore not all current financial service providers, not even all financial centers, can hope to survive. That makes integration a risky project, at least for those not perfectly sure of their competitive strength. To the competition among financial centers and their business communities (whose interests do not always overlap) must be added competition between political institutions at the national and EU level for competences in the financial services field. The result is a 'prisoner's dilemma' type of situation. Despite the fact that the idea of EU financial services reform had achieved hegemony, competition regarding the modalities still posed a threat to the project.

Therefore, once the FSAP was agreed upon, leading policymakers came to the conclusion that they had to do something to reform the process of policymaking. After the EU had largely failed in promoting the formation of political will with a high-level group of senior policy advisers (the Financial Services Policy Group), the French presidency in mid-2000 proposed to appoint a group of 'wise men' to find a new way to structure the policy process. Traditionally, the French government's stance on financial integration had been characterized by a strategy of resistance and claiming national exceptions. This was due to the strong involvement of state and state regulation in financial services, and financial service firms being predominantly oriented toward their home markets. Europe's opening of markets and the expansionist strategy of British firms were perceived as a competitive threat. After the introduction of the FSAP, the old strategy no longer seemed viable and a new one was needed. In other issue areas of standards-setting, French strategies toward the EU have repeatedly been led by attempts to turn French law into European law (Josselin 1997, p. 38). With the FSAP in place, this line of thinking was beginning to be applied to lawmaking in the financial sector. As a result, French economic policymakers opted for an attempt to turn the tables by institutionally reframing the decision-making process for the measures of the FSAP. The plan met with resistance from the governments of Germany and UK. They suspected an element of subterfuge, namely that France was planning to establish a central regulatory and supervisory authority for the EU, thereby paving the way for a heavy-handed approach to regulation, and to place it in Paris. But as the French only proposed to have these 'wise men' think about appropriate responses on current market developments, which also lay at the heart of the whole FSAP, it was hard to argue against it openly. In the negotiations preceding the ECOFIN Council in July 2000, the opponents only managed to get the mandate for the group narrowed and to influence its membership (*Financial Times*, 12 July 2000).

When the group of 'wise men' finally finished their report under the chairmanship of Belgian central banker Alexandre Lamfalussy, it proposed something which was both new and well known: The introduction of 'Comitology' to EU financial services legislation was something the Commission had supported for quite some time.

According to prevailing EU procedures, financial services legislation (mainly in the form of directives, which leave more room in implementation than regulations) was based on proposals by the Commission, then subjected to a co-decision procedure involving the Council (voting with a qualified majority) and the European Parliament, and finally implemented by the member states. According to the wise men's report, this process was inadequate: It took too much time, sometimes resulted in ambiguous directives to accommodate conflicting views, failed to achieve consistent implementation of directives in member states and lacked the flexibility necessary to react to new developments in markets. Blockages were said to exist in four areas: in the Commission due to understaffing, in the Council of Ministers due to its tendency to add unnecessary levels of complexity, in the European Parliament due to delays in approval, and finally in the member states due to late and frequently incomplete and diverging transposition and implementation. The report counts about 40 public bodies in the EU dealing with securities market regulation and supervision, with mixed competences and different responsibilities, leading to fragmented regulation and supervision and thereby inhibiting market integration. To improve things, the report proposes a reformed institutional structure and a streamlining of processes (Committee of Wise Men 2000).

The central feature of the Lamfalussy Procedure is to divide decision making into a four-level procedure: Regulations are to be split into basic political framework decisions and implementation measures containing technical details. Legislation on framework principles (Level 1) is to be decided by the Council and the European Parliament on the basis of Commission proposals. The technical details of framework legislation are delegated to the Commission. This is Level 2, which consists of two expert committees with delegates nominated by member states under Comitology Procedure to assist the Commission, one for advising and one for decision-making. Before the Level 2 regulatory committee is supposed to vote on a proposal, public consultation is to be held on every legislative proposal at Level 2. The Level 3 committee's task is to assist in the implementation of regulations at the national level by ensuring enhanced cooperation and networking among EU securities regulators, thereby achieving the consistent and equivalent transposition of legislation at the national level. Finally, at Level 4, the Commission checks and enforces the compliance of member state laws with EU legislation. The rationale of these changes was to speed up decision-making and achieve a more efficient, comprehensive and consistent legislative procedure.

The main argument in favor of the four-level structure was that faster political decisions can be made at Level 1 if they are not held up by technical details. These technical details should be dealt with by experts at Level 2, which, if left to themselves, could find solutions – and above all regular adaptations to changed market circumstances – faster without being held up by political sham fights. The obvious consequence is that under the Lamfalussy procedure the policy process lies more firmly in the hands of expert committees. They play a decisive role in drafting legislation and collecting comments, and are therefore equipped with high steering power over the regulatory process.

Implementing the proposal proved to be a delicate task. In national governance arrangements, despite differences between member states, national market participants and regulators by and large dominated for a long time. With the exception of crisis situations, financial governance arrangements at the national level are usually dominated by 'low politics' and a high degree of expert influence and technicality (Busch 2004). Initiating EU reform debates is ambivalent from the perspective of these policy elites: It might be necessary in order to achieve desired reforms (opening up foreign markets, changes in regulation, etc.). But it also harbors the risk of 'politicizing' financial governance issues, with the consequence of involving new actors and their agendas, thus weakening the existing policy circles' monopoly over the issue. This fear of a loss of control over the agenda (apart from competition between national policy circles) was part of the problem faced by established policy circles and part of the explanation for deadlocks in previous negotiations on EU financial services legislation. Therefore, a mechanism had to be found in order to ensure that EU discussions on the matter were kept as much a 'low politics' issue as possible. With Lamfalussy, the paradox had to be solved that in order to secure the institutionalization of EU financial regulation as a low politics issue (dominated by expert committees), the issue had to be made subject to high politics for a short time in order to get the Council to agree to Comitology. This was not an easy task, as finance ministers were reportedly not very easily convinced to tackle the issue.

In the debate that followed the Lamfalussy proposal, pressure was mainly exerted by two parties concerned: First, the financial services sector put a great deal of pressure on policymakers to respect its interests and involve it in legislation (Frach 2005). Second, the European

Parliament offered severe resistance to its limited role in the new arrangement. That resistance proved to be tough and brought some publicity to the issue. Parliament members raised the issue of 'democratic legitimacy' in this context, implying that it hinged on their full participation in the legislation process.

The Lamfalussy procedure for securities market legislation was adopted by the Stockholm Council in March 2001. When ECOFIN proposed an extension of the approach to the areas of banking and insurance in 2002, it took two years of negotiation until the European Parliament finally gave its approval (April 2004).

The Lamfalussy arrangement enabled progress toward the common goal – producing decisions on FSAP measures. But it did not eliminate conflict regarding details. Its main achievement was probably the fact that it introduced more control to the policymaking process concerning rules of procedure and participation. Complete satisfaction for all participants of the process is not among its achievements: The UK as the main promoter of financial services integration intended the FSAP as a vehicle to open up foreign markets by the 'mutual recognition' of existing national rules. This was the traditional policy line of the financial service providers united in the 'British Invisibles', an association with a very international outlook which had not been very oriented toward or occupied with European affairs until that time (Rigaut 2001). As the UK's regulatory framework was very much in tune with demands of the City, it hoped to overcome the protective barriers enshrined in other nations' laws concerning consumer protection, national origin, etc. with a 'single European passport' for all aspects of financial service provision. Regulatory competition was seen (as repeatedly proposed by the UK in other areas) as the preferred route for integration (Hertig and Lee 2003). There was reason to hope that the action plan with its tight deadlines would lead to such an outcome and overpower the reluctance of national delegates from other states and reign supreme over the deadlocked status quo. The relevant directorate in the European Commission could be considered an ally of the UK view (*Financial Times*, 27 March 2001). With the Commission as the guardian of the action plan and the committees of national delegates under pressure to meet deadlines, the expansive UK financial market interests could hope for a good outcome.

Five years after the presentation of the FSAP, then considered a victory of the Anglo-Saxon policy approach, the enthusiasm of the UK financial market community for the FSAP and the Lamfalussy process started to fade (Davies 2004; Bishop 2004; *Financial Times*, 4 December 2002). The UK had been voted down in some important areas of FSAP legislation. In addition, market participants, despite being highly involved in initial discussions about regulatory proposals, did not always seem to get what they wanted, partly blaming a lack of transparency in the later stages of the decision-making process (AMCHAM EU 2002, EPFSF 2003, FBE 2002, FESE 2002). At least in some instances, national administrations from continental Europe seemed to be successful in influencing EU legislation, making it conform to their existing national regulatory framework. The acceleration of the legislative process also sometimes seemed to pose problems for many market participants. Short deadlines for consultation and highly demanding specialist texts meant that only industry representatives with the largest resources could cope, leaving smaller interests and 'outsiders' without a chance to influence the process.

These distributional considerations within the group of main actors aside, those in favor and in charge of the FSAP can regard their efforts and the working of the Lamfalussy procedure as a success. As some observers have remarked, 'few other European policy programmes have been completed so comprehensively in such timely fashion' (Freixas et al. 2004, p. 479).

However a wider debate about the substance of the law projects in the FSAP failed to materialize. An indication of the narrowness of the debate about the FSAP project is that the attention to its progress in the public has been confined to a very narrow set of specialized publications, with publicity falling to extremely low levels outside the UK.[2] The consultations on legislative drafts also failed to attract inputs from other sources than the 'usual suspects'.

In the few cases that became politicized, final legislation did diverge from the line preferred by the mainstream of market participants: The takeover directive, which triggered a comparatively broad public debate and led to mobilization beyond the community of the financial sector and its regulators, above all in Germany, was substantially changed after intense debate, much to the disappointment of its proponents (Van Apeldoorn and Horn 2004). In the case of the market abuse directive, in the context of the Enron affair with the ensuing mistrust of financial markets and fear of crisis, less attention was paid to the inputs of market participants than they had desired (Grossman 2004).

For a short time, the fall in confidence among consumers of financial services after the stock market slump following 2000 and the scandals at Enron, Parmalat, etc., raised concerns that something had to be done about the legitimacy of the reform process and confidence in financial services among consumers.

---

[2] A search for the keyword 'Lamfalussy' in the Factiva Database for the period 1 January 2000 to 1 September 2004 yields the following results: *Financial Times* 222 hits, *Financial Times Deutschland* 54, *Frankfurter Allgemeine Zeitung* 57, *Le Figaro* 12, *Le Monde* 3. Obviously, the English-speaking business press dealt far more with the issue than the German one, and discussion in the French press has been nearly absent.

Concerning the possibility of crisis, in 2002 Germany and the UK launched a surprising common initiative to extend the Lamfalussy procedure to the banking and insurance sectors, thereby overcoming the sectoral and national segmentation of supervision and promoting its integration. ECOFIN endorsed the plan in April 2002.

In reaction to criticism concerning the industry-driven regulatory approach, the European Commission called on consumers of financial services to put their perspectives forward in 2003 – after most of the FSAP's agenda was finished. It resulted in some critical remarks concerning the threat the integration agenda poses for consumer protection, the lack of evidence put forward for some policy objectives, and the ignorance of problems such as exclusion, predatory lending, overindebtedness and fraud (FIN-USE 2004), but its consequences for policy remain unclear and seem bound to be neglected.

In summary, the politics of integrating EU financial services governance were dominated by national policymakers and large market participants from the EU's main financial centers (France, Germany, UK) as well as European institutions (Commission, Parliament). Conflict over the design of governance architecture and the substance of legislation was mainly driven by the competitive concerns of market participants. With minor exceptions, the consequences of the policy for interests beyond those concerns did not play a relevant role despite the broad implications of the reforms for the economy, as discussed in the previous chapter.

4. THE CONSTRUCTION OF A FINANCIAL SERVICES POLITY

The Lamfalussy procedure introduced two central elements: first, a new, 'streamlined' process for financial services legislation, as outlined in the previous chapter, and second, a transformation of the polity engaged in the policy process.

In the following, we trace these modifications of the policy community, which emerged from – and in significant ways mirror – the struggles around the policy agenda. In addition to formal decision-making processes, which have seen important modifications, special attention is paid to the composition of the policy community at the stage of sorting out policy proposals and drafting legislation; this goes beyond those eligible to vote. As a result, phenomena of inclusion and exclusion can be detected.

Because financial sector regulation did not feature prominently on the EU agenda until the late 1990s, no coherent policy community had formed, and intergovernmentalism by and large dominated EU financial services legislation. This left room for veto players within member states to block integration in the process leading up to decision-making as well as afterwards due to the considerable latitude in the process of transposing EU legislation into national law (e.g. delays, exceptions, divergent interpretation of clauses). The centers of gravity in the policy process lay within member states, where policy communities were predominantly concerned with their position within nation-states and in international competition. The forces pushing for European integration were weak, and the policy community at EU level was very thin. Conflicts of interest and strategy among governments, as well as dispersed, partly overlapping or blurred governance responsibilities (regulators, supervisory institutions, central banks), and the incoherent stance of market participants stood in the way of shaping a coherent European regulatory framework.

Lamfalussy represents an attempt to transform financial services legislation into a more Europeanized policy field.[3] It envisages a transformation of political institutions as a precondition for transforming policies: the building of a European policy network in order to achieve progress in an integrated financial services agenda suitable for finance-led restructuring of the whole economy. This is due to the likely effects attributed to policy networks: epistemic community building, peer pressure and the gradual shifting of members' priorities from national to common goals. In the financial services field, this was seen as necessary both in order to mobilize and concentrate expertise, as well as to end or channel power struggles.

Because the Lamfalussy process is not mere form but an instrument designed to facilitate implementation of the FSAP, the efforts to construct a policy community were biased in favor of arrangements which promised to achieve this goal. The construction of a policy community was a contested process. This meant deliberately empowering suitable allies, disempowering or neglecting other stakeholders possibly posing a threat to the agenda or holding conflict potential, as well as prudently integrating actors which could act as veto players if left out. The resulting polity is not a neutral form or something which can be considered a fair representation of all stakeholders concerned, but a governance body which increases the likelihood of implementing the agenda of the FSAP.

The main institutions in the EU polity are the Council, the European Parliament (EP) and the Commission. Compared to their usual roles, their positions within the financial services policy process have been subjected to some changes. As mentioned before, under the Lamfalussy procedure,

---

[3] Eberlein and Grande (2005) see the emergence of transnational regulation networks of the Lamfalussy committee type as common trend in EU policymaking.

a committee structure consisting of national representatives, regulators and supervisors is set up which assists the Commission at all stages of the regulatory process.

It has been suspected that the European Commission's underlying goal in promoting Comitology arrangements under Lamfalussy is to strengthen its own role and to use more openness and involvement only as justification for increasing its own power against governments (Almer and Rotkirch 2004).

While it is unclear whether this has been successful from the viewpoint of the Commission considering that member states have created many safeguards against being overruled in the Comitology process, it is certainly true from the viewpoint of the financial services policymaking community comprising the Commission and the financial regulators from member states.

Compared to 'normal' Comitology, the powers of the Commission in the financial services area were more limited, and intergovernmental features strengthened. Due to fears that the new procedure would still unduly favor market interests from the UK (which were suspected to have disproportionate influence on the Commission), not only were Level 3 committees chaired by the member states instead of the Commission, but Germany demanded a safeguard against being overruled in the Level 2 committee with majority voting. Therefore, when the Lamfalussy procedure was finally adopted by the Stockholm Council in March 2001 after months of negotiations, the Commission was forced to give a commitment 'to avoid going against predominant views which might emerge within the Council' in any decision-making at Level 2 (European Council 2001).

In the Lamfalussy procedure, the European Parliament is excluded from the technical details of legislation at Level 2, limiting their co-decision powers, formerly comprising all aspects of legislation, to framework decisions at Level 1 (including decision-making about which aspects of legislation to declare as 'technical details' of regulation). Technical details are to be dealt with at Level 2, where the Parliament only has observer status. But as has been pointed out, behind technicalities there is often political content, so the European Parliament was very reluctant to approve this procedure also in light of the danger that this arrangement could be considered a precedent for other areas (European Parliament 2001). The EP claimed that it was the voice of the public and its exclusion from Level 2 meant excluding public debate in favor of bureaucratic and market interests. Which parts of the public do prevail in the EP? On the one hand, economic policy debates and position-taking in the EP have most of the time been dominated by industry lobbyists (Grossman 2005). In the negotiations preceding the decision on the Lamfalussy process, financial market actors supported the

EP's demand for a greater role in the process (European Shadow Financial Regulatory Committee 2001). The EP has developed a strong reputation for correcting market-insensitive aspects of legislative proposals (Ferran 2004, p. 109). Therefore it cannot be seen as a representative of the general good or a strong counterweight to the dominating forces in the policy process. Also, the membership of its Advisory Panel of Financial Services Experts is dominated by financial industry experts. On the other hand, at least the Advisory Panel also has some members with mixed political and occupational backgrounds (European Parliament 2002). It also has to be mentioned that through the EP's inclusion in the legislative process the publicity of legislation is raised, at least offering chances for public debate.

In the shaping of the polity for financial services legislation, power struggles involving national administrations and market participants as well as European institutions resulted in destabilization, transformation and a rearrangement of existing competences, institutions and arrangements in order to make them more compatible with the goal of achieving progress. The integration of independent institutions, construction and empowerment of actors, and enhancement of expert control can be considered the most important developments in this respect.

Integration of Independent Institutions

One aspect which highlights the construction of the new polity is the changing role of independent official agencies in the financial services field.

One of the aims of the Lamfalussy procedure was the systematic integration of regulation and supervision. Before, banking supervision had been the prerogative of independent central banks in several countries, and they had their own coordination forum at the European level. With the extension of the Lamfalussy framework, central bankers had to fight to even stay in the game. In the end, those in charge of supervision managed to keep a seat in the Level 3 committees (being delegated by their ministries of finance), but their power was reduced (Engelen 2002). Representatives of independent national supervisory authorities can be nominated as experts in the advisory committee at Level 2, thereby becoming members of the policymaking community. The argument for the stronger involvement of finance ministries in supervision was that only governments are democratically legitimated and accountable, and crisis resolution often involves taxpayers' money for rescue operations.

Where the coordination of the international relations of securities exchanges was formerly in the hands of the Federation of European

Securities Commissions (Fesco), consisting partly of independent chairmen of stock exchanges, a follow-up institution was created under the EU umbrella. The independence of Fesco came to an end, and now the reformed institution was more formally integrated into the EU legislation process (Moloney 2003). Allocation of responsibility for the EU policy agenda and control can be considered the main motives for this.

Construction and Empowerment of Actors

In EU policy documents, only the financial services industry as well as its customers are mentioned as stakeholders.[4] Other groups affected by finance-led restructuring are not considered. The former two, which are seen as the main constituencies of the project, are subject to construction efforts.

Apart from national regulators, the dominant players in the polity under Lamfalussy are financial service providers. With Lamfalussy, they obtain explicit influence. Public consultation is a central feature of the legislation process under Lamfalussy, and it is predominantly aimed at (and predominantly used by) the financial services industry. Its expertise, and also its preferences, are formally integrated in policy deliberations. Access to this network is costly for private actors – they have to provide people with expertise. But even expertise is not enough: You may enter only if you accept the rules of the game or the minimum requirements in terms of policy preferences (Grossmann 2005). Opponents to market integration now face heavy pressure to justify their position in terms of common benefits, which means identifying its contribution to financial integration.

Including market participants in the regulation process is in line with a worldwide trend, accompanying a changed approach in which finance is no longer seen so much as something to be either used and controlled by policy or best left alone, but more as something to be nurtured and supported by concerted efforts involving public and private actors with a view to global competitiveness.

While giving way to industry pressure for increased consultation and transparency, the Commission put pressure on industry to 'speak with one voice'. Indeed, in recent years industry associations with a European outlook have proliferated in various financial services sectors. Increased cooperation and coherence among market participants is one of the

---

[4] For instance, in its recent Green Paper on financial services policy the Commission states that 'The FSAP has over the last six years aimed to put integrated, efficient, deep and liquid financial markets at the service of European issuers, investors and financial service providers' (European Commission 2005).

consequences of the EU's integration efforts in the financial services area. There is a tendency to move away from the strictly national organization of interests and patterns of lobbying toward the building of European interest associations (Rigaut 2001, Grossman 2004).

The Commission has been active in calling on 'the investor' when arguing for integration, realizing that the retail investor is a potentially important agent for the construction of the single market and that investor confidence could be as powerful a single market lever as the free movement rights of investment firms (Moloney 2003, p. 824; see also Langley 2005).

Using the well-known strategy of speaking in the name of consumers and their benefit when reforming regulatory arrangements, the Commission underlined benefits for the investor as well as companies (issuers), both allegedly benefiting from a lowering of capital costs brought about by European financial integration.

As an ally for its integration strategy, investors calling for integrated financial services markets would be very much welcomed by the Commission, also in order to avoid blame for promoting only the interests of deep pockets. But there was no audible voice of investors publicly making such claims. So the Commission started attempts to construct such a voice by taking steps to mobilize an end-user perspective in the debate – at least by calling on experts on consumer affairs in financial services (European Commission 2003), with the obvious aim of increasing the legitimacy of legislation. The legislation also relies heavily on empowering the rational investor who is able to decode financial information – transparency rules play a strong role (Ferran 2004).

Enhancement of Expert Control

With the policy process in the hands of standing expert committees which dominate the drafting and implementation of legislation texts, and the area of financial services legislation being subjected to an action plan, decision-making in financial market regulation is now more secure from any linkage with other issues and therefore any dilution resulting from package deals, thus reducing the chances that debates about financial regulation will reach a broader public.

The discussion in the first section indicates that fulfillment of the EU financial integration agenda has implications for a variety of stakeholders outside the financial services area. So what about the chances of the broader public to participate under the Lamfalussy procedure?

While the state and market players do cooperate to design financial market regulation, policy concerns from outside the financial sphere do not feature in this arrangement. In the EU, the Lamfalussy procedure makes financial services legislation more autonomous from other policy areas.

With the confinement of the European Parliament to Level 1, there is no forum for public debate on the 'technical' issues of Level 2, which sometimes involve political content. In the Lamfalussy procedure, participation is interpreted in terms of transparency and consultation, in line with the general trend in the EU. Financial services legislation, especially Level 2 measures, are of such a technical nature and the deadlines given by the FSAP so tight that de facto they are an exclusive experts' domain anyway, confining these debates and the possibility of contributing inputs to the industry. If and how inputs are considered is up to the technical committee to decide, there are no legally binding rules on how inputs in consultation procedures are to be processed (Almer and Rotkirch 2004).

Room for inputs is also constrained in other ways. With its transparency and consultation procedures, the Lamfalussy process simply executes the FSAP. In the consultation procedures, that only leaves room for those inputs which accept the aims of this plan. In that way, deliberation only starts after the main terms of the process have already been decided upon.

Within the remaining confines for argument about details left open by the FSAP, the opportunities for stakeholders other than financial institutions to participate in consultation and benefit from transparency are very limited: Understanding technical consultation documents and providing inputs for their drafting that stand a chance of being taken seriously requires knowledge and resources only found in national administrations, large financial service providers and some industry associations.

While the possibilities for non-specialists' participation in the EU decision-making process are institutionally constrained, the opportunities offered at the national level are also far more limited than before. One of the aims of the Lamfalussy reform is to constrain national leeway in transposing and interpreting EU directives in financial market affairs. This implies strictly limiting the role of national policy processes, such as national parliaments. The process is now firmly in the hands of the European policy network.

The strengthening of the European regulatory process and policy community related to it implies a weakening of actors with only national reach (national parliaments, trade unions, industries with only a local outreach, the general public), which in turn makes it easier to agree among experts largely in isolation from national obligations outside the narrow confines of the financial services industry.

Summing up, in the polity engaged in financial services legislation we can trace signs of exclusion of some of the stakeholders concerned. More often than not, 'exclusion' does not imply an active hindrance to participation. It is undeniable that apart from specialists, matters of financial services legislation do not stir up any interest among wider social groups (Frach 2005, Tsingou 2004). This can be attributed to the fact that by and large finance is viewed and presented as something technical which is best left to the experts. In order to broaden participation in the process, the current transparency procedures are not enough. Empowerment measures would be needed. That this is not too much to demand can be seen in the fact that empowerment techniques are already being employed: The Commission's measures to strengthen the representation of financial services consumers as mentioned above are one obvious example. The current wave of financial literacy initiatives (OECD 2004) provides a further example: While it is widely held that measures are needed in order to enhance knowledge among the population about financial services in order to make them more confident consumers, the possibility that one could promote enhanced literacy also to widen participation in shaping regulation is rarely considered.

5. CONCLUSIONS

The agenda of financial integration as embodied in the Financial Services Action Plan aims at a thorough transformation of the European financial landscape. As the financial services sector provides important infrastructure for the whole economy, apart from producers and consumers of financial services, many groups in society will be affected. When we consider democracy to be an arrangement in which those affected by a decision should participate in it, the groups affected by finance-led restructuring should be involved in the EU policy process engaged in reforming the financial sector. This is not a utopian demand: Financial service providers demanded this participation, and it was granted by policymakers, as reflected in current consultation practice within the Lamfalussy framework. But participation is unbalanced: Analysis of the EU policy process does indicate that it is dominated by a very small circle of experts from member states' administrations (regulators and supervisors, central banks) and financial service providers. This is due to the fact that phenomena of exclusion have arisen in the financial services polity: Due to formal and informal barriers, only specialists take part in deliberations and bargaining over the legislation agenda and its implementation.

In a recent statement about the future of the Lamfalussy process, the European Commission declared its intention of '[s]trengthening even further the democratic accountability of the process' (McCreevy 2004).

While this is obviously intended as a diplomatic gesture toward the European Parliament, one could reflect on what it would imply to take the statement seriously in light of the analysis in this paper. In order to break up the monopoly of experts from industry and national administrations and to broaden participation, empowerment measures already employed for selected constituencies could be used for all groups affected by financial services legislation. If participation is meant to go beyond securing the legitimacy of the existing agenda, it must not be restricted to implementing the legislative agenda envisaged in the FSAP and its follow-up measures (European Commission 2005), but must also encompass discussion about fundamental policy priorities in the financial services field, considering its impact on other areas.

REFERENCES

Almer, Josefin and Matilda Rotkirch (2004), 'European Governance – an overview of the Commission's agenda for reform', Stockholm: Swedish Institute for European Policy Studies.

Almunia, Joacquin (2005), 'The Euro, Financial Market Integration and Structural Reform in Europe', European Commission Speech/05/240, New York, 19 April.

AMCHAM EU – American Chamber of Commerce to the European Union (2002), 'Comments in the consultation process on the "Report of the Economic and Financial Committee on financial regulation, supervision and stability"', December 9.

Barros, Pedro Luis Pita, Erik Berglöf, Paolo Fulghieri, Jordi Gual, Colin Mayer and Xavier Vives (2005), 'Integration of European Banking: The way forward', *Monitoring European Deregulation*, 3, London/Bilbao: Fundacion BBVA/CEPR.

Bieling, Hans Jürgen (2003), 'Social forces in the making of the new European economy: The case of financial market integration', *New Political Economy*, **8** (2), 203–24.

Bishop, Graham (2004), Notes of the European Financial Forum meeting held on 15 March, available at http://www.grahambishop.com.

Busch, Andreas (2004), 'The resilience of national institutions: The case of banking regulation', in Stefan A. Schirm (ed.), *New Rules for Global Markets: Public and Private Governance in the World Economy*, Houndmills, Basingstoke: Palgrave, pp. 87–107

Cerny, Philip (2005), 'Power, markets and accountability', in Andrew Baker, David Hudson and Richard Woodward (eds), *Governing financial globalization*, New York: Routledge, pp. 24–48.

Coleman, William (1999), 'Private governance and democracy in international finance', McMaster Working Paper No. 99/1.

Committee of Wise Men (2000), 'Initial Report of the Committee of Wise Men on the Regulation of European Securities Markets', 9 November, available at http://europa.eu.int/comm/internal_market/securities/docs/lamfalussy/wisemen/initial-report-wise-men_en.pdf.

Davies, Howard (2004), 'Creating a single financial market in Europe: What do we mean?', LSE Financial Markets Group Special Paper No. 155.

Döpke, Jörg and Susanne Lapp (2004), 'Der Finanzmarktrahmenplan der EU', *WisSt Heft*, 11, November, 677–81.

Eberlein, Burkhard and Edgar Grande (2005), 'Beyond delegation: transnational regulatory regimes and the EU regulatory state', *Journal of European Public Policy*, **12** (1), 89–112.

ECOFIN (2000), The Committee of wise men's terms of reference given by the European Union's Economic and Finance Ministers on 17 July 2000, Annex 1 of Committee of Wise Men (2000), available at http://www.eu.int/comm/internal_market/securities/docs/lamfalussy/wisemen/initial-report-wise-men_en.pdf

EEAG – European Economic Advisory Group at CESifo (2003), Report on the European Economy 2003.

Engelen, Klaus C. (2002), 'Europe's post Enron response', *The International Economy*, Fall, 40–3.

EPFSF – European Parliamentary Financial Services Forum (2003), 'The Lamfalussy Process: Does it work and what are the consequences of extension?', 2 December, available at http://www.epfsf.org/ meetings/2003/briefings/briefing_2dec2003_more.htm.

European Commission (1999), 'Financial Services: Implementing the framework for financial markets: Action Plan, Communication of the Commission', COM(1999)232, 11 May 1999, available at http://europa.eu.int/comm/internal_market/en/finances/actionplan/actionen.pdf

European Commission (2003), 'Financial services: Commission to set up expert forum to look at policies from users' point of view (FIN-USE)', IP/03/1119, 25 July 2003, available at http://europa.eu.int/rapid/pressReleasesAction.do?reference=IP/03/1119&format=HTML&aged=0&language=EN&guiLanguage=en.

European Commission (2005), 'Green Paper on Financial Services Policy (2005–2010)', COM (2005)177.

European Council (2000), 'Presidency Conclusions – Lisbon European Council 23 and 24 March 2000', available at http://europa.eu.int/ISPO/docs/services/docs/2000/jan-march/doc_00_8_en.html.

European Council (2001), 'Presidency Conclusions – Stockholm European Council 23 and 24 March 2001', at http://ue.eu.int/ueDocs/cms_Data/docs/pressData/en/ec/00100-r1.%20ann-r1.en1.html.

European Parliament (2001), 'Minutes of the meeting of the European Parliamentary Financial Services Forum on 27 February 2001', available at www.epfs.org.

European Parliament (2002), 'European Parliament launches Advisory Panel of Financial Services Experts', press release, 28 May.

European Shadow Financial Regulatory Committee (2001), 'The Lamfalussy Report', Statement No. 10, 26 March 2001, available at http://www.aei.org/publications/filter.economic,pubID.16961/pub_detail-asp.

FBE – European Banking Federation (2002), 'Financial Services Industry urges proper consultation on Prospectus Directive', 1 August, available at http://www.fbe.be/pdf/fProspectus%20consul.Web%20version.pdf.

Ferran, Eilis (2004), *Building an EU securities market*, Cambridge: Cambridge University Press.

FESE – Federation of European Securities Exchanges (2002), 'European financial sector associations call for consultation on revised draft for Prospectus Directive', 31 July, available at http://www.fese.be/initiatives/european_representation/2002/bolkestein_letter_31jul2002.htm.

FIN-USE Forum (2004), 'Financial Services, consumers and small businesses. A user perspective on the reports on banking, asset management, securities and insurance of the Post FSAP stocktaking groups', 4 October.

Frach, Lotte (2005), 'Participation of interest groups in the Lamfalussy process. A new quality of participatory legitimacy?', Research Group on Equity Market Regulation (REGEM), *REGEM Analysis*, 13, available at http://www.chinapolitik.de/studien/regem/regem_no13.pdf.

Freixas, Xavier, Philipp Hartmann and Colin Mayer (2004), 'The assessment: European financial integration', *Oxford Review of Economic Policy*, **20** (4), 475–89.

Gardener, Edward, Philipp Molyneux and Jonathan Williams (2003), 'Competitive banking in the EU and Euroland', in Andrew Mullineux and Victor Murinde (eds), *Handbook of international banking*, Cheltenham, UK and Northampton, MA, USA: Edward Elgar, pp. 130–55.

Gottwald, Jörn-Carsten (2003), 'Finanzmärkte und Staatliche Regelsetzung', Research Group on Equity Market Regulation (REGEM), *REGEM Analysis*, 2, available at http://www.chinapolitik.de/studien/regem/regem_no2.pdf.

Grossman, Emiliano (2004), 'Bringing politics back in: rethinking the role of economic interest groups in European integration', *Journal of European Public Policy*, **11** (4), 637–54.

Grossman, Emiliano (2005), 'European banking policy: Between multi-level governance and Europeanization', in Andrew Baker, David Hudson and Richard Woodward (eds), *Governing Financial Globalisation. The Political Economy of Multi-Level Governance*, London: Routledge, pp. 130–46.

Heilmann, Sebastian (2003), 'Capital Market Reforms as an Economic and Political Process', *REGEM Analysis*, 1, available at http://www.chinapolitik.de/studien/regem/regem_no1eng.pdf.

Hertig, Gérard and Ruben Lee (2003), 'Four predictions about the future of EU securities regulation', *Journal of Comparative Law Studies* (forthcoming), available at http://www.oecd.org/dataoecd/5/27/18469147.pdf.

Josselin, Daphne (1997), *Money politics in the new Europe*, Basingstoke: MacMillan.

Kleiner, Thibaut (2003), 'Building an asset management industry: forays of an Anglo-Saxon logic into the French business system', in Djelic, Marie-Laure and Sigrid Quack (eds), *Globalisation and institutions. Redefining the rules of the economic game*, Cheltenham, UK and Northampton, MA, USA: Edward Elgar, pp. 57–82.

Langley, Paul (2005), 'The everyday life of global finance', in Andrew Baker, David Hudson and Richard Woodward (eds), *Governing financial globalization*, New York: Routledge, pp. 85–101.

Leyshon, Andrew and Nigel Thrift (1997), 'Geographies of financial exclusion', in Andrew Leyshon and Nigel Thrift, *Money/Space. Geographies of monetary transformation*, London: Routledge, pp. 225–60.

McCreevy, Charlie (2004), 'Assessment of the integration of the Single Market for financial services by the Commission', Speech/04/515 at the CESR (Committee of European Securities Regulators) Conference, Paris, 6 December.

McCreevy, Charlie (2005), 'The future of banking policy in the Union', European Commission Speech/05/191, Brussels, 22 March.

Moloney, Niamh (2003), 'New frontiers in EC capital markets law', *Common market law review*, **40** (4), 809–43.

OECD (2004), 'OECD's Financial Education Project', *OECD Financial Market Trends*, 87 (October), 223–28.

Piccioto, Sol and Jason Haines (1999), 'Regulating global financial markets', *Journal of Law and Society*, **26** (3), 351–68.

Porter, Tony (2001), 'The democratic deficit in the institutional arrangements for regulating global finance', *Global Governance*, **7** (4), 427–39.

Rigaut, Aloys (2001), 'La representation des intérets des places financières dans le contexte de l'intégration européenne', available at http://www.lobbying-europe.com.

Schaub, Alexander (2002), 'The European Single Financial Market: A permanent construction site?', speech at the ELEC Monetary Commission, Kronberg, 15 November, available at http://www.elec.easynet.be.

Smith, Mitchell (2001), 'In pursuit of selective liberalization: single market competition and its limits', *Journal of European Public Policy*, **8** (4), 519–40.

Tsingou, Eleni (2004), 'Policy preferences in financial governance: Public-private dynamics and the prevalence of market-based arrangements in the banking industry', University of Warwick, CSGR Working Paper 131/04.

Underhill, Geoffrey (2002), 'Global integration, and monetary governance in the EU: The political economy of the "Stability culture"', in Kenneth Dyson (ed.), *European States and the Euro*, Oxford: Oxford University Press, pp. 31–52.

Van Apeldoorn, Bastiaan and Laura Horn (2004), 'Levelling the playing field for whom? The European takeover directive and the European marketisation project', paper for Deutsche Vereinigung für Politische Wissenschaft, Sektion "Politik und Ökonomie", Sektionstagung 'Die politische Ökonomie der Wirtschafts- und Währungsunion', 3–4 December, Cologne.

Verdier, Daniel (2002), 'How and why financial systems differ: A survey of the literature', European University Institute, Working Paper SPS No. 2.

6. Financial Education for the Poor in the United States

Martin Schürz*

INTRODUCTION

In February 2002, former US Treasury Secretary Paul H. O'Neill argued in his testimony before the Senate Committee on Banking, Housing and Urban Affairs, 'Financial education can be compared to a road map to the American dream. I believe that we need to teach all Americans the necessary skills to read that map, so that they can reach the dream'. The US Treasury Secretary is quite explicit on the value of programs which enhance financial literacy; it 'permits people to believe that their ambitions do not have to be limited' (US Senate Committee on Banking, Housing and Urban Affairs 2002, p. 16).

Financial education involves providing financial information and supporting consumers to develop the relevant skills and confidence in order to make informed financial decisions. It makes consumers aware of financial opportunities, choices and consequences, and tries to ensure that consumers acquire the skills to understand financial concepts. It also involves changing behavior and ensuring that consumers feel confident in making decisions. This definition refers to the information, knowledge and behavior of individuals. In particular, financial education comprises the development of skills, the ability to transform knowledge into action, the awareness of choices and the ability to choose self-assuredly among various options. Financially educated consumers should make better decisions for their families, and 'financially literate consumers enable increasingly complex financial markets to operate efficiently' (OECD 2004, p. 8).

In general, financial consumers are often not well-informed when making decisions about financial products. Research shows that a substantial percentage of the population (in the US, UK, Australia, etc.)

* The views expressed in the paper are those of the author and do not necessarily represent those of the OeNB.

has inadequate knowledge about concepts related to personal finance (Fannie Mae Foundation 2000, FSA 2000b, Braunstein and Welch 2002, FSA 2004b).

The aim of this chapter is to outline what we know about the effects of financial literacy programs on low-income households in the United States. The first main section examines the official justification of financial literacy programs. The second part concentrates on the question of whether low-income households definitely face problems that can be cured by financial literacy programs. Finally, the third section considers financial education as a cultural governance mechanism that provides an alternative to income-support policies.

1. OFFICIAL JUSTIFICATION OF FINANCIAL LITERACY PROGRAMS

Financial market innovations, the increasing complexity of financial products, and changes in personal finance have been important developments in the financial landscape. Capital markets have become more sophisticated. Innovations allow consumers broader access to financial products, but the characteristics of such products are sometimes difficult to comprehend.

Social and political changes leading to the broader involvement of consumers in financial markets have contributed to the – perceived – need for greater financial awareness. The importance of individual autonomy in society is growing. The consumers' responsibility for their own retirement savings has also grown. Changes in welfare reform have transformed low-income consumers from government benefit recipients into permanent job seekers.

The characteristics of actual financial markets differ from those of purely competitive markets. Financial education is meant to help create the conditions necessary to approach purely competitive markets. Another goal stated in all financial literacy rationales is that informed consumers help to avoid the predatory practices of unscrupulous financial firms (Greenspan 2003, OECD 2004).

In OECD countries, numerous actors are increasingly emphasizing the importance of financial education (Braunstein and Welch 2002, Hogarth et al. 2003, Roy Morgan Research 2003, OECD 2004). In the US, the Federal Reserve Board has addressed the topic on numerous occasions, and Congress held a two-day hearing on the subject in 2002 (US Senate Committee on Banking, Housing and Urban Affairs 2002, Greenspan 2002, Pitt 2002).

Up to now, the bulk of educational efforts have drawn their rationale from more or less plausible inferences concerning the impact of literacy programs on knowledge and behavior. Thus, many literacy programs work under the implicit assumption that enhancing information and knowledge will lead to positive changes in financial behavior.

Many organizations and institutions have included financial literacy education on their agenda. The financial education industry is large (Americans for Consumer Education and Competition, American Savings Education Council, Cooperative Extension System, Consumer Literacy Consortium, Jump Start Coalition for Personal Financial Literacy, and so on). A study conducted by Fannie Mae found that two thirds of the 90 financial literacy programs under investigation were established in the 1990s (Fannie Mae Foundation 2000). The providers of these programs are diverse, including employers, the military community, colleges, faith-based groups and community-based organizations. The scope of financial literacy programs and the number of people they reach varies enormously.

In the US, most state consumer education requirements are aimed at high schools (US Department of the Treasury 2002). School programs, which vary in goals from state to state and in practices from school to school, reach the largest number of people. However, many of the high school students who seem to need financial education most have already dropped out by their junior year. Credit counseling agencies that target people with specific financial troubles reach far smaller numbers, and faith-based educational initiatives get through to even fewer people.

2. EFFECTIVENESS OF FINANCIAL LITERACY PROGRAMS

At a hearing of the US Senate Committee on Banking, Housing and Urban Affairs on the 'The State of Financial Literacy and Education in America', Securities Commissioner Denise Voigt Crawford had to admit: 'On average, the general public is financially illiterate. Despite numerous, well-intentioned efforts over the last few years to increase investor knowledge, recent surveys on financial literacy are finding nearly the same dismal results that were found in surveys five or more years earlier'.

The OECD has recently launched efforts to identify sound practices for effective financial education programs. However, a striking feature of financial literacy programs is the extent to which they have proceeded without much hard evidence of any kind. There are only a few evaluations of their success, and all of them have to be interpreted cautiously. Evaluating the effectiveness of financial literacy programs cannot reveal a direct impact, as there is no credible way to estimate outcomes in the absence of participation.

Looking at the problems identified by the extensive literature on financial education, one could easily conclude that almost everybody today is in need of continuing education. However, different groups are considered more vulnerable (FSA 2000a). The most common argument in the literature is that financial education is of particular importance for three specific groups: the unbanked, credit users and retirement savers (Hogarth et al. 2003).

Evidence suggests that people sign up for training when they have a specific problem or a particular goal. There is not much evidence that financial literacy courses offered outside that context, or outside a captive situation such as the workplace, will attract much interest. Empirical data demonstrate that part of the problem lies in the fact that consumers do not seem to act on the information provided to them in the expected manner (Jump Start 2004). In many cases, they do not make use of or understand the information provided.

Analytically, three types of financial education problems are often distinguished: information problems, knowledge problems and inadequate financial behavior. Financial education is meant to ensure that information will become knowledge; however, even adequate financial knowledge does not ensure adequate behavior.

2.1 Financial Information

The supposed key to getting people to improve their financial behavior is to give them information, which will subsequently form knowledge that they can use to guide their financial behavior. There has already been an explosion of finance-related Internet sites and magazines about money and investing, which means that a wealth of information is available. 'Years ago', said Arthur Levitt, Chairman of the Securities and Exchange Commission, 'the problem was a lack of information. But the irony is: Do people have the foundation in the financial basics that will allow them to use that information?'

Classroom-style programs taking a 'one-size-fits-all' approach may be too little for some participants and too much for others (Braunstein and Welch 2002, p. 448). Suitable ways of delivering financial literacy programs are a topic of scientific investigation (Toussaint-Comeau and Rhine 2000c). There are several ways to realize financial literacy initiatives: organizing seminars, distributing pamphlets, using radio, television and newspapers, or posting information on the Internet. Each of these different types of delivery system has its merits and potential drawbacks. Consumers are more receptive to informal seminars held in their community. Resources such as pamphlets, booklets and videos are more useful to consumers when disseminated at these informal programs. Using radio and television media is an effective way to provide information to consumers, but these media are expensive delivery mechanisms. Information offered on web sites may be less effective for lower-income households that do not have convenient access to the Internet (Toussaint-Comeau and Rhine 2000a). However, the most important source of information about personal finance is personal experience (Braunstein and Welch 2002, p. 455).

2.2 Financial Knowledge

Surveys of financial knowledge in several OECD countries (Roy Morgan Research 2003, Consumer Bankers Association 2003, OECD 2004, Jump Start 2004) have shown that consumers are in need of financial education. But 'there is a difference between providing information and providing education. Education may require a combination of information, skill-building, and motivation to make the desired changes in behaviour' (Hilgert and Hogarth 2003, p. 321). Most surveys found that financial knowledge varied with socio-economic conditions such as income, education and race. While the questions varied, the standard suggestions regarding behavior seem to follow the financial education messages of the US Treasury: build savings to avoid high-cost debt and improve payment options, pay bills on time and pay more than the minimum payment, compare credit offers and obtain only the credit you need, and understand your credit history and how it affects you (US Treasury 2004).

Surveys in the United States found that half of adults and two thirds of high school students had failing scores on a basic economics test. The respondents did not understand economic concepts such as inflation and interest rates. Results from the Jump Start Coalition's biennial financial literacy tests of high school seniors in 2004 show that on average students answered 52 per cent of the questions correctly. In 1997, the corresponding figure was 57.3 percent. Hispanics and African Americans tended to have below-average financial literacy scores. The majority of the participants said they learned most of their skills at home (Jump Start 2004).

While financial consumers generally lack the knowledge they need to make informed choices about a range of products, for poor people a lack of knowledge is claimed to be a barrier to using financial services at all. Low-income families generally have less financial knowledge than wealthier families. This is even true of children: Those from low-income families have fewer opportunities to learn about the role financial institutions play as they do not observe their parents using banks or non-cash methods of payment (FSA 2000a).

2.3 Financial Behavior

There is a correlation between financial knowledge and behavior: Those with better results in financial tests follow recommended practices such as paying all their bills on time, balancing their checkbooks every month and having an emergency fund. However, the direction of causality is unclear (Hogarth et al. 2003). Either the increased knowledge improves people's behavior, or those who save their money gain financial knowledge, or a third variable such as economic socialization affects both.

- How do people make financial decisions? There are empirical indications that the common-sense observation of human actions is not that wrong. Behavioral economics has revealed different kinds of anomalies (Thaler and Benartzi 2001). Vice-Chairman of the Federal Reserve Roger W. Ferguson (2002) points to the regular tendency toward myopic financial behavior even among sophisticated individuals. Ferguson concludes that neoclassical economics, with its strong assumptions on rational behavior, is of limited explanatory value for real behavior. Most studies on the effects of financial literacy programs show that households do not act as required by orthodox economists' models. Even in the presence of reliable information, self-destructive behavior can be observed. The self-destructive aspects of consumer behavior in financial matters are not cured by information alone.
- In the first systematic study on the long-term behavioral effects of high school financial curriculum mandates, Bernheim et al. (1997) show that such mandates elevate the rates at which individuals save and accumulate wealth.
- Hirad and Zorn (2001) show that the average 90-day delinquency rate of borrowers receiving homeownership counseling is 19 per cent lower. However, they cannot confirm whether this reduction comes from the counseling itself rather than the selection of borrowers in these programs.
- Recent surveys show that in 2004 high school seniors in the US knew even less about credit cards, retirement funds, insurance and other personal finance basics than they did five years before. Despite all the educational efforts, the knowledge of high school students has declined (Jump Start 2004).
- After a seminar for potential participants in a 401(k) pension plan, 100 per cent of those in attendance said that they would join the plan after the seminar, but half a year later only 14 per cent had done so (Choi et al. 2001). Another survey demonstrated that 68 out of 100 employees

in a US company believed that they were not saving enough. 24 of the 68 mentioned that they would start saving more within three months, but only three of the 24 actually did.

- In a study of defined contribution plans (Choi et al. 2001), one third of self-reported 'under-savers' said they intended to increase their saving rate in the next few months, but almost none made a change in their 401(k) saving rate.
- Thaler and Mulainathan (2000) suggest, for instance, that the lack of self-discipline among financial consumers necessitates strategies that force savings (e.g. automatic enrollment in 401(k) investment plans).
- Madrian and Shea (2001) show the difference in participation rates in a 401(k) pension savings scheme for two different groups of new employees in a firm. When employees were enrolled automatically unless they deliberately opted out, the participation rate was 30 per cent higher than when enrollment required them to opt in.
- Asset allocation decisions are influenced by the choices presented: If a financial advisor asks individuals to choose freely among four equity funds and two bond funds, the choices made will be more equity-focused than if two equity funds and four bond funds are on the list of available investments. Moreover, too many choices make people avoid a decision. People faced with 20 product or fund choices will be less likely to make a savings decision than if presented with only three choices (Pensions Commission 2004, p. 210).

Thus, there is evidence of procrastination, that is, people are persuaded by information and advice that saving is desirable, but they delay implementation often indefinitely. Even when people recognize that saving is in their best interest, there are barriers which prevent them from doing so. Another key finding is inertia. People often prefer the status quo or choose the alternative that requires the least decision-making. Those who have already started to save usually keep saving, and people who do not save usually do not start (Thaler and Benartzi 2001).

3. FINANCIAL EDUCATION FOR THE POOR IN THE US?

How effective are financial literacy efforts for the poor? As financial products are not only complex but transactions are also rare, the issue should be more severe for people with low resources and no second choices. Unfortunately almost no empirical data are available to evaluate the effectiveness of these specific programs. However, the literature on the problems of the poor in the financial field is abundant (Bird et al.

1997, Hogarth and O'Donnell 1999, Jacob et al. 2000, Martin et al. 1999, Miller-Adams 2002, Barr 2004, Greene et al. 2003). Moreover, articles on the programs provided by financial institutions and public authorities are also numerous (see Federal Reserve 1999, Toussaint-Comeau and Rhine 2000a, Carr and Schuetz 2001, Caskey 2002).

In the next section, we study whether poor people in the US actually require financial literacy. Our analysis will focus on capabilities. If the source of the exclusion problem is an asymmetric information problem, financial literacy might be of help. However, if resources and capabilities are lacking, the importance of education is likely to be limited. In addition, if there are rational motives not to participate in the financial field, then we should ask whether the existing financial education initiatives fulfill other functions.

3.1 The Unbanked

In 2001, about 9.1 per cent of all American families had no transaction accounts of any kind. This is a drop of only one half per cent since 1998. Of the families in the lowest income quintile, only 62.5 per cent had a transaction account in 2001. 54 per cent of Mexican immigrants are unbanked (Survey of Consumer Finances (SCF), Federal Reserve Board 2001).

Table 6.1 Reasons why low-income households do not have deposit accounts

Reasons given	Percentages giving this reason
Do not need account because we have no savings	53.3
Bank account fees are too high	23.1
Banks require too much money just to open an account	22.1
Want to keep our financial records private	21.6
Not comfortable dealing with banks	17.6
Banks won't let us open an account	9.5
No bank has convenient hours or location	8.5

Source: Caskey (1997).

Having a deposit relationship with a financial institution allows consumers greater access to credit for the purpose of purchasing a house or other consumer goods. What are the reasons for bank exclusion?

Unfortunately, the SCF does not ask people why they do not have a deposit account (see Annex I). A survey of 900 low-income households showed that 53 per cent of respondents cited 'Do not need an account because we have no savings' (see Table 6.1).

Thus, most households without deposit accounts do not complain about inadequate access to savings facilities because they rarely have significant regular savings. They only need an instrument to satisfy their payment needs – cashing checks and making long-distance payments.

Table 6.2 Primary reasons why households do not have checking accounts (in %)

Reason	1992	1995	1998	2001
Do not write enough checks	30.4	25.3	28.4	28.6
Minimum balance is too high	8.7	8.8	8.6	6.5
Do not like dealing with banks	15.3	18.6	18.5	22.6
Service charges are too high	11.3	8.4	11.0	10.2
Cannot manage or balance a checking account	6.5	8.0	7.2	6.6
No bank has convenient hours or location	0.8	1.2	1.2	0.4
Do not have enough money	21.2	20.0	12.9	14.0
Credit problem	0.7	1.4	2.7	3.6
Do not need/want an account	3.2	4.9	6.3	5.3
Other	1.9	3.5	3.1	2.1
Total	100	100	100	100

Source: Survey of Consumer Finances (2001).

Access to transaction accounts can be difficult for consumers with a bad credit history. The most widely used credit database in the US is ChexSytem (a clearing house that identifies customers who have had banking problems in the past). An entry in this system, which is used by an estimated 85 per cent of US banks, is seen by many banks as sufficient reason to refuse to allow a potential customer to open an account. About 9 million people in America are listed on ChexSystem (Kempson et al. 2004, p. 44).

People excluded from using banks often turn to alternative providers for services such as cashing paychecks or benefit checks. Many receive and make few non-cash payments. 83 per cent of the unbanked spent less per year on cashing checks and buying money orders than the fees a bank would charge to provide them with a basic account (estimated at USD 100 per year).

3.2 Credit-Constrained Low-income Households

Lenders score loan applications using credit histories. Over the past two decades, computerized databases and scoring methods have allowed lenders to classify loan applicants with greater accuracy. This corresponds to an increase in the number of mainstream lenders (deposit institutions and non-bank financial institutions such as mortgage companies and finance companies) willing to provide credit to subprime and sub-subprime applicants. Since the default risk and monitoring costs are higher, these institutions charge a higher interest rate for subprime loans than for prime borrowers.

Table 6.3 Disposition of conventional home purchase loan applications by characteristics of applicant in 2002 (percentage distribution by number of applications, in %)

Applicant characteristics	Approved	Denied
Race/ethnic identity		
Black	61.9	26.3
Hispanic	70.5	18.2
White	80.7	11.6
Income (percentage of metropolitan area median)		
Less than 50	61.7	28.8
50–79	74.2	16.5
80–99	78.5	12.3
100–119	80.4	10.3
120 or more	82.6	8.0

Source: Federal Financial Institutions Examination Council 2003. The metropolitan area median is the median family income of the metropolitan area in which the property related to the loan is located.

The 2002 data include a total of 31 million reported loans. The denial rate for black people is higher than the one for Hispanics, and far higher than for white people (lenders are required to ask all applicants about their ethnicity). Furthermore, differences in income account for differences in denial rates. Low-income households are substantially less likely to have home-secured loans than other households, and they are somewhat less likely to have installment loans. The low incidence of credit granted to low-income households may be caused by a lower level of loan applications or a higher level of loan denials. The extent to which low-income households receiving credit belong to a higher-cost subprime or sub-subprime sector is unclear. The only credit market for which there are good empirical data is the home mortgage market. Access to mortgage credit is particularly important for most families in the US, as homeownership among the population is high compared to continental Europe. Table 6.3 shows that mortgage denial rates are higher for low-income households. Moreover, the data show that subprime loans are disproportionately represented among low-income people.

Homeownership is the main saving vehicle for most American households. Two thirds of Americans own their homes, and a majority of those who do not own a home rank homeownership as their highest priority (Fannie Mae National Housing Survey 2001). Despite all the educational effort to make the American dream of owning a house accessible to the poor as well, it remains a dream for low-income families. The share of poor households with housing debt declined from 9.5 per cent in 1992 to 8.9 per cent in 2001 (Table 6.4).

Table 6.4 Share of households with housing debt (mortgage, home equity loans, HELOCs, in %)

Income deciles	1989	1992	1995	1998	2001
1	4.8	9.5	8.7	8.5	8.9
2	10.6	11.5	13.0	14.3	18.4
3	17.1	18.1	23.8	22.9	26.4
4	29.6	25.0	27.1	25.2	27.7
5	37.0	31.2	32.4	38.8	40.1
6	38.8	40.0	44.0	47.5	49.1
7	50.9	53.1	54.3	56.5	57.5
8	62.1	59.8	63.8	70.6	66.4
9	69.7	68.3	69.9	73.9	76.6
10	74.1	74.8	72.8	72.8	75.5

Source: SCF. HELOC stands for home equity line of credit, a loan set up as a line of credit for a maximum draw rather than for a fixed dollar amount.

Lenders in the US practiced racial discrimination until the late 1960s, but there is much disagreement among researchers about its significance today (Urban Institute 1999, FSA 2000a). Almost all households excluded from mainstream credit have alternative sources of credit. Low-income households help one another out at the end of the week, but only few have someone they can ask for larger sums in emergency cases.

Thus, they have to use money lenders or pawnbrokers and pay higher charges. In a number of US states, regulations permit lenders to charge annualized interest rates of 200 per cent or more. Even licensed money lenders are reluctant to lend to some groups of people (the long-term unemployed, single parents, people living in high-crime areas). Payday lenders commonly charge a fee of about 20 per cent for cashing a check, and annualized interest rates on such loans are often 500 per cent or more (FSA 2000a, p. 74). Still, if these groups need credit, they have informal alternatives (family, friends and community organizations). These networks have cost advantages in information gathering, can utilize effective enforcement mechanisms, and provide access to short-term financing and smaller loans.

3.3 Wealth of the Poor

The trend in the wealth data of the poor shows huge differences compared to the development of the average. In particular, the situation of single black parents with no high school education has shown dramatic change (see Table 6.5).

Table 6.5 Net worth of vulnerable groups (mean, 1989 dollar)

	1989	**1992**	**1995**	**1998**	**2001**
Average	181 061	160 340	169 360	214 020	276 270
Single parent	51 678	27 861	43 770	60 068	55 566
Single parent, black	24 354	18 502	15 243	17 465	12 612
Single parent, black, no high school	10 110	2 622	5 804	5 922	1 421
Black	37 443	38 901	32 317	46 155	48 204
Hispanic	40 482	44 297	45 292	62 666	58 197

Source: SCF, own calculations.

At present, the most important reason to save for people in the US is retirement (see Table 6.6). While liquidity was stated as a more important reason in the 1990s, retirement has gained in importance in recent years. And financial knowledge should help people make good choices in finding the best way to save for retirement.

However, a disproportionate percentage of low-income households do not have pension accounts to supplement social security. In the 1990s, the share of households with any type of pension in the lowest income decile even decreased to 13.5 per cent (see Table 6.7).

Table 6.6 Reasons for saving (in %)

Reason	1992	1995	1998	2001
Education	9.1	10.8	11.0	10.9
For the family	2.6	2.7	4.1	5.1
Buying own home	4.0	5.1	4.4	4.2
Purchases	9.7	12.8	9.7	9.5
Retirement	19.4	23.7	33.0	32.1
Liquidity	33.9	33.0	29.8	31.2
Investments	7.6	4.2	2.0	1.0
No particular reason	1.7	0.8	1.3	1.1
When asked for a reason, reported do not save	12.0	6.8	4.9	4.9
Total	100	100	100	100

Source: SCF, Federal Reserve Board.

Table 6.7 Share of households with any type of pension (in %)

Income deciles	1989	1992	1995	1998	2001
Decile 1	19.6	12.6	16.5	19.3	13.5
Decile 2	26.6	24.5	24.5	24.3	27.6
Decile 3	38.2	43.4	41.2	39.2	44.1
Decile 4	46.8	48.4	47.1	49.0	50.1
Decile 5	58.8	57.5	58.7	57.6	58.2
Decile 6	65.3	65.2	68.9	68.0	66.9
Decile 7	73.0	75.9	70.6	75.1	75.4
Decile 8	78.0	75.5	78.9	80.8	78.6
Decile 9	81.3	83.3	81.7	78.0	80.6
Decile 10	76.5	75.9	80.2	78.9	76.3

Note: Either the head of household or spouse/partner has any type of pension.

Source: SCF, Federal Reserve Board, own calculations.

4. FINANCIAL EDUCATION PROGRAMS AS PART OF ASSET-BUILDING POLICIES

The notion that assets can play an important role in combating poverty is a relatively new one. The traditional discourse on poverty focused on income. The idea of asset-based development was partly a response to perceived inadequacies in the traditional welfare system. This system was said to prevent the poor from moving into the middle class by means-testing benefits and limiting asset accumulation. Recipients of Aid to Families with Dependent Children were prohibited from keeping more than USD 1 000 in a savings account. Asset-building, as the argument goes, can put out the flame of poverty and economic despair.

In the US, most subsidies for asset accumulation such as Individual Retirement Accounts (IRAs) or 401(k) plans disproportionately favor the non-poor because they directly or indirectly require wealth, and because the rich generally have a higher saving rate than the poor (Dynan et al. 2000). One asset-building program that exclusively aims at the poor is the establishment of Individual Development Accounts (IDAs). These programs, which combine financial incentives (subsidies in the form of matching funds upon withdrawal) with the requirement to attend financial education classes, are among the most prominent ones in the financial literacy debate and have been studied extensively with respect to their impact on financial behavior (e.g. Sherraden 2000, Stegman et al. 2001, Bernstein 2003, Center for Community Capitalism 2003, Schreiner 2004). The uses of matched IDA withdrawals typically include homeownership, post-secondary education, and microenterprise or job training expenses. Hence, participants accrue funds as they save for goals that are perceived to increase long-term wealth and financial self-sufficiency. Although there are 40 states with an IDA policy and some 400 community-based IDA programs, coverage is quite limited (20 000 participants).

The focal point of IDAs and their evaluation in the United States is the American Dream Demonstration (ADD). Run by the Corporation for Enterprise Development with private and public funding, ADD has enrolled 2 400 participants in 14 programs across the United States since its start in 1997. Approved expenditures are typically matched at a two-to-one or three-to-one ratio. IDA programs generally provide at least ten to 20 hours of training on topics such as credit repair, budgeting, consumption, retirement savings options and investments. Participants receive a monthly statement to remind them of their goals.

A cross-sectional survey by the ADD came up with a number of interesting results (Schreiner 2004):

- Participants who said that the economic education class helped them increase their savings accumulated about USD 9 less per month than those who did not find the class helpful.
- The most common strategies for setting money aside for IDA deposits were changes in consumption behavior. 70 per cent of the poor said they shopped more carefully for food, and 68 per cent ate out less.

The proponents of IDAs read these findings as an indication that participants are willing to alter consumption choices for the possibility of improved well-being through asset accumulation. Some participants may be close to subsistence and have high and variable expenses in relation to their income.

- The positive effects reported by most respondents were those related to psychological status. 93 per cent felt more confident about their future, 84 per cent felt more economically secure, and 85 per cent felt more in control of their lives because they had IDAs.
- The average monthly net deposit (AMND) – defined as net deposits divided by months of participation – was USD 19. The median average monthly net deposit was USD 9.8. On average, the AMND was 1.6 per cent of monthly income (median: 0.7 percent).
- A few hours of general financial education increase savings, although the effects of additional hours have diminishing returns. On average, participants had attended 12 hours of general financial education. More than 8 hours had no additional effect.
- Participants did not take full advantage of their match eligibility. The average participant saved 51 cents for every dollar that could be matched.
- IDA seems to be a policy instrument for the working poor (almost 90 per cent of participants worked or were students). The mean monthly household income of participants in ADD was USD 1 496, and household income was 116 per cent of the family size-adjusted poverty threshold. Thus, participants seem likely to represent the upper end of what most low-income people can save. Compared to all low-income families, the ADD participants studied were better educated and more likely to be employed.

The preliminary findings of research on the impact of IDAs are discouraging. Even in the context of the supportive institutional structure of IDAs, savings do not increase very much, and this is too little to change the economic trajectory of a poor family. The assets accumulated in IDAs can hardly be believed to make a difference. Furthermore, IDAs reach a relatively small number of people in spite of noticeable policy activity. Even though savings incentives are combined with redistribution, the program's effectiveness remains limited. However, proponents claim that 'what matters is not only the amount but also the existence of accumulation' (Schreiner 2004).

5. FINANCIAL EDUCATION AS A CULTURAL GOVERNANCE MECHANISM

Policies affect the incentives, skills and beliefs of citizens and shape issue framing. The idea that education rather than explicit redistribution is the crucial factor in fostering opportunity is a touchstone of American thinking (Hacker et al. 2004). And policies to improve the behavior of poor people have dominated the post-war approach to poverty in the US (Bell and Wray 2004). Thus, how does financial education compare to other initiatives in combating poverty?

President Johnson's 'War on Poverty' from 1964 to 1968 initially put more resources toward education and training in order to increase the marketable skills of the poor than toward redistributing money in order to bring them above the poverty line. The Social Security and Medicare programs have shaped the organizational landscape of American politics (Hacker et al. 2004). They have given rise to important watchdog groups which represent senior citizens (e.g. the American Association of Retired Persons). The focus of the War on Poverty was on civil rights and political participation. It challenged racial inequalities more directly than previous social policies. The Civil Rights Act of 1964 outlawed racial discrimination in public institutions. Thus, the political framework tried to affect the capacities of lower-income citizens through programs of political empowerment.

Robert Reich, a proponent of promoting asset ownership, remembers meetings in the 1990s with President Bill Clinton, who concluded that the public would never again support a welfare system that requires more money (Reich 2004). Financial education is less expensive for public providers, as it often relies on public-private partnerships. Financial education is also politically uncontroversial (Beeferman 2002, OECD 2003). Today's advocates of the poor have no strength compared to the civil organizations of the 1960s (Gilens 1999). They are a heterogeneous coalition whose activities can be based either on profit interests, public interests or altruism. But there is no political representation of the interests of the poor as they have no political voice.

Therefore, compared to prior policy initiatives financial literacy has two distinguishing characteristics: It is cheaper and it does not politically empower the poor. However, there is a third element. Financial literacy programs reframe an economic problem as a cultural one. Although economic studies controlling for an income variable demonstrate that saving does not depend on racial differences (Gittleman and Wolff 2004), financial education literature often cites an influence of culture on people's willingness to save (Toussaint-Comeau and Rhine 2000c). Immigrants and minorities are more reluctant to use mainstream financial products. The reasons can be negative historical experience (racial discrimination) and/or different cultural preferences. Twice as many African Americans are part of the lowest-net-worth quartile as their share of the population would suggest (see Annex II, Table 6A.3). Besides these analytical references to cultural factors, there are two further links that point to a cultural framework of financial education initiatives.

5.1 Public-Private Partnership in Financial Education

Financial education is less expensive for public providers as it often relies on public-private partnerships. The instructors are often experts who are recruited from the community and who volunteer their services. Identifying the self-interest of the educators is thus a complex issue. In any case, the altruistic motivation of faith-based communities and individuals will matter as well.

The intellectual proponents of IDAs (in particular Michael Sherraden, whose book *Assets and the Poor* was published in 1991) sought institutional support in order to realize their ideas. Before turning to politicians for support, evidence of success was needed, and for this purpose sponsoring institutions (private foundations) were necessary.

The first private foundation to become interested in Sherraden's ideas was the Joyce Foundation, which focuses in particular on entrepreneurial efforts. The Ford foundation created a new division called Asset Building and Community Development in 1996 and placed asset building at the center of its work on poverty. The director of this division, Thomas Shapiro, co-authored the book *Black Wealth/White Wealth*. He argues: 'Wealth is a special form of money not used to purchase milk and shoes and other life necessities. More often it is used to create opportunities, secure a desired stature and standard of living, or pass class status along to one's children' (Oliver and Shapiro 1995, p. 2). The division made a USD 3 million grant commitment for a nationwide IDA demonstration.

By mid-1997, other major private foundations had joined these efforts, and the Downpayments on the American Dream Demonstration started a nationwide demonstration. The Ford Foundation, Charles Stewart Mott Foundation, F.B. Heron Foundation, John D. and Catherine T. MacArthur Foundation, Citigroup Foundation, Fannie Mae Foundation, Levi Strauss Foundation, Ewing Marion Kauffmann Foundation, Rockefeller Foundation and the Moriah Fund were also involved. Local partners such as churches, corporations and banks also provided support. The demonstration was led by the Corporation for Enterprise Development, and evaluations were carried out by the Center for Social Development, the institution which had launched the initiative. This underlines the value orientation of financial education initiatives and the role of ideas rather than that of coherent interests.

5.2 Value of Responsible Financial Behaviour

The official aim of asset building is to enable poor people to save and to accumulate modest stocks of wealth (OECD 2003, p. 9). Asset-building programs try to stimulate poor people to save for more than precautionary objectives and rather for goals that have more to do with investment in order to enhance their unstable incomes. Financial assets such as savings and checking accounts as well as investments such as stocks, bonds and homeownership are claimed to be critical sources of economic security. The language of asset building promotes the values of work and individual responsibility.

Financial education programs approach economic troubles using one particular solution among a set of alternatives. The fact that a majority of US households have failed to save enough for retirement can be attributed to the fact that they do not act rationally or that they do not have enough money. The data concerning IDAs suggest that it would be crucial to focus on low income and low wealth.

Financial education teaches that asset building is good for numerous things. The hope is to encourage the poor to acquire the financial habits of the middle class.

Financial education could shape the way citizens perceive their economic problems and what they consider to be the appropriate role of the state in dealing with it. 'Poor people – even very poor people – do save, not because it is easy or they have extra income, but because saving is the price of stability, hope, progress' (Bob Friedman, quoted in Miller-Adams 2002, p. 189).

Popular ideology in the US assumes that behavior is mainly driven by adherence to values: Good behavior results from good values and bad behavior from bad values. The idea that behavior is also largely generated by economic, political and other structural conditions to which people must react is rarely recognized (Gans 1995). As a result, if poor people behave in ways that diverge from those thought to be mainstream, it is ascribed to their rejection of the mainstream and not to their inability (mainly rooted in adverse economic conditions) to act according to mainstream values.

Policies shape the degree of unity among citizens and delineate groups within society, thus defining boundaries and infusing them with political connotations. The financially illiterate would not exist without financial literacy programs. Asset-based policies try to endow low-income people with ownership consciousness. Implicitly, this should mean less working class solidarity. While wage-related policies unify the working class via common interests, financial literacy programs construct common interests among a coalition of middle-class shareholders and low-income debtors and savers. As their knowledge, resources, perceptions and behavior differs, this coalition may be rather loose.

The financially illiterate poor are said to be deficient in knowledge and behavior. However, the causes cited for these supposed deficiencies are motivational problems: They do not calculate their financial capacity rationally, and in particular they fail to recognize the difference between short-term and long-term interests. In short, the poor do not behave according to the rules of the financial mainstream in America. Because they practice bad values, they are considered the 'undeserving poor'. If poor people were willing to give up their (bad) values, financial mainstream America would be prepared to help them and their poverty should decline. When the undeserving poor violate financial mainstream patterns, they help to reinforce the desirability of the underlying values. Emile Durkheim stressed nearly a century ago that norm violation is also norm preservation. The norm of ownership (mainly homeownership) gains new prestige when it is dishonored and the violators are stigmatized. If the undeserving poor can be effectively depicted as responsible for not owning a home, they help to reaffirm the American dream of homeownership. Norm reinforcement facilitates the active preservation of values. The mandatory nature of financial education in IDA programs brings the focal point of these initiatives to the fore: Before the undeserving poor receive financial help (matching in IDAs), the prerequisite is a visible indication of their readiness to practice mainstream values (which implies saving for particular purposes).

Financial education is a questionable recipe for the poor to emerge from poverty (see Annex II). While informed choices are an indispensable prerequisite for the middle and upper classes investing in the stock market, the suggestion that low-income households should save more and behave differently is a rather ethical one. If people worked more and spent less, they would be able to save more. However, the recommendation to save more at very low income levels is one made by people who themselves do not have to practice it and might object to practicing it if they had to do so.

In the SCF, we can find ethnic distinctions concerning financial behavior and financial assets. The financial literacy narrative has the following paradoxical structure: African Americans and Hispanics are more likely to be poor, and the poor are more likely to adhere to bad values and make unwise, undisciplined financial decisions, as some would expect minorities to do. Poverty thus becomes ethnicized.

A specific middle class behavior is taken as a guideline to be followed by the financially illiterate poor. The supposed way to broaden personal wealth is to broaden the habits of entrepreneurship – self-discipline and responsibility. Asset accumulation indicates a higher sense of personal responsibility. Holding assets is strongly associated with middle-class values (Miller-Adams 2002, p. 190). In surveys, asset accumulators list their goals as retirement security, education, health care, homeownership and business startups. The act of saving – deferring consumption for a long-term goal – is an emblem of responsibility. Asset holders are more likely to be married than non-asset holders. The American dream of homeownership is a goal that will be more relevant to married people than to singles. Asset holders are more likely to identify with the interests of employers; they favor policies which cut taxes on savings and investments, and they are more likely to vote conservative.

Financial education programs also address individual motivation problems. The motivational purpose of financial literacy programs is to signal that responsible behavior is a way out of poverty. Financial responsibility is understood in an economic and a therapeutic sense. In the economic sense, it signifies rational behavior. In the therapeutic sense, it aims to change people's mind-sets (Beeferman 2002).

Unemployment compensation, employer-guaranteed pensions, and social security harm the project of spreading wealth because they deter the habits of self-reliant saving and investment. Moreover, a broad community of private investors should imply that the constituency for a welfare state will diminish. Richard Nadler of the Cato Institute, a prominent US think tank, is quite outspoken on the political aims of asset building: 'We are attracted by the concept of a nation of asset holders, because we believe that an electorate so constituted will be anti-socialist' (Nadler 2000, p. 14).

CONCLUSIONS

There are different rationales which support financial education for low-income households. Financial education can serve as an incentive instrument for inclusion in the financial mainstream. In this case, financial knowledge should permit social mobility. Income and wealth poverty would mainly be an individual motivation problem to be resolved by enhanced knowledge.

Financial education can also work as a legitimizing substitute for non-existent or diminishing redistribution. In line with the second argument, financial education may legitimize the uneven playing field as it creates the undeserving financially illiterate. Financial education focuses on values (the notion of the American dream was not chosen accidentally) and ethnic habits. As it does not concentrate on economic problems, it also works as a cultural governance mechanism. The notion of responsibility – reformulated as individual freedom of choice – is gaining broad social acceptance. Poverty is considered a sign of a diverse pluralistic society, not the effect of an unjust economic order. The aims of financial education reconfirm the values of the middle class. However, as long as the wealth of the poor does not increase, the middle class will not expand, only its values will.

The problem that keeps low-income households away from finance is not primarily their lack of personal knowledge or their lack of desire to save or to get a loan, but their lack of resources. And this deficit results from a lack of power in the political arena and a lack of bargaining power in the labor market. As the poor have no lobby and the working poor have jobs with no union representation, they hardly receive a living wage. As IDAs obviously fail to shift the power dynamic to alter the primary distribution of income, their effects remain rather symbolic. These programs demonstrate that poor people can also save, but they also show clearly that the poor cannot save their way out of poverty.

ANNEX I

The Survey of Consumer Finances (SCF) is a nationally representative survey of household finances in the US. The Board of Governors of the Federal Reserve System sponsors this survey, which is conducted every three years. The most recent survey (2001) asked more than 4 000 families extensive questions about their assets and liabilities.

Definition of **net worth** (calculated according to the SCF definition minus the value of vehicles). As public transport – in particular in the US – is of poor quality, cars can be considered necessary to get to work and cannot be considered part of wealth:

Value of primary residence
+ Other residential real estate: includes land contracts/notes household has made, properties other than principal residence, time shares and vacation homes
+ Net equity in non-residential real estate: real estate other than the principal residence, properties coded as 1–4 family residences, time shares, and vacation homes net of mortgages and other loans taken out for investment in real estate
+ Checking accounts (other than money market accounts)
+ Savings
+ Money market accounts
+ Certificates of deposit
+ Bonds
+ Quasi-liquid: sum of IRAs, thrift accounts and future pensions
+ Stocks
+ Total directly held mutual funds, excluding money market mutual funds
+ Business interests
+ Call accounts at brokerages
+ Savings bonds
+ Annuities
+ Trusts
+ Other financial assets: includes loans from the household to someone else, future proceeds, royalties, futures, non-public stock, deferred compensation, oil/gas/mineral investments
+ Other non-financial assets: defined as the total value of miscellaneous assets minus other financial assets
– Housing debt (mortgage, home equity loans and HELOCs)
– Other loans
– Credit card debt
– Installment loans not classified elsewhere

– Other debt (loans against pensions, loans against life insurance, margin loans, miscellaneous).

ANNEX II

Table 6A.1 Weighted shares of families who do not/cannot save in the lowest income quintile (in %)

	1989	1992	1995	1998	2001
White non-Hispanic	17.1	22.1	14.1	11.9	14.0
Black/African American	28.8	33.0	15.7	11.6	14.3
Hispanic	17.6	21.4	13.7	18.3	17.4
Other	21.6	32.3	10.3	20.7	4.7
All	20.9	25.0	14.3	11.8	14.0

Source: SCF, own calculations.

Table 6A.2 Share of households where either the head or spouse/partner has a DB plan in current job or from a past job to be received in the future (in %)

Income Decile	1989	1992	1995	1998	2001
Decile 1	17.3	11.6	14.8	16.3	11.4
Decile 2	24.7	22.7	22.2	19.5	21.8
Decile 3	33.2	36.8	34.1	30.1	30.3
Decile 4	41.7	37.3	34.0	33.8	34.3
Decile 5	49.6	46.5	43.9	34.1	31.6
Decile 6	53.5	47.1	45.3	41.7	40.7
Decile 7	55.2	57.1	47.1	46.2	44.5
Decile 8	59.7	58.9	51.4	49.5	46.2
Decile 9	68.4	64.7	53.7	49.4	50.3
Decile 10	62.5	55.4	59.1	46.6	49.0

Source: SCF, own calculations.

Table 6A.3 Share of minorities in the lowest-net-worth quartile / share of overall population in 2001 (in %)

	Share of lowest-net-worth quartile	Share of overall population
White non Hispanic	55.5	76.2
Black/African American	23.9	13.0
Hispanic	16.4	8.0
Other	4.2	2.8

Source: SCF, own calculations.

Table 6A.4 Share of households with negative net worth (in %)

Year	1989	1992	1995	1998	2001
	17.6	17.9	17.9	18.4	18.7

Source: Survey of Consumer Finance, own calculations.

REFERENCES

Barr, Michael S. (2004), 'Banking the Poor', *Yale Journal on Regulation*, **21** (1), 121–237.

Beeferman, L. (2002), 'The Promise of Asset Development Policies', Massachusetts: Asset Development Institute.

Bell, S. and R. Wray (2004), 'The War on Poverty after 40 years. A Minskyan Assessment', Working Paper 404, Blithewood: Levy Economic Institute.

Bennett, Jane and Michael J. Shapiro (2002), *The Politics of Moralizing*, New York: Routledge.

Bernheim, Douglas B., Daniel M. Garrett and Dean M. Maki (1997), 'Education and Saving: The Long-Term Effects of High School Financial Curriculum Mandates', Working Paper No. 97012, Stanford University Department of Economics.

Bernstein, J. (2003), 'Savings Incentives for the Poor. Why the scale doesn't match the promise', available at http://www.prospect.org/print/V14/5/bernstein-j.html.

Bird, Edward J., Paul A. Hagstrom and Robert Wild (1997), 'Credit Cards and the Poor', Discussion Paper No. 1148-97, Madison: Institute for Research on Poverty.

Braunstein, Sandra and Carolyn Welch (2002), 'Financial Literacy: An Overview of Practice, Research, and Policy', *Federal Reserve Bulletin*, November 2002, 445–57.

Carr, J.H. and J. Schuetz (2001), 'Financial Services in Distressed Communities: Framing the Issue, Finding the Solutions', Washington, DC: Fannie Mae Foundation.

Caskey, John P. (1997), *Lower Income American, Higher Cost Financial Services*, Madison: Filene Research Institute.

Caskey, John P. (2002), 'Bringing Unbanked Households into the Banking System', Washington DC: The Brooking Institution.

Center for Community Capitalism (2003), 'Financial Institutions and individual development accounts: results of a national survey', available at http://www.kenan-flagler.unc.edu/assets/documents/CC_Financial_Institutions_and_IDAs.pdf.

Choi, J., D. Laibson, B. Madrian and A. Metrick (2001), 'Defined Contribution Pensions: Plan Rules Participant Decisions, and the Path of Least Resistance', NBER Working Paper No. 8655.

Clark, Robert L. et al. (2003), 'Financial Education and Retirement Savings', Federal Reserve Bank Paper, 27–28 March 2003.

Consumer Bankers Association (2003), '2003 Survey of Bank-Sponsored Financial Literacy Programs', April 2003.

Dynan, K.E., J. Skinner and S.P. Zeldes (2000), 'Do the Rich Save More?', NBER Working Paper No. w7906, available at http://papers.nber.org/papers/w7906.

Fannie Mae Foundation (2000), 'Personal Finance and the Rush to Competence: Financial Literacy Education in the U.S.', available at http://www.isfs.org/rep_finliteracy.pdf.

Fannie Mae Foundation (2001), 'Fannie Mae National Housing Survey 2001'

Federal Financial Institutions Examination Council (2003), Data regarding mortgage lending transactions according the Home Mortgage Disclosure Act (HMDA).

Federal Reserve (1999), 'Banking Relationships of Lower-Income Families and the Governmental Trend toward Electronic Payment', *Federal Reserve Bulletin*, July 1999, 459–73.

Federal Reserve Board (2001), 'Survey of Consumer Finances' (SCF).

Ferguson, Roger W. (2002), 'Reflections on Financial Literacy. Remarks before the National Council on Economic Education', 13 May, Washington, DC.

FSA (2000a), 'In or Out? Financial Exclusion: a literature and research review', Consumer Research No. 3, London: Financial Services Authority.

FSA (2000b), 'Better Informed Consumers', Consumer Research No. 1, London: Financial Services Authority.

FSA (2004a), 'Young People and Financial Matters', Consumer Research No. 25, London: Financial Services Authority.

FSA (2004b), 'Building Financial Capability in the UK: The Role of Advice', London: Financial Services Authority.

Gans, H.J. (1995), *The War against The Poor. The underclass and antipoverty policy*, New York: Perseus Books.

Gilens, Martin (1999), *Why Americans Hate Welfare, Race, Media, and the Politics of Antipoverty Policy*, Chicago: University of Chicago Press.

Gittleman, M. and Edward N. Wolff (2004), 'Racial differences in patterns of wealth accumulation', *Journal of Human Resources*, **39** (1), 193–227.

Greene, William H., Sherrie L.W. Rhine and Maude Toussaint-Comeau (2003), 'The Importance of Check-Cashing Businesses to the Unbanked: Racial/Ethnic Differences', Working Paper 2003-10, Chicago: Federal Reserve Bank of Chicago.

Greenspan, Alan (2002), Testimony of Alan Greenspan, Chairman of the Federal Reserve Board, concerning Financial Literacy before the Committee on Banking, Housing and Urban Affairs, United States Senate, 5 February 2002.

Greenspan, Alan (2003), 'Financial education', 33rd Annual Legislative Conference of the Congressional Black Caucus, Washington, DC, September 2003.

Hacker, Jacob et al. (2004), 'Inequality and Public Policy', Washington, DC: APSA Task Force on Inequality and American Democracy, available at http://www.apsanet.org/Inequality/feedbackmemo.pdf.

Hilgert, Marianne and Jeanne M. Hogarth (2003), 'Household Financial Management: The Connection between Knowledge and Behavior', *Federal Reserve Bulletin*, July 2003.

Hirad, Abdighani and Peter M. Zorn (2001), 'A Little Knowledge is a Good Thing: Empirical Evidence of the Effectiveness of Pre-Purchase Homeownership Counseling', Freddie Mac, available at http://www.freddiemac.com/corporate/reports/pdf/homebuyers_study.pdf.

Hogarth, Jeanne M. and Kevin H. O'Donnell (1999), 'Banking Relationships of Lower-Income Families and the Governmental Trend toward Electronic Payment', *Federal Reserve Bulletin*, July 1999, 459–73.

Hogarth, Jeanne M., Sondra G. Beverly and Marianne Hilgert (2003), 'Patterns of Financial Behaviors: Implications for Community Educators and Policy Makers', discussion draft for Federal Reserve System Community Affairs Research Conference, February 2003.

Jacob, K., S. Hudson and M. Bush (2000), 'Tools for Survival: An Analysis of Financial Literacy Programs for Lower-Income Families', Chicago: Woodstock Institute.

Jump Start (2004), Survey Results, April 2004, available at http://www.jumpstartcoalition.com/upload/SurveyResultsApril2004.doc

Kempson, Elaine, Adele Atkinson and Odile Pilley (2004), 'Policy level response to financial exclusion in developed economies: lessons for developing countries', Bristol, UK: Personal Finance Research Centre, University of Bristol.

Madrian, B. and D. Shea (2001), 'The power of suggestion: inertia in 401(k) participation and savings behaviour', *Quarterly Journal of Economics*, **116** (4), 1149–87.

Martin, Imran, David Hulme and Stuart Rutherford (1999), 'Financial Services for the Poor and the Poorest: Deepening Understanding to Improve Provision', Working Paper No. 9, Institute for Development Policy and Management, University of Manchester.

Miller-Adams, Michelle (2002), *Owning up, Poverty, Assets, and the American Dream*, Washington, DC: Brookings Institution Press.

Nadler, R. (2000), 'The Rise of Worker Capitalism', Cato Policy Analysis No. 359.

OECD (2003), 'Asset Building and the Escape from Poverty: A New Welfare Debate', OECD Code 842003051E1, November 2003.

OECD (2004), 'Progress Report on the OECD Financial Education Project', DAFFE/CMF (2004) 9.

Oliver, Melvin and T. Shapiro (1995), *Black Wealth/White Wealth*, London: Routledge.

Pensions Commission (2004), 'Pensions: Challenges and Choices, The first report of the Pensions Commission', London.

Pitt, Harvey (2002) Testimony of Harvey Pitt, Chairman of the US Securities and Exchange Commission, concerning financial literacy before the Committee on Banking, Housing and Urban Affairs, United States Senate, 5 February 2002.

Reich, R. (2004), 'What Ownership Society?', *The American Prospect Online*, 2 September 2004, available at http://www.prospect.org/web/page.ww?-section=root&name=ViewWeb&articleId=8447

Roy Morgan Research (2003), 'ANZ Survey of Adult Financial Literacy in Australia', May 2003, ANZ Banking Group.

Schlozman, Kay L. et al. (2004), 'Inequalities of Political Voice', Washington, DC: APSA Task Force on Inequality and American Democracy, available at http://www.apsanet.org/Inequality/voicememo.pdf

Schreiner, M. (2004) 'Match Rates, Individual Development Accounts, and Saving by the Poor', http://www.microfinance.com/English/Papers/Match_Rates.pdf.

Sherraden, Michael (1999), *Assets and the poor: A new American welfare policy*, New York: M.E. Sharpe.

Sherraden, Michael (2000), 'From Research to Policy: Lessons from Individual Development Accounts', *Journal of Consumer Affairs*, **34** (2), 159–81.

Stegman, M.A., R. Faris and O.U. Gonzalez (2001), 'The Impacts of IDA Programs on Family Savings and Asset-Holdings', available at http://www.kenan-flagler.unc.edu/assets/documents/CC_ida.pdf

Thaler, R.H. and S. Benartzi (2001), 'Naïve Diversification Strategies in Defined Contribution Saving Plans', *The American Economic Review*, **91** (1), 79–98.

Thaler, R.H. and S. Benartzi (2004), 'Save More Tomorrow: Using Behavioral Economics to Increase Employee Saving', *Journal of Political Economy*, **112** (1), Part 2, 164–87.

Thaler, R.H. and S. Mulainathan (2000), 'Behavioral Economics', Working Paper 00-27, Massachusetts Institute of Technology Department of Economics.

Toussaint-Comeau, M. and S.L.W. Rhine (2000a), 'Access to Credit and Financial Services among Black Households', Consumer Issues Research Series, Paper No. 2000-1, Federal Reserve Bank of Chicago.

Toussaint-Comeau, M. and S.L.W. Rhine (2000b), 'Increasing Participation in Mainstream Financial Markets by Black Households', Consumer Issues Research Series, Paper No. 2000-4, Federal Reserve Bank of Chicago.

Toussaint-Comeau, M. and S.L.W. Rhine (2000c), 'Delivery of Financial Literacy Programs', Consumer Issues Research Series, Paper No. 2000-7, Federal Reserve Bank of Chicago.

Urban Institute (1999), 'What we know about mortgage lending discrimination in America', report issued by the US Department of Housing and Urban Development, Washington, DC.

US Department of the Treasury (2002), 'Integrating Financial Education into School Curricula', October 2002, available at http://www.treas.gov/press/releases/docs/white.pdf

US Senate Committee on Banking, Housing and Urban Affairs (2002), hearing on the state of financial literacy and education in America, 5–6 February 2002.

7. The Governance of OTC Derivatives Markets

Eleni Tsingou

INTRODUCTION

Over-the-counter (OTC) derivatives markets are an important component of transnational financial transactions and are thus significant when we consider the governance of the financial system. The volume of the market is a considerable part of global financial activity and is rapidly growing. Statistics on the OTC market show that at the end of 1990, the amount of outstanding contracts was an estimated USD 3.45 trillion. By the end of 1994 the amount had increased to USD 11.3 trillion (Bank for International Settlements 1996) and by the end of 1999 had reached USD 88.2 trillion (Bank for International Settlements 2000). In the most recent survey, the amount of outstanding contracts at the end of 2004 stood at USD 248 trillion (Bank for International Settlements 2005).[1] The nature of the instruments has puzzled practitioners and regulators alike. Derivatives carry leverage: Most users are interested in derivatives because they allow them to hedge against risks, such as market and credit risks linked to interest and exchange rate variations or the solvency of counterparties. However, some users are undoubtedly taking some risk in handling them and arguably embrace risk in the pursuit of gains. Finally, derivatives contracts have over the years become increasingly complex and the OTC market has allowed the development of ever more specific and 'personalized' instruments; this has technical implications for oversight.

Interest in OTC derivatives, both regulatory and in the private sector, grew in the early years of the 1990s as the instruments became increasingly popular and widely embraced by more or less sophisticated

[1] Notional amounts outstanding refer to the notional value of deals not settled at that date; these refer to overall market size. The gross market value of the OTC derivatives market at the end of 2004 was USD 9.1 trillion. For more information, see Bank for International Settlements (2005).

users. This analysis shows, however, that the rules and practices governing OTC derivatives were initially developed in relative technocratic isolation, relying on expertise and encouraging financial innovation. The more general, and occasionally public unease with the use of derivatives and their potential regulation came later, when some high-profile failures and near-failures implicating US investment banks (as well as the collapse of Barings Bank, though this originated in the use of exchange-traded derivatives) hit the headlines. At that point, however, the banking policy community (regulators, supervisors and private practitioners), best practice principles at hand, was able to prevent, if not criticism, regulatory intervention.

Indeed, the governance of OTC derivatives has evolved from a series of private-sector initiatives and is indicative of complex patterns of interaction between public and private actors. Practitioners in banks and securities firms were quick to realize the potential of derivatives as useful instruments to hedge against risk, and, less conservatively, for financial gain. In the early 1990s, first through the Group of Thirty (G-30) and later through the Derivatives Policy Group (DPG), the private sector acted to ensure a regulatory framework that reflected its interests and remained unobtrusive. At the same time, it formed a private organization, the International Swaps and Derivatives Dealers Association (ISDA), which placed the function of minimizing legal uncertainties in private hands. The industry was keen to establish that OTC derivatives required no special treatment but instead constituted one of several instruments used by financial institutions for risk-management purposes. In this context, the private sector seized the initiative and appeared to be dealing with the subject of OTC derivatives responsibly, thus pre-empting regulatory interference.

In this endeavor, the industry was successful. A study by the G-30, a private organization, part think tank, part interest group, which brings together thirty influential individuals from the world of economics and finance, set the tone for the debate by producing high-quality recommendations that went beyond the status quo, thus lending extra credibility to the private-sector proposals and the self-regulatory approach they advocated. The report produced and transmitted crucial knowledge on OTC derivatives and demonstrated that the private sector had the expertise, capacity and incentive to self-regulate. The report hit the mark and was instrumental in pre-empting additional regulation and legislation, particularly in the United States, where the topic was most hotly debated. As subsequent reports from major international organizations and national regulatory authorities demonstrate, G-30 recommendations were adopted and promoted by all relevant policy actors. No immediate action was taken with respect to OTC derivatives in the aftermath of the report, despite some well-documented losses and the move of the debate to the political arena, where congressional hearings sought to emphasize the politically controversial element of derivative instruments: In focusing on the high loss potential of derivatives, the systemic impact of possible failures and the risk and cost of public bailouts, legislators unsuccessfully endeavored to re-examine the regulation of such financial activities. This created a trend that continues today and fits within the wider development of self-regulatory practices and reliance on market discipline and institutions' own risk-management procedures.

This chapter starts with a background discussion on derivatives and the main policy arguments. In the context of a discussion of the nature of and the actors involved in financial governance, it proceeds with an analysis of the policy actors and debates that were instrumental in putting the current governance arrangements in place: It looks at the work of the G-30 and the DPG and how it was taken up by the relevant public-sector institutions, as well as its influence on US legislative debates. The analysis continues with an overview of later developments and explains that the trend to view OTC derivatives as an integral part of risk management continues, thus the governance of this market essentially amounts to self-regulation and self-supervision.

Finally, the chapter concludes with some observations on the significance of the private sector's success in offsetting intrusive regulation and legitimizing self-regulation. The analysis shows that in the governance of financial markets in general and OTC markets in particular, policy is in the hands of a transnational policy community of public and private actors; it explains that not only are public and private officials comfortable in cooperating on technical issues, but they also work together in de-politicizing matters such as the treatment of OTC derivatives; policy-relevant issues such as the off-balance-sheet nature of a growing market in OTC derivatives or the systemic risk potential of the possible failure of risk-management techniques were seldom discussed.

OTC DERIVATIVES: A NEW POLICY ISSUE?

A derivative is 'a financial contract whose value depends on one or more underlying assets or indexes of asset values' (Institute of International Finance 1993, p. ii). They come in several types: forward contracts, where one party agrees to buy something from another party at a particular future date and at an established price; futures contracts, which are similar to forwards with the exception that quantities and dates are standardized and that trading takes place on an organized exchange; option contracts, where it is agreed that one party has the right, but not the obligation, to buy or sell something at a future specified date and at a fixed price; additionally, there are swaps, which are more a technique than an instrument and entail an exchange between parties of their respective liabilities or interest on their liabilities. These instruments are not new; in the seventeenth century, a market for future delivery of rice functioned in Osaka. Options have an even longer history; Aristotle refers to them in *Politics*, and a tulip options market operated in Amsterdam in the 17th century (*Economist* 1999). But it is the latest developments in the use of derivatives that have put the instruments at the center of financial markets and policy concerns.

In their contemporary incarnation, derivatives come in two forms. First, there are exchange-traded derivatives, where contracts are standardized and where the clearing house of the exchange is one of the parties. These became widespread in the 1970s and have been traded at exchanges such as the Chicago Board of Trade (originally an agricultural exchange created in 1848) and later at the London International Futures and Options Exchange, among others. Second, there are OTC derivatives, where parties trade directly with one another and often customize products to suit their individual needs; it is these instruments that are the focus of analysis. OTC derivatives became available in the 1980s, the first currency swap taking place between the World Bank and IBM in 1981. By the mid-1980s, advances in computer technology allowed an increasing number of quantitative analysts or 'quants', mathematicians who were soon dubbed the 'rocket scientists' of Wall Street, to develop OTC derivatives. Having created 'plain vanilla' straightforward instruments, they moved towards more complex, composite derivatives, that is, increasingly tailor-made to the parties' circumstances, or simply more complicated.

The primary purpose of derivatives is to hedge against risk, 'offsetting an existing exposure by taking an opposite position in the same or a similar risk' (Steinherr 1998, p. 399). Derivatives are essentially an effective way to transfer risk from those who are exposed to it but would rather not be, to those that are not but would like to be. As a result, risk is said to be redistributed in an efficient manner. Concern about derivatives arises when the instruments are used not for hedging, but for speculation. The leverage that the instruments carry can make them a source of significant profit for a financial institution, but also one of potential loss. Further problems include the difficulty some end-users may face in achieving a clear understanding of the instruments, the high concentration of derivatives trading among a small cluster of institutions – which could cause financial instability if one firm fails – and the perceived lack of transparency of derivatives trading both within and outside an institution (Dale 1996, p. 157). Yet these are issues that apply to the regulation and workings of financial markets in general, and not derivatives in particular. Banks are already regulated and supervised and 'derivatives are a natural extension of banks' traditional risk intermediation activities' (Institute of International Finance 1993, p. 2). Indeed, an early report of the Bank of England concluded that 'there is little that can be clearly said to be unique about derivatives in so far as supervisory interest is concerned' (Bank of England 1993, p. 4).

PRACTICES OF GLOBAL FINANCIAL GOVERNANCE

Germain has defined global financial governance as the 'broad fabric of rules and procedures by which internationally active financial institutions are governed' (2001, p. 411). This definition is indicative of three important trends in global finance: (i) the focus on a core group of large and transnational financial institutions; (ii) the absence of a clear actor or set of actors setting the rules; and (iii) the emphasis on rules and procedures in an evolving and flexible regulatory framework. Governance is about practice and standards as much as it is about rules: In concrete terms, financial governance relates to a list of activities: regulation and supervision, decision-making, but also information-gathering and dispute settlement. How these activities are undertaken depends, both practically and analytically, on the actors involved (public, private, a mix of both), the level at which most policy processes evolve (national or transnational), the nature of regulation (predominantly state or market-based) and the evolving state-market relationship. In this context, global financial governance refers to transnational policy processes of rule and standard formulation, implementation and monitoring by a policy community of public and private actors who continually interact, and is made up of a series of policy decisions on different financial issue-areas. Several actors, and several types of actors, are in charge of global financial governance. At the heart of the process is a robust and more or less formalized practice of public and private-sector interaction. Policy formulation, implementation and enforcement are based on this interaction. The ensuing governance arrangements are characterized by a mix of public and private authority, and thus an accepted policy role for the private sector.

Private-sector authority in global finance rests primarily on three sets of sources: expertise, economic weight and the power of ideas. Expertise and specialist knowledge are central to the governance of financial markets, where innovation brings about new and complicated products and transnationalization rapidly alters the range of an institution's operations. The 'growing intellectual complexity of issues related to economic regulation' has long been acknowledged (Hancher and Moran 1989, p. 294). The necessity of up-to-date information on practices and instruments makes public authorities 'captive of knowledge specialists' (Lindblom 1977, p. 120). The private sector's role is further enhanced through its ability to 'translate' its knowledge for the benefit of public officials (Sell 2003, p. 99). Business often has an advantage in claiming access to, and influence over, policymakers: There is a 'privileged class of market agents' (Cohen 1999, p. 135). This position is also based on economic strength, the importance of financial institutions in the running of the national economy, as well as their significance for the stability of the financial system as a whole. The third category of sources concerns ideas. 'Economic ideas provide agents with an interpretative framework . . . [and] both a "scientific" and a "normative" account of the existing economy and polity, and a vision that specifies how these elements *should* be constructed' (Blyth 2002, p. 11). Smith in the eighteenth century, Ricardo in the nineteenth, Keynes and Friedman in the twentieth have all been 'intellectual icons' in this respect (Braithwaite and Drahos 2000, p. 123). And while Keynes's economic ideas 'provided a rationale for more active government management of the economy' (Hall 1989, p. 363), Friedman and the Chicago School of Economics were at the heart of an ideological shift to neoliberal economic principles which favored a greater policy role for the private sector (Helleiner 1994, p. 15).

How do these sources of influence translate into authority? In his analysis of the political influence of economic ideas, Hall explains that it is 'congruence between the ideas and the circumstances that matters', that complex ideas need to be interpreted in a particular manner and that 'an idea must come to the attention of those who make policy . . . with a favourable endorsement from the relevant authorities' (Hall 1989, p. 370). In the 1980s, the embracing of neoliberal economic ideas in the making of policy was consistent with particular economic and political circumstances (the end of the fixed exchange rate system and stagflation, as well as the election of a Republican administration and Conservative government in the United States and the United Kingdom, respectively). At the same time, developments in financial markets made private-sector expertise key: As public authorities struggled to keep up with new financial instruments and methods; private actors relied on their (perceived) ability to manage complexity in order to command authority. Furthermore, the trend towards the consolidation of financial activity among a small number of transnational institutions gave the latter great leverage in their dealings with the public sector.

This analysis uses the concept of 'transnational policy community' to best capture financial governance arrangements. 'Policy communities are stable networks of policy actors from both inside and outside government which are highly integrated with the policy-making process' (Stone 2002, p. 132). The term refers to 'experts and professionals that share their expertise and information and form common patterns of understanding regarding policy through regular interaction' (Stone 2001, p. 6). The transnational character of global finance and its governance means that the relevant policy community also operates at that level.

The concept is key to understanding global financial governance and the role of the variety of actors involved, as it best captures the process of public and private actor interaction in the making of financial policy, as well as the variety of settings within which this interaction takes place. The concept focuses on the expertise of community members, the stable, often formal and accepted as legitimate nature of interactions, and is thus a significant analytical tool in explaining the formation of shared understanding and therefore agreement over policy. Moreover, the concept does not explicitly distinguish between public and private actors, or their respective interests. The community maintains some links with respective national systems, but its strongest (and often predominant) ties and perceived constituency are at the transnational level. It is also associated with a particular understanding of 'good governance' that follows neoliberal economic principles; the interests of the community are defined and articulated without explicit reference to public goods and private priorities but in terms of the widely accepted economic principles of efficiency and stability. The officials who make up this community are mostly educated (both academically and professionally) in an Anglo-American context and, crucially, have experience of both the public and private sector, thus further blurring traditional public-private boundaries. These characteristics often make for a coherent community that is surprisingly exclusionary. The case of the governance of OTC derivatives markets provides evidence of the workings and practices of this community.

THE GOVERNANCE OF OTC DERIVATIVES MARKETS: THE POLICY DEBATE

The G-30 brings together officials from the public and private sectors and represents one instance of public-private sector interchange, and of growing private authority in a vital public policy domain.[2] The G-30, despite its non-official status, has played a key role in the regulatory

---

[2] The membership of the G-30 is undoubtedly prestigious; it currently counts among its members the governors of the central banks of Israel, Mexico, Poland, Spain (also Chairman of the Basel Committee) and the United Kingdom as well as of the European Central Bank and a Vice-Chairman of the Federal Reserve Board; senior executives of Goldman Sachs, JP Morgan Chase and Morgan Stanley; and several prominent economists. For a complete list of current members as well as an overview of the groups' reports, see www.g30.org.

outcome of certain policy issues by being purposefully involved in governance processes through explicit delegation of authority or informal assigning of functions. Its recommendations have often been openly adopted by relevant bodies, and the group has been widely and publicly acknowledged for its governance role and its contribution to shaping policy by the wider transnational policy community of public and private practitioners.

The G-30, a private organization made up of public and private-sector officials, published a report entitled *Derivatives: Practices and Principles* in 1993.[3] This privately financed study was motivated by the interest of public and private actors to better understand OTC derivatives and by the realization that in order to take full advantage of the opportunities offered by these instruments, derivatives needed to be an integral part of an effective risk management policy. Another purpose of the study was to demonstrate that responsible and efficient self-regulation was key to the use of derivatives, as intrusive rules-based regulation can render these instruments rigid and hamper financial innovation. To make this point, the private sector, through the G-30, took the initiative of producing an authoritative expert report.

The G-30 commissioned the study on OTC derivatives to a group of experts, including the chairmen and senior executives of the major financial institutions. Among those involved were the chairman of J.P. Morgan, which first took the initiative to make elements of its risk-management techniques public, and the director of the ISDA.[4] The study focused on the role of derivatives in providing 'new ways to understand, measure and manage financial risk' and insisted that they should not be differentiated from other financial instruments. Its 24 recommendations, directed at dealers and end-users, supervisors and legislators, address the role of senior management, managing different types of risk through sophisticated techniques and sound risk management methods, and the proliferation of master agreements. The report also makes an early reference to operational risk and finally concentrates on disclosure; in

---

[3] For a comprehensive analysis of the G-30 and the role of its report, see Tsingou (2003).

[4] The influence of the private sector on the report and its recommendation was clear from the outset. The chairman of J.P. Morgan and G-30 member Dennis Weatherstone chaired the Steering Committee following from J.P. Morgan's initiative to publicize its model for measuring market risk free of charge; RiskMetrics became available to banks and securities firms as part of the overall G-30 effort. The report was written by a working group chaired and largely populated by private-sector representatives (24 out of 26 participants), and the study was mostly financed by the private financial institutions. This context is important as it testifies to the private-sector commitment to the initiative; it contributed human and financial resources and expertise but was also represented by officials of the highest level. The G-30 initiative was of great interest to the private sector, which both financed and shaped it, assuring that its interests would be well represented in debates over OTC derivatives.

order to enhance responsible self-regulation, financial firms are to provide additional qualitative information on the use of derivatives and the management of subsequent risks in their statements.

The report's authors researched the practices of financial institutions and also used data provided by two major industry groups, the Institute of International Finance (IIF) and ISDA. There is thus further evidence of reliance on the private sector, which explains both that the study deals with the topic of OTC derivatives as essentially a practitioners' issue and the self-interested aspect of the industry's incentive to self-regulate.

The G-30 report made a significant impact. In the immediate aftermath of its publication, regulators and practitioners examined the recommendations and debated their merits. Among the enthusiastic responses of supervisors and legislators, as well as those of industry representatives, a voice of caution came forward, with Brian Quinn, at the time Deputy Governor at the Bank of England, arguing that the G-30 contention that the supervisory framework was adequate as it stood was 'somehow complacent' (Quinn 1993, p. 536). He argued that knowledge of derivatives remained partial and that practitioners and public officials alike were still both excited and alarmed by the instruments. This was an important point, especially considering the transnational scope of the report and of the financial institutions that use OTC derivatives. A systemic crisis could come about as a result of 'default by a major institution; a sudden shift in the prices of derivatives in the financial markets sufficient to undermine the viability of a major institution; or the inability to net out obligations or receipts' (Tickell 2000, p. 90). Yet as subsequent analysis shows, this factor was overshadowed and did not prevent widespread acceptance of the study or its principles, mostly because of the strong impetus for the adoption of G-30 proposals and the agreement among the policy community about the self-regulatory thrust of these proposals.[5]

The G-30 study set the tone for other reports on the subject of OTC derivatives. It affected the policy discussion and made responsible self-regulation the focal point. The G-30 promoted its conclusions by addressing its audience, part of which was already within the G-30 community (either as members, study group participants or invited guests). The timing of the study also meant that the work of the group was sought at a time of uncertainty. The G-30 relied on the implicit

[5] Not all public bodies were equally enthusiastic about a self-regulatory approach: In addition to Quinn's reservations, the research arms of the US Congress and the European Parliament produced reports that raised some concerns about the regulatory status of OTC derivatives. The General Accounting Office report is discussed later in this chapter. The European Parliament also commissioned a study which maintained a more critical approach to the instruments, recommending clearer disclosure and accounting procedures, stopping short, however, of advocating a different type of regulation (European Parliament 1995).

understanding among public and private-sector officials that private-sector involvement in the global financial governance was both desirable and necessary. Agreement on this issue suggests that the nature of regulatory arrangements had started to shift. The private sector had the incentive to self-regulate in a drive to pre-empt intrusive and costly rules; at the same time, the public sector welcomed such initiative as it lacked specialized expertise and would have been reluctant to introduce regulation harmful to innovation and the competitiveness of the industry. Yet the widespread acceptance of the self-regulatory approach advocated by the G-30 goes beyond instrumental and mutually beneficial arrangements and is indicative of the development of common, shared sets of principles and interests relating to regulation and supervision. This willingness of public authorities to support self-regulation is in line with Anglo-American practices of self-regulation in the financial industry and, with the bulk of OTC derivatives activity concerning US financial institutions, there were perhaps few opportunities for alternative regulatory traditions to make their mark in the debate.

In this context, and judging from the exposure and the positive response that it received, it is hardly surprising to see the recommendations of the G-30 study replicated in the reports of major international organizations. Dealing specifically with this topic, two major reports were made public a year after the work of the G-30 was put forward. The reports were produced by the Basel Committee on Banking Supervision (Basel Committee 1994) and the Technical Committee of the International Organisation of Securities Commissions (IOSCO 1994). They closely followed the recommendations of the G-30 and both based their findings on consultation with the public and the private sector; moreover, both reports exhibit a reluctance on the part of regulators and supervisors to interfere in the derivatives markets, believing indeed that 'global financial services corporations should govern themselves' (Coleman 2003, pp. 287–88).

This approach permits and even encourages self-regulation and has been carried through in subsequent reports of international organizations. The Basel Committee, in particular, has taken a very active role in the oversight of derivatives activity, producing regular comprehensive statistics and reviews of practices. Importantly, the reports show that both the Basel Committee and IOSCO have accepted a role of limited involvement; they have centered their work on promoting a better foundation for self-regulation, which amounts to reviewing progress in the area of disclosure. Throughout this series of documents, emphasis is put on meaningful information and reliable figures that are put in context. Authorities are also encouraging further detail on the overall risk management strategy of financial firms. This approach has most recently been manifest in Basel II, the new revised capital measurement framework (Basel Committee 2004); there is nothing in these documents to suggest that officials are looking at more forceful regulation.

Following the lead of the Basel Committee and IOSCO, regulatory and supervisory authorities in the European Union have mostly focused further discussion on OTC derivatives on questions of harmonization across the internal market and improvements in disclosure; regulatory activity has thus treated OTC derivatives in the context of the regulation and supervision of financial institutions (Investment Services Directive and Capital Adequacy Directive). Indeed, the bulk of reactions to OTC derivatives took place in the United States, both as a consequence of the losses that will be subsequently discussed but also as a result of the high concentration of OTC derivatives activity among a small cluster of New York-based financial institutions.

A pattern of emphasis on self-regulation and disclosure is evident in the evolution and outcome of regulatory and legislative debates on OTC derivatives in the United States, where an increasingly like-minded policy community comprised of a coalition of private and public actors, financial institutions, regulatory and supervisory agencies and central banks came into focus. As shaped in the US, the debate on OTC derivatives took place between a policy community favorable to self-regulation on the one hand, and the legislators, supported by the 'dangerous' public image and the genuine problems associated with OTC derivative instruments on the other.

The approval of private efforts and lack of interest in more dynamic intervention can be seen in the guidelines issued by a series of agencies including the Federal Reserve (Board of Directors of the Federal Reserve System 1993), the Office of the Comptroller of the Currency (OCC 1993) and the Commodity Futures Trading Commission (CFTC 1993). A dissenting voice did emerge, however, in the form of the General Accounting Office's report to Congress (GAO 1994). This report relied heavily on the G-30 study, and its data mirrored G-30 recommendations; however, it reached rather different conclusions with respect to the effectiveness of private-sector efforts without the 'weight' of actual regulation and possibly legislation.

There was indeed reason to suspect that the argument for increased and derivatives-specific regulation could gain support. The year 1994 was especially bad for the reputation of OTC derivatives, with some high-profile losses hitting the headlines. Financial institutions were portrayed as irresponsible and risk-taking, and the public perception of derivatives suffered a great deal. Three cases in particular highlighted all that can go wrong when the instruments are used unwisely: They involved Gibson Greetings and Bankers Trust, Procter & Gamble and Bankers Trust, and Orange County and Merrill Lynch.

Bankers Trust became involved in derivatives activity early and with great success, attracting highly qualified people who could create and trade in increasingly complex products. One commentator observes that 'competitors admitted that Bankers probably had the highest collective IQ on Wall Street' (Thomson 1998, p. 112). In 1991, the bank first became involved in dealings with Gibson Greetings of Cincinnati, the second biggest greeting card manufacturer in the US. The first two derivative contracts arranged with the firm were plain vanilla deals and did make money, but subsequent deals performed less impressively, going well beyond the USD 3 million limit set by Gibson. Bankers Trust lied about the losses, which ultimately amounted to USD 27.5 million. The case was investigated by the SEC and CFTC, which determined that Bankers Trust had lied to its client. Eventually, Bankers Trust settled with Gibson, paid a large fine and parted with several employees.[6]

Procter & Gamble, arguably a more sophisticated player, did not fare a lot better in its dealings with Bankers Trust. The company agreed deals with major loss potential in 1993 and 1994, which did indeed result in losses of USD 160 million. This was a source of great embarrassment to the treasury department of Procter & Gamble, but telephone conversations indicate that Bankers Trust officials were aware that Procter & Gamble did not fully understand the risks involved: 'It's like Russian roulette, and I keep putting another bullet in the revolver each time I do one of these [trades]', said one Bankers Trust salesman. Procter & Gamble launched litigation against Bankers Trust and an out-of-court settlement was finally agreed.[7] Bankers Trust did not come out of these dealings unscathed. Its shares did not open on the New York Stock Exchange on 2 March 1994, but though it suffered large losses, it did survive.[8]

Orange County, a traditionally Republican group of wealthy municipalities in California, also found itself in an unenviable position after dealing with OTC derivatives. The county treasurer, aiming to balance conflicting citizens' expectations of lowering taxes and maintaining or increasing services, became more adventurous with the county's investment fund, pursuing an aggressive, risky and complex strategy. Merrill Lynch sold many of the products that contributed to losses of over USD 1.5 billion in 1994. This time, however, the fault lay mostly with the end-user. A California state special committee report

---

[6] Information based on Thomson (1998) and The Washington Post (1995a).

[7] Information based on Thomson (1998) and The Washington Post (1995b).

[8] Bankers Trust survived this series of episodes but was eventually taken over in the wave of mergers and consolidation in the financial industry of the late 1990s; it was bought by Deutsche Bank in 1999.

found that the county's strategy was knowingly risky and put much of the blame on the county's practices.[9]

It is important to note that while the impact of these events was short-lived, they provided the background for what was a hot policy issue in the mid-1990s and were at the center of Congressional initiatives to 'tame' OTC derivatives. Indeed, through several rounds of hearings and attempts at legislation,[10] the advocates of self-regulation and those favoring a more interventionist approach converged in Congress. The financial policy community brought its knowledge and influential position to the table and stuck together through the shared belief in self-regulatory and self-supervisory practices. The legislators tried to understand the subject and, alarmed by the behavior of financial institutions, pushed for stricter regulations that could restore public confidence in the industry behaving itself. In particular, in the context of *H.R. 4503, The Derivatives Safety and Soundness Supervision Act of 1994* (House of Representatives 1994), legislators attempted to push for stringent legislation. Regulatory and supervisory agencies, however, denied that legislation was necessary, and did so quite forcefully. The community supported their position by reiterating that OTC derivatives did not require special treatment and that the existing regulatory and supervisory framework was both strong and adequate in dealing with the issues arising from the instruments; for the most part, they also focused on the advantages offered by the flexibility of best practice standards for financial innovation. The private sector was also invited to provide input and, unsurprisingly, was similarly hostile to legislation. In presenting their case, they used and relied on the G-30 study. In the end, attempts at legislation fell through. Derivatives were not subjected to separate and restrictive legislation, and the idea of self-regulation became more established.

How did this happen? The House committee was adamant in its attack on derivatives. One of the bill's sponsors, Representative Gonzalez, often used the word 'casino' in his references to derivatives. More generally, congressmen were particularly worried that they would be accused of inaction should a derivatives disaster strike, and were convinced that it would (Peltz 1994, p. 100). Legislation was never going to be easy as it is in itself a lengthy process; nevertheless, the failure of the House committee to find support among public agencies further decreased its chances.

---

[9] Information based on The Wall Street Journal (1994) and The Wall Street Journal (1995).

[10] In all, there were in both houses three failed attempts at legislation: the Derivatives Safety and Soundness Supervision Act of 1994 (House – Gonzalez/Leach bill), the Derivatives Dealers Act of 1994 (House – Markey Bill) and the Derivatives Supervision Act of 1994 (Senate – Riegle Bill).

The willingness of regulatory and supervisory agencies to accept self-regulation as a best practice standard, or according to Tickell, their 'regulatory neglect' (2000, p. 91) does indeed require some explanation. On the basis of the evidence, regulators and supervisors appear to have been impressed by the quality of the work produced by the private sector and the G-30 in particular. Moreover, they focused on the question of expertise and accepted the primacy of the private sector in this matter. The main explanation, however, lies in the fact that the debate on the regulation of derivatives came at a time of a 'high degree of co-ordination among US regulators and private market participants' (Levin et al. 1994, p. 15). Public authorities, and in particular the Federal Reserve, did not just accept self-regulation but believed in it.[11] The Fed was confident in its ability to supervise and was firmly part of the policy community favoring the promotion of standards as opposed to rules. They also understood that in such a dynamic market, regulation was bound to be rigid, and were concerned about the risk of regulatory arbitrage, that is, losing business to more flexible markets (Peltz 1994, p. 102). The fact that most of the institutions dealing with derivatives are banks and securities firms further reinforced their views that OTC derivatives were part of already properly overseen activities. As for non-bank derivatives dealers, some felt that 'affiliates of non-banks are not beneficiaries of government deposit insurance, and taxpayers are not at risk for losses incurred by failed non-bank dealers' (Edwards 1995, p. 271). This is, of course, debatable and ignores the risk of contagion, as was made evident at the time of the Long-Term Capital Management crisis (LTCM); however, the argument was used to maintain the regulatory status quo.[12] Finally, it might be useful to consider that self-regulation probably benefited from agency overcrowding in the US. It is possible that turf battles among the relevant agencies also served the self-regulation cause.

Beyond these reasons, however, the debate over OTC derivatives shows a determined public-private coalition which has been developing common understandings, preferences and policies not just on OTC derivatives, but on the nature of global financial governance in general.

[11] This point was made in an interview with an official at the Federal Reserve Board. In a separate interview with Gary Parker, an aide to Representative Leach in the House Banking Committee, this 'free market type of attitude' was also acknowledged (Washington, DC, USA, 22 October 1999).

[12] Reliance on traditional regulation and supervision practices relating to banks and securities firms is further challenged through the continuous growth of hedge fund activity: A recent report states that the hedge funds accounted for 50 per cent of plain vanilla option OTC contracts in the United States in 2004 and have funds valued at USD 1 trillion under their management. While these figures remain a fraction of overall OTC derivatives activity, they are becoming increasingly significant (Financial Times 2005).

This case also shows that there are different types of 'public'. Public regulators and supervisors are much closer to the private sector and their counterparts in other countries than they are to other national public actors such as legislators. This has serious implications with respect to the interests that they represent and the extent to which private-sector interests are internalized by the transnational policy community to the detriment of public interests and concerns.

THE GOVERNANCE OF OTC DERIVATIVES MARKETS: CONSOLIDATING PRIVATE AUTHORITY

The self-regulatory and self-supervisory arrangements in the governance of OTC derivatives were further consolidated with the work of another major private-sector initiative on derivatives. The Derivatives Policy Group (DPG) was formed, involving six major dealers[13] which got together and agreed to voluntarily set detailed standards and promote meaningful disclosure. The DPG report, *A Framework for Voluntary Oversight of the OTC Derivatives Activities of Securities Firm Affiliates to Promote Confidence and Stability in Financial Markets* (DPG 1995), took on previous G-30 recommendations and produced a detailed structure, following up on each one with concrete guidelines for practice and disclosure. The DPG emphasized management controls and the clarification of accountability, enhanced reporting and counterparty relationships, and tackled the issue of evaluating risk in relation to capital, proposing that such calculations should be based on banks' internal models. The DPG accepted that industry self-regulation would include cooperation with regulators, including the accommodation of ad hoc requests for information. This was another instance of responsible private-sector initiative. The DPG took into account regulatory concerns and addressed them seriously. Their report was authoritative: Participants were major players, with all the necessary expertise, whose opinions mattered. In addition, having the main firms involved meant that even if less sophisticated players took longer to implement recommendations, those institutions with the greater exposures were already adhering to high-quality best practice standards.

A parallel development has been the growing significance of ISDA, which by providing model contracts for OTC derivatives, has established a secure legal background against which transactions can take place. This

---

[13] The institutions that participated in the DPG project were: CS First Boston, Goldman Sachs, Lehman Brothers, Merrill Lynch, Morgan Stanley and Salomon Brothers.

has allowed OTC markets to grow further and has intensified their relative importance in global financial activities. The fact that the organization is essentially a private-sector actor looking after the interests of private financial institutions is largely considered to be an efficient arrangement that is not questioned.

The governance practices generated through this series of private-sector initiatives were quickly established and have not been the subject of substantial scrutiny or rethinking despite the central role of OTC derivatives in some major financial 'disruptions' such as the failure and bailout of LTCM and the collapse of Enron. Some voices maintain that these instances have underlined the risk of OTC derivatives as sources of vulnerability to the financial system by augmenting speculation activity, presenting opportunities for fraud and manipulation, accentuating liquidity risk as well as causing risks at the systemic level (Dodd 2004). These concerns can only be accentuated by recent trends of consolidation,[14] especially as there are significant worries that banking institutions are adopting hedge fund practices (*Economist* 2004). The policy community remains unmoved: In the words of Alan Greenspan, Chairman of the Board of Governors of the Federal Reserve, 'although the benefits and costs of derivatives remain the subject of spirited debate, the performance of the economy and the financial system in recent years suggests that these benefits have materially exceeded the costs'. Any risks that remain should be addressed through 'prudential regulation [as] supplied by the market through counterparty evaluation and monitoring rather than by authorities' (Greenspan 2003, pp. 2–5). There are, however, significant limits to reliance on market discipline, such as the existence of safety nets and deposit insurance, and the central bank function of lender of last resort, especially for institutions that are 'too big to fail'. These are strong political functions and considerations which also provide a great degree of security to the private sector. As a result, concerns remain as to how responsibly the private sector takes its policy role, as well as with regard to the safeguards that are in place should something go wrong. The probability of failure for a financial institution cannot and should not be driven to zero, but in the current financial environment, the private sector enjoys a great degree of autonomy without assuming a corresponding level of responsibility; the public sector is (or will be) thus left with the task of picking up the pieces when private-sector decisions prove detrimental to the stability of the financial system. In some instances, this financial structure can lead to moral hazard; global banks can reap the benefits of their involvement in the making of regulation and the conducting of supervision but also fall back

[14] According to an OCC report, in the United States, seven banks hold more than 95 per cent of the US system's notional derivatives exposure (OCC 2002).

on the state in times of problems. Public authorities have traditionally assumed the functions of lender of last resort for illiquid institutions and provided a safety net for depositor protection. More awkward is the more unofficial role of central banks as rescuers of insolvent institutions that are considered 'too big to fail'. Indeed, because of the tradition of providing liquidity support, central banks can find that they are providing a 'significant subsidy to the risk management industry' (Steinherr 1998, p. 276). The rescue of the LTCM in 1998 with private money but Federal Reserve logistical support indicates that there may be an increasing number of big players that matter to systemic stability. The Federal Reserve may not have used public money that time, but its intervention still hints that it is prepared to act decisively to avoid a crisis. This may leave some in the private sector off the hook. It remains to be seen whether potential changes to the reporting requirements relating to OTC derivatives will make the use of derivative instruments more transparent, thus adding a layer of responsibility to the private sector.

GLOBAL FINANCIAL GOVERNANCE: ASSESSMENT AND IMPLICATIONS OF CURRENT ARRANGEMENTS

In a governance setup that diffuses functions among public and private actors, what happens to interests? In the current regulatory and supervisory arrangements, there is 'heavy emphasis on technical reports and virtually no reference to politics' (Porter 2001, p. 248). Indeed, the focus on knowledge and the presumed neutrality of technical expertise de-politicizes financial issues (Cutler et al. 1999, pp. 346–47; Radaelli 1995, p. 176). The current arrangements, though, are not interest-free. Knowledge controls mechanisms of inclusion and exclusion, and a knowledge structure 'determines what knowledge is discovered, how it is stored, and who communicates it by what means to whom and on what terms' (Strange 1988, pp. 119–21). Therefore, the governance setting matters; in the current framework, under the pretext of efficiency, private interests are internalized in the policy process and 'financial institutions decide which state policies are acceptable and which are not' (Boyer and Drache 1996, p. 1).

The legitimacy of global financial governance arrangements is also affected. The transnational policy community focuses on efficiency and stability; other public goods such as social or distributive justice are largely neglected (Kapstein 1999). In practice, this means a shift of economic policies, such as the phasing-out of the welfare role of the state in favor of support of the private sector (Prakash and Hart 1999, p. 15). As Kirshner (2003) also explains, economic ideas define the 'feasible' and the predominance of a particular policy discourse has led to an impression of inevitability of both policy and outcomes.

Unavoidably, these policy priorities produce winners and losers. In other aspects of economic governance, policy outcomes in terms of winners and losers are easily apparent; Sell's analysis on the influence of private actors over the regime of intellectual property protection shows a clear impact on the ability of states in the developing world to tackle health issues and the HIV/AIDS crisis in particular (Sell 2003). The identification of 'losers' in global finance is more subtle; the failure of regulation and supervision can have an impact on workers who become unemployed as a result of a currency crisis or taxpayers who have to bail out insolvent financial institutions (Porter 2001, p. 428). More generally, Cutler et al. argue that private actor authority leads to decisions about 'who gets to play, what are the limits on play, and often who wins' (Cutler et al. 1999, p. 369). Increasingly, the winners are the 'key domestic interest groups . . . which are tied in most closely to the international economy' (Cerny 1996, p. 92). This leaves a progressively under-represented group that includes state employees, welfare recipients, farmers, small businesses and workers in traditional industries (Cox 1996, p. 200). As a result, the 'notion of the state's commitment to the general interest of society as a whole . . . risks becoming eroded in a *sauve qui peut* among rival claimants for whatever returns' (Cox 1996, p. 206).

Finally, what is the legitimacy of the structure of global financial governance? Clark (2003) distinguishes between two discourses of legitimacy. One relates to the systems of rule, while the other focuses on the normative principles that determine who is included: Concerns should not only focus on who governs, but also whose voices are heard. This analysis shows that the loudest voices are those articulating private-sector preferences. Recent work has focused on such issues; Germain proposes the principles of inclusion and globalized accountability as a way to enhance legitimacy (Germain 2001 and 2004). While it is the case that the institutional framework, primarily in the implementation process, did become more inclusive in the aftermath of the Asian financial crisis, the core of governance arrangements is still inhabited by a relatively small number of financial institutions and public authorities with a strong North American and European bias. Furthermore, such processes of inclusion remain narrow and do not take into account the social, economic and political implications of regulation.

The legitimacy of non-state actor influence and authority becomes more problematic when we examine accountability patterns relating to the activities of these actors. Agnew and Corbridge argue that 'the trend from boundaries to flows that is associated with globalisation is also bound up with a more general crisis of representation' (Agnew and

Corbridge 1995, p. 216). This is particularly true in global finance, where policymaking remains 'esoteric' and leads to a 'limited democracy' (Coleman 1996, p. 10). Against this background, the 'power of the vote in shaping public policy decreases' (Reinicke 1997, p. 3), while at the same time the private actors that hold authority are not part of a mechanism that assigns appropriate responsibility. 'Market actors are neither elected nor politically accountable' (Cohen 1999, p. 135). An apparent democratic deficit has emerged, highlighted in the reality of 'substantial decisions . . . frequently [being] taken by unaccountable officials operating in arcane and secretive forums [and exerting] strong pressure on, even if they do not formally bind, national decision-making processes' (Picciotto 1996, p. 118). Policymakers (public and private) 'are not accountable to any citizens, but are accountable only to the market itself'. But there are currently no procedures to guarantee that the policies decided with more or less private-sector and non-state actor input are 'fair' or 'equitable' (Cutler et al. 1999, p. 369). Financial governance patterns have been left outside democratic political debates because of the low visibility of finance with the exception of crisis moments; financial matters are of a technical nature and 'no specific popular social group [is] directly affected in a negative way' (Helleiner 1994, p. 203).

So, if accountability in global financial governance does not follow processes traditionally associated with democratic representation, is the transnational policy community at least accountable to the 'market'? When losses happen, or crises occur, market mechanisms do not always take over by inflicting 'punishment' or 'discipline'. Instead, the public sector does act to remedy problems, and its interference affects a wider set of actors in ways that are not explicitly recognized by the governance framework.

CONCLUSIONS

This chapter has argued that the governance arrangements for OTC derivatives are predominantly based on private sector-inspired practices of self-regulation and self-supervision. The analysis shows that this is the result of an increased shared understanding among a transnational policy community of public and private actors of what constitutes efficient governance and is an example of wider global financial governance patterns. The case of OTC derivatives indicates that self-regulation in this market did face hurdles, not least the very public losses incurred by end-users and dealers from using OTC derivatives and the associated private-sector misconduct; indeed, it could be argued that self-regulation had *already* failed as the policy debate went on. The instruments had and retain a reputation for risk, and this has significant implications for policy. Yet the transnational policy community maintained that for the markets to thrive, instruments and techniques need to be flexible. It thus helped de-politicize an otherwise politically controversial topic and prioritize private-sector interests. It also substantially altered the nature of regulation and supervision by delegating significant elements of these functions to the private sector, essentially 'privatizing' them (Tickell 2000, p. 95). This case study shows how the transnational policy community has grown close to the private sector and its concerns, a trend most obviously manifested in the Congressional hearings where the community literally stood together in opposition to domestically based accountable actors and public institutions. The relative 'novelty' of the instruments assisted the process as it allowed the policy issue to be debated outside discussions on the nature of regulation. This, in turn, helped alter regulatory practices and gave the private sector an official role. The chapter argues, however, that the endurance and relative 'success' of these arrangements should not detract from the serious legitimacy, accountability as well as economic efficiency issues that follow from the internalization of private interests in the policy process.

REFERENCES

Agnew, John and Stuart Corbridge (1995), *Mastering Space: Hegemony, Territory and International Political Economy*, London: Routledge.

Bank for International Settlements (1996), *International Banking and Financial Market Developments*, Basel: Bank for International Settlements.

Bank for International Settlements (2000), 'The global OTC derivatives market at end-December 1999', press release, 18 May.

Bank for International Settlements (2005), 'OTC derivatives market activity in the second half of 2004', Basel: Bank for International Settlements.

Bank of England (1993), *Derivatives: Report of an Internal Working Group*, London: Bank of England.

Basel Committee on Banking Supervision (1994), *Risk Management Guidelines for Derivatives*, Basel: Bank for International Settlements.

Basel Committee on Banking Supervision (2004), *International Convergence of Capital Measurement and Capital Standards – A Revised Framework*, Basel: Bank for International Settlements.

Blyth, Mark (2002), *Great Transformations – Economic Ideas and Institutional Change in the Twentieth Century*, Cambridge: Cambridge University Press.

Board of Directors of the Federal Reserve System (1993), *Guidelines on Derivatives Activities*, Washington, DC: Federal Reserve Board.

Boyer, Robert and Daniel Drache (1996), ' Introduction', in Robert Boyer and Daniel Drache (eds), *States Against Markets*, London: Routledge, pp. 1–27.

Braithwaite, John and Peter Drahos (2000), *Global Business Regulation*, Cambridge: Cambridge University Press.

Cerny, Philip G. (1996), 'International Finance and the Erosion of State Policy Capacity', in Philip Gummett (ed.), *Globalisation and Public Policy*, Cheltenham, UK and Brookfield, US: Edward Elgar, pp. 83–104.

Clark, Ian (2003), 'Legitimacy in a Global Order', *Review of International Studies*, 29, Special Issue, 75–95.

Cohen, Benjamin J. (1999), 'The new geography of money', in Emily Gilbert and Eric Helleiner (eds), *Nation-States and Money, The past, present and future of national currencies*, London: Routledge, pp. 121–138.

Coleman, William D. (1996), *Financial Services, Globalisation and Domestic Policy Change*, London: Macmillan.

Coleman, William D. (2003), 'Governing global finance: financial derivatives, liberal states, and transformative capacity', in Linda Weiss (ed.), *States in the Global Economy – Bringing Domestic Institutions Back In*, Cambridge: Cambridge University Press, pp. 271–92.

Commodity Futures Trading Commission (1993), *OTC Derivative Markets and their Regulation*, Washington, DC: Commodity Futures Trading Commission.

Cox, Robert W. with Timothy J. Sinclair (1996), *Approaches to World Order*, Cambridge: Cambridge University Press.

Cutler, A. Claire, Virginia Haufler and Tony Porter (1999), 'The contours and significance of private authority in international affairs', in A. Claire Cutler, Virginia Haufler and Tony Porter (eds), *Private Authority and International Affairs*, Albany: State University of New York Press, pp. 333–76.

Dale, Richard (1996), *Risk and Regulation in Global Securities Markets*, Chichester: John Wiley & Sons.

Derivatives Policy Group (1995), *A Framework for Voluntary Oversight of the OTC Derivatives Activities of Securities Firms Affiliates to Promote Confidence and Stability in Financial Markets*, Washington, DC: Derivatives Policy Group.

Dodd, Randall (2004), 'Derivatives markets: Sources of Vulnerability in US Financial Markets', Financial Policy Forum – Derivatives Study Center.

Economist (1999), 'Schools brief – future perfect', 27 November.

Economist (2004), 'Trading wars', 28 August.

Edwards, Franklin R. (1995), 'Off-Exchange Derivatives Markets and Financial Fragility', *Journal of Financial Services Research*, 9, 259–90.

European Parliament (1995), 'Derivative Financial Instruments', *Economic Series*, E-4, External Study.

Financial Times (2005), 'Hedge funds dominate distressed debt trading', 17 January.

General Accounting Office (1994), *Financial Derivatives – Actions Needed to Protect the Financial System*, GAO/GGD-94-133, Washington, DC: United States General Accounting Office.

Germain, Randall (2001), 'Global Financial Governance and the Problem of Inclusion', *Global Governance*, **7** (4), 411–26.

Germain, Randall (2004), 'Globalising Accountability within the International Organisation of Credit: Financial Governance and the Public Sphere', *Global Society*, **18** (3), 217–42.

Greenspan, Alan (2003), 'Corporate governance', *BIS Review*, 21.

Group of Thirty (1993), *Derivatives: Practices and Principles*, Washington, DC: Group of Thirty.

Hall, Peter A. (1989), 'Conclusion: The Politics of Keynesian Ideas', in Peter A. Hall (ed.), *The Political Power of Economic Ideas*, Princeton: Princeton University Press, pp. 361–91.

Hancher, Leigh and Michael Moran (1989), 'Organising regulatory space', in Leigh Hancher and Michael Moran (eds), *Capitalism, Culture, and Economic Regulation*, Oxford: Clarendon Press, pp. 271–99.

Helleiner, Eric (1994), *States and the Reemergence of Global Finance – From Bretton Woods to the 1990s*, Ithaca: Cornell University Press.

House of Representatives (1994), *H.R. 4503; The Derivatives Safety and Soundness Supervision Act of 1994*, Hearing before the Subcommittee on Financial Institutions Supervision, Regulation and Deposit Insurance of the Committee on Banking, Finance and Urban Affairs, House of Representatives, 12 July 1994, Serial No. 103-153, Washington, DC: US Government Printing Office.

Institute of International Finance (1993), *An Integrated Bank Regulatory Approach to Derivatives Activities*, Washington, DC: Institute of International Finance.

International Organisation of Securities Commissions (1994), *Operational and Financial Risk Management Control Mechanisms for Over-The-Counter Derivatives Activities of Regulated Securities Firms*, taken from James Hamilton and Kenneth R. Benson, *Federal Regulation of Derivatives*, Chicago: CCH Incorporated, pp. 69–78.

Kapstein, Ethan B. (1999), 'Distributive Justice as an International Public Good', in Inge Kaul, Isabelle Grunberg and Marc A. Stern (eds), *Global Public Goods*, New York: Oxford University Press, pp. 88–115.

Kirshner, Jonathan (2003), 'Money is Politics', *Review of International Political Economy*, **10** (4), 645–60.

Levin, Peter, Jordan Luke and Pimkaeo Sundaravej of Davis Polk & Wardwell, New York (1994), *International Financial Law Review*, November, 10–16.

Lindblom, Charles E. (1977), *Politics and Markets – The World's Political Economic Systems*, New York: Basic Books.

Office of the Comptroller of the Currency (1993), *Risk Management of Financial Derivatives*, Banking Circular 277, Washington, DC: Office of the Comptroller of the Currency.

Office of the Comptroller of the Currency (2002), *OCC Bank Derivatives Report, Second Quarter*, Washington, DC: Office of the Comptroller of the Currency.

Peltz, Michael (1994), 'Congress's lame assault on derivatives', *Institutional Investor*, December, 99–102.

Picciotto, Sol (1996), 'The Regulatory Criss-Cross: Interaction between Jurisdictions and the Construction of Global Regulatory Networks', in William W. Bratton, Joseph McCahery, Sol Picciotto and Colin Scott (eds), *International Regulatory Competition and Coordination, Perspectives on Economic Regulation in Europe and the United States*, Oxford: Clarendon Press, pp. 90–123.

Porter, Tony (2001), 'The democratic deficit in the institutional arrangements for regulating global finance', *Global Governance*, **7** (4), 427–39.

Prakash, Aseem and Jeffrey A. Hart (1999), 'Globalisation and governance: an introduction', in Aseem Prakash and Jeffrey A. Hart (eds), *Globalisation and Governance*, London: Routledge, pp. 1–24.

Quinn, Brian (1993), 'Derivatives – where next for supervisors?', *Bank of England Quarterly Bulletin*, **33** (4), 535–38.

Radaelli, Claudio M. (1995), 'The Role of Knowledge in the Policy Process', *Journal of European Public Policy*, **2** (2), 159–83.

Reinicke, Wolfgang H. (1997), 'Global Public Policy', *Foreign Affairs*, **76** (6), 127–38.

Sell, Susan K. (2003), *Private Power, Public Law*, Cambridge: Cambridge University Press.

Steinherr, Alfred (1998), *Derivatives – The Wild Beast of Finance*, Chichester: Wiley.

Stone, Diane (1996), *Capturing the Political Imagination: Think Tanks and the Policy Process*, London: Frank Cass.

Stone, Diane (2001), 'Learning Lessons, Policy Transfer and the International Diffusion of Policy Ideas', CSGR Working Paper No. 69/01, April.

Stone, Diane (2002), 'Knowledge networks and policy expertise in the global polity', in Morten Ouggard and Richard Higgott (eds), *Towards A Global Polity*, London: Routledge, pp. 125–44.

Strange, Susan ([1988] 1994), *States and Markets*, 2nd edition, London: Pinter.

Thomson, Richard (1998), *Apocalypse Roulette: The Lethal World of Derivatives*, London: Macmillan.

Tickell, Adam (2000), 'Dangerous derivatives: controlling and creating risks in international money', *Geoforum*, 31, 87–99.

Tsingou, Eleni (2003), 'Transnational policy communities and financial governance: the role of private actors in derivatives regulation', CSGR Working Paper No. 111/3.

Wall Street Journal (1994), 'Derivatives lead to huge loss in public fund', 2 December.

Wall Street Journal (1995), 'As Orange County blames others, guess where latest report points', 7 September.

Washington Post (1995a), 'Guess what? The loss is now… $s million', 11 June.

Washington Post (1995b), 'Derivatives "Like Russian Roulette"', 5 October.

8. Risks, Ratings and Regulation: Toward a Reorganization of Credit via Basel II?

Vanessa Redak*

1. INTRODUCTION

On 26 June 2004, the Group of Ten (G-10) finally agreed on the new capital accord commonly known as Basel II. Implementation of the new Basel accord can be expected – at least in the EU – in 2007 at the latest. This paper will analyze the political and economic consequences of Basel II with special attention to the relationship between regulatory authorities and financial market actors. Their role will be analyzed with regard to the process of shaping the accord and to the future implications of the accord for both groups of actors. The driving questions are whether the power or authority of either the industry or regulators will increase or decrease with Basel II, who was able to influence the accord manifestly, and which actors were left aside. Concerning the relationship between the industry and regulators with regard to Basel II, opposing views can be found: Whereas on the one hand a number of critical analyses highlight the significant influence of private industry actors (notably financial interest groups and banks), on the other hand several positions state that regulatory intervention by public authorities has never been so high as with Basel II. In the first step, the article will investigate the role of these agents based on the three pillars of Basel II. It can be shown that both regulators and industry actors were and will be able to increase their authority according to the specific pillar in question. Their interests

* I would like to thank Eleni Tsingou and Brigitte Unger for their well-reasoned comments on my presentation at the conference 'The Political Economy of International Financial Governance' at the Oesterreichische Nationalbank, 26 November 2004, Vienna. Helene Schuberth, Stefan W. Schmitz, Martin Schürz, Elisabeth Springler, and Beat Weber also provided fruitful insights on this paper. The views expressed in the paper are those of the author and do not necessarily represent those of the OeNB.

converge in the Basel II process several times, and thus a mere confrontation of their roles and interests is not enough to grasp the qualitative change in banking regulation due to the Basel II process. Therefore, in the second step the paper will not only single out the leading agents of the accord and analyze their roles but also try to capture the entire regulatory framework within the politico-economic environment in which it developed. The findings of the first step will help to focus on the extent to which the changes in the relationship between public and private actors will lead to a transformation of the organization, regulation, and governance of bank lending to date. I will argue that Basel II, with its emphasis on risk measurement and on market discipline, acts as a catalyst, promoter, and accelerator of lending practices based on ratings and risk-adjusted pricing. Borrowers, especially firms, will therefore feel the pressure to adjust to new norms in the credit business as their activities will be scrutinized by banks more intensely.

2. BASEL II AND FINANCIAL MARKET REGULATION: A RACE TO THE TOP

In the literature on International Relations (IR) and International Political Economy (IPE), the Basel Accord is very often described as one of the most successful examples of international policy cooperation (cf. Genschel and Plumper 1997; Lütz 1999, p. 12; Simmons 2001; Porter 2004, p. 12). Already with Basel I in 1988, a process of harmonization in banking regulation started on a worldwide level based on the mutual recognition of national particularities and on coordinated negotiation under the guidance of the Basel Committee on Banking Supervision (BCBS). This successful multilateral negotiation of the first as well as the second capital accord and the impacts it had on capital adequacy contrasts with commonly held beliefs that regulation initiatives face downward pressure in an era of globalization and liberalization, as regulation is assumed to harm international competitiveness at the global level and to scare away investors at the national level. The Basel capital accord, however, shows that a regulatory *race to the top* instead of the bottom is possible even in financial markets, a domain not expected to be open to strict regulation these days. This is demonstrated in the rise of banks' capital cushions – the main target of the Basel accord – in the past decades. Measured as the portion of the capital base (own funds) in the banks' risk-weighted assets, the capital ratios of internationally active banks were very low in the pre-1988 era, demonstrating a very low level of capitalization of banks vis-à-vis their risky assets. After the 1988 accord, however, capital ratios increased steadily. Today the 8 per cent minimum capital requirement is a target that banks in the EU easily reach: In fact, many banks in the EU have capital buffers well above the 8 per cent requirement. In contrast to tax harmonization, for example, countries who have less strict rules on capital adequacy do not achieve any advantages. On the contrary, they (or rather their banks) are likely to be punished with higher refinancing costs as important actors on financial markets, especially rating agencies, take capital provisions as a main indicator in their assessments of banks and countries. Banks themselves consider high capital cushions a good way to cope with risks and have therefore increased capital in order to maintain higher safety buffers.

3. FROM BASEL I TO BASEL II

The need for a revision of the first accord (Basel I) was primarily created by an ongoing deregulation and liberalization process on financial markets, leading to more competitive markets and a whole new series of innovations in financial services, such as asset securitization, derivatives trading and so on. These innovations were not covered by the old accord and left loopholes for regulatory arbitrage. At the same time, the risk management techniques of banks improved, so that a revision of the capital accord seemed necessary in the eyes of banking supervisors in order to realign supervisory regulation and industry practice.

The launch of the new capital adequacy accord differs from Basel I in several respects: The importance of own funds reserves is now no longer questioned by the countries negotiating the capital accord. The 1988 negotiations (Basel I) were heavily influenced by the United States and the United Kingdom supporting stricter capital rules for competitive reasons. Especially the United States deemed higher capital requirements necessary for two reasons: First, in the wake of several bank crises regulators were facing increasing criticism of their inactivity and felt the pressure to regulate in a more proactive way. Second, by increasing capital ratios on a worldwide level, US banks could regain a competitive advantage over Japanese banks, which had become fierce competitors to US banks in the US home market. 'The U.S. proposal for capital adequacy regulations was not motivated by concern about international financial stability, but by a need to satisfy competing interest group and voter pressures' (Oatley and Nabors 1998, p. 36). As US and UK banks were better capitalized than their Japanese counterparts, raising capital requirements seemed one way to penalize Japanese banks. Japan finally agreed to higher capital requirements, but only after substantial concessions had been made to them.[1] In the Basel II negotiations, however, there is unanimous belief among the BCBS members that minimum capital requirements are an appropriate way to deal with banks' risks. Therefore, conflicts arose not on the principal objective but on the details of the new accord.

As far as the leading role of the United States in the 1988 accord is concerned, the country's influence lessened during the Basel II negotiations. The preferential treatment of small and medium-sized enterprises and residential mortgage loans, the need to calculate capital requirements only for unexpected loss, the prevention of unfavorable treatment of long-term loans (abandonment of maturity adjustments), and several relief measures for small and medium-sized banks were achievements of the European negotiators.

Although the elaboration of the Basel II framework was primarily the task of the G-10[2] representatives in the BCBS, the comments on the various consultation papers and the empirical quantitative impact studies (QIS) have been delivered and carried out by a far larger number of countries not represented in the G-10 group, including South America, Central and Eastern European countries, and Africa.

Another difference concerns the need for change in industry practices due to the introduction of a new regulatory framework for banks. In contrast to the situation before Basel I, on an aggregate level banks will not need to change their current level of own funds as they are already sufficiently capitalized. Recent empirical research shows that due to the incentives in the Internal Ratings Based (IRB) Approach, in which banks can use their own internal risk models, a fall in capital requirements can be expected for the majority of banks (cf. BCBS 2003). For banks using the simpler Standardized Approach, capital requirements will stay approximately the same. As the majority of assets[3] in the EU and in the US will be treated under the IRB Approach, capital requirements will decrease on an aggregate level. In contrast to 1988, the implementation of Basel II will therefore not lead to a great need to adjust bank capital.

[1] Meticulous documentation of these negotiations can be found in Reinicke (1995).

[2] In fact, the G-10 consists of 13 states: Apart from the original members – Belgium, Canada, France, Germany, Italy, Japan, the Netherlands, Sweden, the United Kingdom and United States – Switzerland, Luxembourg and Spain have joined the group in recent years.

[3] Taking into account the volume of assets and not only the number of banks under Basel II is an important aspect when discussing the quantitative impacts of the new accord.

4. BASEL II IN A NUTSHELL

Before our analysis of the relationship between private and public actors along the three pillars of Basel II, a short description of the main features of the new framework will be presented here.

Both Basel I and Basel II regulate banks primarily via the calculation of capital requirements. Banks should be adequately capitalized in order to cope with the risks arising from their banking activities. This should be accomplished by three pillars (BCBS 2004)[4]:

Pillar 1 deals with minimum capital requirements. Here, banks are required to hold enough capital cushions against various business risks, which comprise the following:

Credit risk – the risk that a borrower will default,
Market risk – the risk of a change in the value of a bank's assets, and (newly introduced)
Operational risk – a risk category including management failure, technical deficiencies, etc.

In order to quantify capital requirements, each asset is multiplied – depending on its assessed risk – by a so-called risk weight, resulting in risk-weighted assets. In contrast to Basel I, the new accord increases differentiation among asset classes as well as risk weights. Whereas the 1988 accord only had one asset class for corporates, for example, the new framework now differentiates corporate clients by size (SMEs, total sales, etc.) and intrinsic risk. Substantial concessions have been made to SMEs: Under an exposure threshold of EUR 1 million, they receive lower risk weights than other companies. Under Basel I, countries were only categorized into OECD member and non-member states, whereas in the new accord each country will be given its own risk assessment and accordingly its own risk weight. Lower risk or a better rating will bring about lower risk weights and consequently lower capital requirements. In general, 8 per cent of risk-weighted assets must be held in the form of own funds.

Pillar 2 refers to the supervisory review process and defines the tasks of financial supervisors as well as banks with regard to the requirements of banks' risk management systems. The following main lines of action are required by supervisors in Pillar 2: controlling for the risk management system's consistency with the risks identified in Pillar 1,

[4] Due to the 'stranding process' in EU legislation, the three pillars have 'disappeared' in the EU draft directive. The draft directive is organized in Articles with general clauses and Annexes with technical details; see http://europa.eu.int/comm/internal_market/regcapital/docs/com-2004-486/how-to-read_en.pdf

calculating those risks not captured by the bank's risk management system, and supervising the banks' stress tests, in which the banks have to assess the reaction of their capital base to the economic cycle. Pillar 2 can impose further capital requirements in addition to Pillar 1.

Finally, Pillar 3 contains the rules and regulations for the disclosure and reporting of bank data and information under the heading of 'market discipline'.

These three pillars will serve as a reference framework for analyzing potential new relationships between the public and the private in the financial and banking sector. By analyzing each of the three pillars, I will try to identify the extent to which Basel II represents a new mode of financial regulation, and to what extent it fits current trends in regulatory policy concerning financial markets. In particular, these trends include worldwide legal and regulatory harmonization in order to further competition, the introduction of market discipline and corporate governance mechanisms, a change in supervisory style towards risk-oriented supervision, and the consideration of industry representatives as allies in the regulation process.

5. PUBLIC AND PRIVATE AGENTS AND THE THREE PILLARS OF BASEL II

Concerning the role of the banking industry and regulators in the Basel II process, opposing views can be found: Whereas on the one hand a number of critical analyses highlight the significant influence of private actors (notably financial interest groups and banks), on the other hand several positions maintain that regulatory intervention by public authorities has never been so high as with Basel II. This chapter will therefore investigate their roles, first with reference to their appearance during the negotiation process. The driving questions will be how open the negotiation process was to the public, who was able to influence the accord manifestly, and which actors were left aside. In the second step, I will address the question of what implications Basel II will have for the power and authority of industry and supervisory agents in the future by analyzing each of the three main pillars of Basel II.

5.1 Negotiating the Accord

The relationships between the industry and regulators have been intense throughout the Basel II process: The preparation of the Basel Accord has seen high industry involvement in shaping the new framework. Each round of Basel II negotiations at the BCBS was accompanied by intense industry consultation. For example, Porter (2004, p. 12) argues that the main influence on the BCBS proposals came from the Institute of International Finance (IIF). Underhill (in this volume) also sees private think tanks like the Group of Thirty or finance associations like the IIF as the main drivers of Basel II or the sole interlocutors of the BCBS. At the EU level, banking associations such as the recently founded European Banking Industry Committee (EBIC) were frequently consulted via the EU Commission for the purpose of preparing the EU directive on capital adequacy by which Basel II will be implemented in the EU. The EBIC was founded in January 2004 with the explicit aim of facilitating industry consultation by EU institutions and consists of the main European banking industry federations such as the European Savings Bank Group, the European Association of Cooperative Banks, the European Mortgage Federation, etc. Soon after the EBIC was established, the legislative process for the Basel II directive in the EU started at the EU Commission level, and the EBIC was soon invited to advise the Commission's expert group on Basel II issues. In an EBIC position paper released in March 2005, the Committee congratulates the EU Commission for the 'high quality' of the proposal for the Basel II directive and 'feels that the quality of the draft legislation reflects the *unprecedented* level of consultation . . . during the process of converting the Basel rules into EU law' (EBIC 2005, emphasis added by author). Porter (in this volume) therefore concludes that the accord 'was skewed in favor of the largest banks relative to other banks, indicating that there were problematic exclusionary elements in the process'. As a result, the policy preferences of international financial institutions have been extensively incorporated into the new framework.

Concerning the relationship between the industry and regulators, market actors were not seen as adversaries by public authorities during the negotiation process, but as partners. This was made clear several times in the public statements of the BIS (Bank for International Settlements) or EU officials. In the making of Basel II, for example, current Chairman of the Basel Committee on Banking Supervision Jaime Caruana proclaimed: 'Bank regulators in recent years have begun to view markets as an ally to our system of supervision' (Caruana 2003, p. 1). This is partly justified by a belief in the paramount expertise of market actors as far as their business activities are concerned. It was not unusual, therefore, that regulators acted on behalf of their national industries in the Basel and EU negotiations. Finally, it can be concluded that each amendment to or recalibration of the accord at least had the approval of the major banks if it was not implemented in the accord due to initiatives from the banking industry.

Still, the dissemination of the Basel II proposals was conducted in a far more open way than the first accord. Whereas the '1988 Accord was negotiated in relative secrecy by regulators, . . . the Basel II negotiations involved direct interaction between the Basel Committee and the private sector. Hundreds of pages of comments from private sector and public sector actors were posted on the Basel Committee's website'[5] (Porter 2004, p. 12). Whether this has also led to a more integrating process in general is questionable. Consumer and labor groups have clearly been absent from the negotiating process. They have neither been invited by the regulators to voice their concerns, nor have they participated in the consultation rounds.[6] Moreover, in the EU it is questionable whether the European Parliament, which will debate on the Basel II directive in 2005, will meet its proclaimed intention to 'improve the democratic legitimacy of G10 decisions' (quoted in Grossmann 2004). The Parliament's *rapporteur* on the Basel II issue, Alexander Radwan, sees the Basel Committee on Banking Supervision as acting without democratic legitimization and control, and denounces the lack of integration of the Parliament in the Basel negotiations: 'Politics is in danger of losing its active role in policy shaping and becoming an ex-post rubber stamp for each piece of financial market legislation set out on an international level'.[7]

Summing up, in terms of inclusion and exclusion the negotiation process of Basel II can be described in the following way: Basel II is a further example of a change in regulatory style since the liberalization processes of the 1980s and 1990s. Embracing market actors as allies in the regulation process is a marked shift away from former regulatory practices. At the same time, financial markets seem to be a domain where consumer and labor groups are not included in shaping and negotiating the relevant political and legal processes.

5.2 Implications of Basel II for the Future Roles of Banking Industry and Regulators

Along the three pillars of Basel II, we can now analyze the implications of the new framework for the future roles of banking industry and regulators.

---

[5] For these comments, see: http://www.bis.org/bcbs/cp3 comments.htm

[6] Behind some of the organizations taking part in the consultation process (see Footnote 5), consumer interests might have played a role (e.g. in consumer mortgage associations), but they are clearly outnumbered by industry organizations.

[7] See http://www.alexander-radwan.de/ger/arPage000103.asp (author's translation).

Pillar 1: Rating agencies as norm setters in bank lending

Once again, Pillar 1 defines how much capital a bank must hold against its risks. Risk can fundamentally be assessed in two ways: using the Standardized Approach and the Internal Ratings Based Approach. In the Standardized Approach, the risk of borrowers can be assessed externally, that is, by an external rating agency. One particular strand of literature therefore sees an increase in the role and importance of private rating agencies (King and Sinclair 2001, King and Sinclair 2003, Coffee 2001). As far as redistribution effects are concerned, King and Sinclair (2003, p. 357) see rating ágencies as winners in the Basel II process because 'credit rating agencies will capture rents in the form of expanded requirements for their services by all participants in the bank lending markets. Given the number of unrated entities in this market, the potential further revenues from this business are large'.

This purported increase in the power of rating agencies has to be modified in two respects: Critics of Basel II and of the role of rating agencies ignore the possibility of maintaining unrated assets in the banking book under Basel II. Unrated companies will be assigned a 100 per cent risk weight, and therefore their capital requirements will not differ from the current accord. Research estimates that the majority of European non-financial firms will remain unrated in the Standardized Approach (Resti 2004). Ratings are costly, with fees coming to as much as EUR 50 000 per rating. This leaves a number of smaller and medium-sized companies out of the rating market. The number of companies subjected to rating by private agencies is likely to be overestimated by critics. Still, the pressure to obtain a (naturally good) rating will increase among larger companies, and price differentials in loans due to ratings might disadvantage unrated firms.

Furthermore, under Basel II rating agencies not only enter into new relationships with the clients to be rated but also with supervisory authorities. In order to be able to bring rating assessments into line with Basel II, rating agencies or *External Credit Assessment Institutions* (ECAIs), as they are called in Basel terminology, have to be approved by the national supervisor. Supervisory authorities have to address the question of the circumstances and criteria under which ECAIs should be allowed. The Basel Committee remains vague in its list of criteria for ECAI approval (cf. BCBS 2004, p. 23), but it is obvious that the criteria reflect recent criticism regarding rating agencies by introducing elements such as transparency, objectivity and so on. Although this will not call into question the rating mechanism per se, it will temporarily shift some power to public authorities, remarkably in times where several states and supervisors, for example in the US, France, Germany, and Austria, have addressed increasing concerns about the market behavior of rating agencies. Concerns about the reliability of ratings have even led to a reconsideration of the current rating agencies' regulation in Europe and the United States (cf. Sanio 2004). In the process of Basel II negotiations, for example, the Banque de France decided to build its own rating model so that it can make its own 'independent' rating assessments of corporates. It is therefore possible that rating agencies will see not simply an increase in their role in banking regulation, but possibly competition from public authorities on the market for ratings as well as reinforced scrutiny of their methods by public and private agents.

Given these two lines of reasoning, I would argue that under the Basel II regime rating agencies will not gain momentum in banking regulation via direct economic gains due to an expanded requirement for their services. Their power will at first stem less from a sharp increase in rating clients and thus profits than from the *political and ideological acknowledgement* of their (rating) practices. Their authority as *reputational intermediaries* in shaping the behavior of the rated agents will lead to more uniform behavior among market participants according to the rating agencies' opinions of what is appropriate or not. In banking,[8] for example, banks feel that their so-called Tier 1 ratio (or core capital ratio) must be at least 8 per cent in order to get a good rating. 'This is what rating agencies expect', says a manager at a large German bank. This yardstick is clearly higher than for regulatory purposes, where a 6 per cent Tier 1 ratio is regarded as sufficient in the eyes of supervisors.

As the Basel II framework puts more emphasis on private-sector assessments of risks and thereby substitutes traditional bank examiners from financial market authorities and central banks by rating agencies, the nature of banking regulation is changing. Through their judgments on credit and market risk, rating agencies are becoming private makers of global public policies (King and Sinclair 2003). 'Rating agencies' views on what is considered "acceptable" shape the decision making and actions of those dependent on ratings, due in large part to the inclusion of ratings in regulation. This process of interaction between private actors in the capital markets narrows the expectations of creditors and debtors to a set of norms shared among all parties' (King and Sinclair 2003, p. 357). By appreciating the role of ratings in the lending process, the BCBS has enforced the standardization of credit lending mechanisms and questioned former lending practices. This will potentially threaten countries with a tradition of relationship lending (e.g. Germany, Austria, Japan) where risk assessment and in particular risk-adjusted pricing is not customary.

---

[8] Another example of rating agencies' judgments is the disqualification of pension reserves as equity, which in the past led to a downgrade of the German company Thyssen-Krupp to 'junk status'.

Pillar 1: The rise of the technical authority of markets

Whereas the role of rating agencies within the Basel II framework is very often highlighted in analyses of the role of private actors in the Basel II process (*see above*), another aspect of the role of private agents is mentioned less frequently. This aspect concerns the more sophisticated approaches to risk assessment: The Internal Ratings Based (IRB) Approaches allow banks to use their own risk assessment models in order to calculate the resulting capital requirements. Banks then are no longer dependent on external credit assessment by rating agencies, but instead they can implement their own risk management techniques which best fit their business practices and activities. On the one hand, the internal model has to be approved by the banking supervisors and thereby gives new authority and control to public institutions (see Pillar 2 below). On the other hand, by allowing these internal risk models, the public has reacted to a private market mechanism by acknowledging business practices as a sufficient way to cope with risk. The use of risk management models is not prescribed by the state or public authorities. Those models, like CreditMetrics, Credit Risk+, Credit Portfolio View, or the KMV model[9] were introduced mainly by internationally active banks themselves after severe banking crises in the 1980s jeopardized the banks' profits or even their existence. Advancements in financial and actuarial mathematics and statistics have been used increasingly for ever more sophisticated risk modeling techniques in banks and other financial institutions.

The acknowledgment of these internal risk assessment models by Basel II will have several implications for the parties involved.

With its stimulus for the continuous improvement of risk modeling, Basel II will spur regulatory processes which encourage 'self control and self learning [rather] than direct intervention' (Larsson 2003, p. 440) by public authorities. The responsibility for monitoring banks' risks will be shifted away from regulators to the banks themselves. This will upgrade the technical authority of market actors. However, this recognition of risk management techniques ignores criticism from within the finance community on risk management techniques and their formal foundations (cf. Daníelsson et al. 2001, Daníelsson 2003). At present, financial market data do not allow an exact determination as to when risk occurs. Risk factors cluster with no regularity or specific pattern and are thus difficult to forecast. Financial market disruptions are infrequent but severe, thus contradicting the attributes of a normal distribution function underlying many risk models. 'This implies that the financial system,

[9] Specifically, CreditMetrics was developed by JP Morgan, Credit Risk+ by Credit Suisse, and Credit Portfolio View by McKinsey.

especially in the aggregate, is not easily amiable to be described by a set of engineering equations describing risk. Such modeling of risk is much akin to the old-style Macro models where the entire economy was described by a relatively small number of equations' (Daníelsson 2003, p. 159). The widespread thrust in risk modeling by regulators thus involves the risk of imagining the safety and soundness of the banking system in a misleading way and of underestimating other threats to financial stability like systemic risk.

Smaller banks with less sophisticated risk management methods will be punished by higher capital requirements, as the accord provides incentives for the use of IRB approaches by lowering capital requirements for IRB banks. The methods used by smaller banks for screening clients' creditworthiness will be downgraded. For example, the relationship lending approach of many small banks in local markets will be seen as anachronistic, although the information and knowledge these banks have about their customers is not necessarily inferior to credit assessment based on default probability calculation.

Finally, a shift in the authority of different departments within banks is conceivable, as we can expect a downgrade of loan officers vis-à-vis the risk management branches of a bank.

In summary, it therefore depends very much on the rating approach a bank chooses when determining the implications for regulatory and industry agents and the political consequences of regulatory reforms arising from Pillar 1. On the one hand, in the case of the Standardized Approach and the increasing role of rating agencies, some authors conclude that this encourages a more private form of banking regulation (Sinclair 2001, p. 442) when the monitoring of creditors is delegated to private market agents. Still, recent initiatives for the reform of rating agencies also carry signs of an increased engagement of public authorities in the rating market. However, the ideological and political *aggrandizement* of rating agencies' practices is indisputable.

In the case of the Internal Ratings Based Approach, the monitoring of risks will be shifted away from regulatory bodies to the industry by reference to the superior technical expertise of market actors. This has implications for several parties involved and might challenge the ultimate goal of financial stability by uniquely relying on risk modeling techniques of individual banks, without taking into consideration systemic risk. Still, in both approaches not only private actors gain new momentum in regulatory practice, but the mechanisms of credit lending and credit monitoring change as well (see Section 6).

Pillar 2: Cooperation leading to the formation of technocratic elites

Whereas Pillar 1 is rather criticized for the rise of new private power over banking regulation (see the discussion of rating agencies above), Pillar 2 faces the opposite criticism. Pillar 2 defines the way in which supervisors will assess the risk management techniques mentioned in Pillar 1. It also lays the foundations for the ICAAP (Internal Capital Adequacy Assessment Process), in which banks must stipulate their internal capital requirements irrespective of regulatory requirements.

A massive increase in public authority over the way banks manage their risks is the focus of several complaints (e.g. BBA 2004, European Shadow Financial Regulatory Committee 2003, Fritz-Aßmus and Tuchtfeldt 2003). Hahn (2003, p. 148; author's translation), for example, argues that 'supervisory agencies will be given competences which exceed the current state of supervisory authority by far' because in particular Pillar 2 requires the elimination of any constraints on the scope of discretion of supervisors. This argument is backed by ordo-liberals who also consider Basel II to be a framework which sharpens supervisory tools and their authority (e.g. Fritz-Aßmus and Tuchtfeldt 2003). Especially when assessing the internal rating systems of banks (Pillar 2), ordo-liberals fear 'arbitrary decisions' of supervisory authorities and subsequently untransparent and nationally uneven regulatory practices, a view also supported by the self-proclaimed European Shadow Financial Regulatory Committee (2003), a body of academics and experts in the field of banking and finance which comments regularly on developments in European financial market regulation.

In fact, the discretionary components of Pillar 2 arise because many parts of Pillar 2 are set out as principles and only broad, industry-wide standards and regulations for risk management approval exist. The approval of the internal risk management methods of banks will therefore rely very much on a dialog between regulators and banks. Much will be done in consultations and talks with banks on an individual basis. Supervisors are therefore willing to accept the industry's own knowledge and expertise concerning risk management, whereas advantages of this form of regulation arise for banks out of its principles based on co-evolution, cooperation, and flexibility.

Regulation will therefore be based on negotiation instead of command and control, leading to a much closer relationship between banks and regulators based on mutual learning. Despite the complaints of the banking industry about the lack of rule-based regulation and the possible arbitrariness of supervisory decisions, the regulation process offers individual banks more room and flexibility in implementing their risk management models.

Apart from negotiating skills, both sides – private institutions as well as public regulators – will need technical skills in order to understand or elucidate the risk models in question. Regulators 'are expected to build a substantial quantitative and qualitative expertise and to work closely with banks' (Ayadi and Resti 2004, p. 1). Lütz (2002, p. 328) therefore sees advantages for both sides of the regulatory process and regards both of them as winners in the new regulatory regime, as together they form a 'technocratic elite' with exclusive knowledge and expertise as well as a privileged relationship. This creates disadvantages not only for smaller banks with less sophisticated risk management techniques but also for the clients of banks which are rated who are not able to understand the rating mechanism on which their creditworthiness depends.

In summary, the assessment of internal rating and capital calculation methods will see an intensification of the relationships between banks' risk management employees and regulators. Together they will form a technocratic elite with exclusive knowledge, thus excluding other parties from shaping the lending business.

Pillar 3: Individual responsibility and self-discipline

Under the heading of *market discipline*, the third pillar determines the disclosure requirements for banks as well as supervisory authorities. Market discipline is not a Basel-specific topic in financial market regulation. It has been the centerpiece of many recent financial market reform proposals and policies and is – together with corporate governance codes – considered a very industry-friendly form of regulation (cf. Davies 2003, Fritz-Aßmus and Tuchtfeld 2003). With Basel II, market discipline will also be applied broadly to banks. After all, the banks were the ones granting loans to corrupt companies such as Enron even after suspicions about Enron's accounting practices had arisen.

The motivation behind market discipline is the assumption that opacity is the cause for financial instability.[10] Hiding relevant information from market participants leads to imbalances in market perceptions and expectations, and thus to a misallocation of capital and subsequent crises. By disclosing more relevant information, the market in question will increasingly resemble a market with perfect information where rational agents can easily follow their buying and selling strategies according to their risk preferences on the basis of their judgement of "fundamentals".

With its focus on market discipline, Pillar 3 is very often acknowledged even by critics of (excessive) regulation of banks. Decamps et al. (2004, p. 132), for example, justify Pillar 3 regulations 'to encourage monitoring of banks by professional investors and financial analysts as a complement to banking supervision'. De Ceuster and Masschelein (2003, p. 750) see positive effects in Pillar 3, as 'it adds a dimension to the first Capital Accord, since within the old Accord the regulator was officially the sole institution who disciplined the banks'.

[10] For a critique of this rationale, see Lordon (2001).

With the introduction of market discipline mechanisms, other actors, namely market actors, will also monitor banks' behavior. Disclosing information to monitoring stakeholders is further justified when it safeguards the interests of depositors.

Advocates of market discipline thus admit on the one hand that market failure is possible and that institutional response is required. On the other hand, however, '(s)uch responses should be kept to the minimum necessary, in order to allow for the maximum freedom of market forces' (Best 2003, p. 583).

Whether market discipline works in the way it is directed is still questionable. Several academics question the working of a regulatory mechanism which primarily consists of simply issuing information to the public: 'Despite banking industries concerns about cumbersome requirements . . . disclosure often involves a few extra paragraphs and additional figures in institutions' annual reports and supervisory statements' (Tsingou 2004, p. 6) which do not automatically provide relevant and significant information about the risk appetite of financial institutions or their business strategies and the markets they are in. By looking at potential stakeholders, De Ceuster and Masschelein (2003) question from a supportive view the effectiveness of disciplining banks via disclosure requirements as laid down in the new capital accord. Whereas the Basel Committee leaves it open who the relevant monitors are, De Ceuster and Masschelein identify three main parties: equity holders, subordinated debt holders, and depositors. Equity holders, especially large ones, can rely on various corporate governance mechanisms to discipline bank managers: They can create circumstances for hostile takeovers, exercise their voting rights accordingly and thereby influence managerial decisions and management compensation, etc. De Ceuster and Masschelein concede, however, that these disciplining efforts are restricted to large shareholders only. Furthermore, if equity holders behave as suggested in standard option pricing theory, they might even favor a more risky strategy on the part of the bank, as the option-like character of their stake limits the extent of losses they might experience, while at the same time benefiting them when higher risks also lead to higher profits. Much of the same can be said of subordinated debt holders: "Whenever subordinated debt is representing only a minor portion of a bank's total liabilities, the bank is not dependent on it for its funding. Hence, small proportions of subordinated debt will not generate any market disciplining incentives' (De Ceuster and Masschelein 2003, p. 755). Finally, depositors can discipline banks' risk behavior with the threat of deposit withdrawal. In reality, the majority of depositors are too small to have the necessary ability to monitor banks' activities or to pose any threat to banks – although at least in Germany and Austria banks rely heavily on deposits for (cheap) funding – when they withdraw their deposits. De Ceuster and Masschelein (2003, p. 757) conclude that 'banks in difficulties may be confronted with only a very small funding limitation'. Moreover, exhibiting financial distress may even deepen banks' problems when stakeholders overreact to difficulties which are possibly only temporary. Therefore, even from a supportive point of view it is questionable whether market discipline really works in the direction it was supposed to.

In summary, in contrast to supporting views market discipline will not lead to a broader involvement of parties monitoring banks. Whereas institutional investors with experience and instruments for market monitoring and banking analysis may be able to exploit the additional information on banks, the broader range of depositors will not be able or willing to use the increase in disclosed information in order to monitor banks and to react accordingly.

To conclude the assessment of all three pillars, we can say that the involvement and role of public and private actors in the Basel II process gives us a mixed picture: There is no clear advantage for either the public or private agents in terms of political gains. Whereas rating agencies can increase their authority as their mechanisms and practices are widely acknowledged by the BCBS, and whereas international banks and their associations have been able to influence the Basel negotiations to a great extent, at least under Pillar 2 of the framework public regulators will also see their supervisory authority increase and benefit from being part of a technocratic elite. As with all political processes, the shaping of the Basel Accord was by no means a uniform or coherent process. A plethora of national, public, and private interests tried to influence the regulatory framework. Although a general tendency toward a more liberal regime can be observed in Basel II, the concrete policies or reform steps were developed casually or through trial and error. Much of the complexity of the accord is due to the willingness of the BCBS to bring Basel II to a successful end, thereby integrating manifold requests from various actors into the accord. In the end, it thus becomes increasingly difficult to single out private or public interests in the regulatory regime. In the next sections, therefore, the analysis of the role of public and private agents will be complemented by an assessment of how much this change in the relationship between public and private agents under Basel II will also have implications for the organization of bank lending and how this fits in with current political economic trends in financial markets regulation.

6. IMPLICATIONS OF BASEL II FOR BANK LENDING AND BANK REGULATION

6.1 Basel II: A Reorganization of Bank Lending?

Basel II is an example of how new developments in banking and new modes of regulation change the banking system from within. My argument here is that the Basel Committee on Banking Supervision acts as a condenser and catalyst for a new organization of bank lending. Basel II creates pressure for a reorganization of bank lending in the following ways.

By boosting the role of rating agencies, appreciating quantitative ratings as the basis for creditworthiness assessment and pushing for more risk-adjusted pricing of loans, the BSBC has reorganized and standardized the mechanism of credit lending and thereby questioned previous lending practices. This will potentially threaten countries with a tradition of relationship lending (e.g. Germany, Austria, Japan) where risk assessment and in particular risk-adjusted pricing are not customary. Long-term lending relationships have been prevalent in such countries, and banks have been willing to finance companies throughout the cycle, still funding them in times of economic distress. The risk-averse principles of Basel II might lead to a refusal of credit in times of an economic downturn. They might also serve as an excuse for not lending to less developed countries as they are estimated to be too risky. This obsession with risk as the main factor in granting a loan leads to a rhetoric of justification for the denial of credit to disadvantaged groups.

By harmonizing banking regulation on a worldwide level, the Basel accord furthers the intersubjectivity and observability of creditworthiness on a global level. Thus, commonly shared views on borrowers' risk and the increasing transparency of lending practices on a global level favor the internationally active banks who complained about the obscurity and incomplete competitiveness of several 'difficult' banking markets (e.g. Germany, Japan). Basel II will not lead to a complete reversal of loan financing by companies and other clients as some critics fear, but it may change lending practices and subordinate credit relationships under market scrutiny (ratings, risk-adjusted pricing). Although small and medium-sized enterprises will – due to their favorable treatment under Basel II – probably not face difficulties in obtaining loans in comparison to larger corporates, they will feel pressure to adjust to new norms in the credit business. Their information and accounting activities will be scrutinized by banks more intensely as the companies will have to prove they are (still) creditworthy.

6.2 Basel II in a Politico-Economic Setting

The relationships between different social actors, between the public and the private, are historically variable. Contingent coalitions and power relations shape specific political regimes. These power relations always materialize in the form of specific institutions or practices; for example, with regard to financial systems they materialize in the form of accounting rules, corporate governance codes and other regulatory practices. At the same time, the analysis of those manifestations should allow conclusions about the current overall politico-economic setting in which they are embedded. Institutions and apparatuses are not analyzed as simple technical instruments of diverse governments but as a concretion or condensation of social relationships (cf. Sablowski 2003, Röttger 1998).

A detailed analysis of the individual elements of Basel II above should therefore allow inferences about general tendencies in the currently observable politico-economic processes. A first conclusion is that Basel II fits into the current political and economic setting as it is generally a liberal regime and furthers the political objective of financial market liberalization. According to a ranking established by Abiad and Mody (2005), banking systems can be qualified as fully repressed if credit controls coexist with interest rate controls, entry barriers, operational restrictions, the nationalization of banks and restrictions on international financial transactions. The less such instruments are used, the more liberalized a banking system is considered. As the introduction of capital requirements in the 1980s represented a move away from interest rate ceilings and credit controls, and as it did not inhibit business lines or international transactions, the Basel accord represents a more liberal banking regime than those which had prevailed in former regulation periods.

As with general regulation, banking regulation can be classified either as regulation of structure or as regulation of conduct. Whereas regulation of structure deals with the type of banking activity (e.g. universal banking, investment banking, etc.), regulation of conduct targets the behavior of banks (cf. Freixas and Rochet 1997, pp. 258f.). Capital requirements can be considered instruments of conduct regulation. Their aim is not to restrict banking activities (via market entry barriers, separate banking, interest rate ceilings, credit rationing, and so on), but to guide the behavior of banks toward a more risk-sensitive approach to managing their activities. What regulators are telling the banks is that they can practically engage in whatever business they like (investment banking, commercial banking, securitizing loans, etc.) as long as they assess their risk and manage it accordingly.

Basel II is also a more liberal regime, as it follows current market regulation trends by incorporating market discipline as one of the main pillars in the regulatory framework. With its reliance on market discipline and corporate governance, Basel II contributes to the enhancement of financial discipline – one of the cornerstones in a finance-led economic environment[11] in which the dominance of financial affairs over various aspects of daily life (retirement planning, insurance, etc.) is increasing (Froud et al. 2001). This requires a developed financial market, including banks, which offers adequate financial products and investment alternatives. In such an environment, a possible mismatch between the interests of households and the finance industry has to be addressed by regulatory reforms. This is where market discipline and corporate governance come into play: Via regulations and laws like the post-Enron Sarbanes-Oxley Act, but also the Basel II framework, regulators demonstrate their willingness to enforce trust and confidence in financial markets. In times of several new initiatives to promote financial markets and to incite more and more private households and companies to participate in financial markets (retirement savings, share issues, etc.), raising confidence in financial markets is an important political task. Market discipline therefore serves the purpose of building trust[12] in financial markets without doing extensive harm to market players at the same time.

Within the EU context, Basel II helps to push forward the integration of financial markets, which is among the main political objectives at least in the EU (cf. Lamfalussy 2003). The new framework pushes integration via establishing homogenous rules, thus creating a level playing field for banks (cf. Grossmann 2004). The harmonization of banking law will facilitate cross-border mergers and acquisitions which in the past have threatened jobs and the availability of financial services when bank outlets have been closed due to the consolidation process.

Territorially based compromises and bargains will be scrutinized as the emergence of larger and internationally active banks will increase their bargaining power vis-à-vis other stakeholders, such as local policymakers, trade unions and consumer groups mostly acting on a local basis (cf. Weber in this volume).

Finally, in contrast to former banking regulation, private industry has gathered momentum under Basel II at least from an ideological perspective. Private-sector concerns have increasingly been internalized in the Basel II process. The adoption of industry proposals by regulators

[11] For an elaborate account of such transformations in the European Union with attention to banking regulation, see Bieling (2003).

[12] 'Building Trust' was also the slogan for the 2003 World Economic Forum in Davos after worldwide protests challenged globalization, (see also: World Economic Forum 2002).

was not based on enforcement by the industry but on a mutual understanding and agreement on common interests and political ideas. This, together with the approval of rating agency techniques, increases the structural power of financial industry interests. 'This structural power is made concrete when policy-makers incorporate the decisions of these private actors into regulation at the domestic and the international level' (King and Sinclair 2003, p. 358).

At the same time, the absence of labor and consumer groups is obvious in the Basel II process. From a purely technical or economic point of view, this is not so much a problem because consumers (households) will be treated in the retail and residential mortgage categories, which receive preferential risk weights and are therefore advantaged vis-à-vis other assets classes. But it is problematic from a political point of view: It is worrying in terms of democracy when labor and consumer groups are not involved in negotiation processes in banking and finance. Financial market stability does affect consumers and employees, for example regarding the need to secure household deposits or jobs in the banking industry. With the absence of consumer and labor groups, Basel II is a further indication that these groups have increasing difficulties in exercising democratic control over financial market issues or even determining financial market outcomes (Grahl and Teague 2003, Mooslechner 2004, p. 13). The European Union recently showed some concern about the marginal involvement of consumer groups as far as financial market regulation is concerned in the EU. In 2004, a report on consumers' views on the Financial Services Action Plan (FSAP) – FIN-USE – was published by the European Commission. Moreover, the post-FSAP agenda places emphasis on consumer protection and – given the rejection of the European Constitution in France and the Netherlands – EU politicians are feeling increased pressure to realign union politics with the concerns of EU citizens. Up to now, Basel II has not concerned itself with such legitimacy problems.

7. CONCLUSION

As far as the relationships between public and private agents are concerned, Basel II provides a mixed picture. Whereas private agents like rating agencies will see an increase in their authority as their ideological judgments and mechanisms are acknowledged by the Basel II framework, at the same time supervisory discretion will increase at least in Pillar 2. Furthermore, Basel II is an example of private industry interests becoming more important as its concerns have been internalized in the Basel II regulations based on mutual understanding and agreement on common ideas shared by the industry and regulators. At the same time, it is democratically worrying that labor and consumer groups have been absent in the Basel II process. As changes in financial market regulation are not isolated from other policy areas and 'appear to be related to other key institutional features of the economies, including the degree of corporatism, social security and distribution of income, wealth and risk in the society' (Mooslechner 2004), future political processes should take into consideration that such regulations concern a wider range of social groups than those included in negotiation. It is therefore democratically desirable to enhance the possibility of consumer and labor groups to take part in policy shaping as far as financial markets are concerned.

REFERENCES

Abiad, A. and A. Mody (2005), 'Financial Reform: What Shakes It? What Shapes It?', *The American Economic Review*, **95** (1), 66–88.

Ayadi, R. and A. Resti (2004), 'The New Basel Accord and the Future of the European Financial System', CEPS Task Force Report No. 51, Brussels.

BBA – British Bankers' Association (2004), *Prudential Newsletter*, October 2004, London.

BCBS – Basel Committee on Banking Supervision (2003), *Quantitative Impact Study 3 – Overview of Global Results*, Basel.

BCBS – Basel Committee on Banking Supervision (2004), *International Convergence of Capital Measurement and Capital Standards. A Revised Framework*, Basel.

Best, J. (2003), 'Moralizing Finance: the new financial architecture as ethical discourse', *Review of International Political Economy*, **10** (3), 579–603.

Bieling, H.J. (2003), 'Social forces in the making of the new European economy: The case of financial market integration', *New Political Economy*, **8** (2), 203–24.

Caruana, J. (2003), 'The importance of transparency and market discipline approaches in the New Capital Accord', keynote speech, Market Discipline Conference, Federal Reserve Bank of Chicago and BIS, Chicago.

Coffee, J. (2001), 'The Acquiescent Gatekeeper: Reputational Intermediaries, Auditor Independence and the Governance of Accounting', Working Paper No. 191, Columbia Law School, Columbia University, New York.

Daníelsson, J. (2003), 'On the Feasibility of Risk Based Regulation', *CESifo Economic Studies*, **49** (2), 157–80.

Daníelsson, J., P. Embrechts, C. Goodhart, C. Keating, F. Muennich, O. Renault and H.S. Shin (2001), 'An Academic Response to Basel II', Special Paper No. 130, Financial Markets Group, London School of Economics.

Davies, H. (2003), 'Managing Financial Crises', in P. Booth and D. Currie (eds), *The Regulation of Financial Markets*, London: Institute of Economic Affairs, pp. 27–43.

De Ceuster, M. and N. Masschelein (2003), 'Regulating Banks Through Market Discipline: A Survey of the Issues', *Journal of Economic Surveys*, **17** (1), 749–66.

Decamps, J., J. Rochet and B. Roger (2004), 'The three pillars of Basel II: optimizing the mix', *Journal of Financial Intermediation*, **13**, 132–55.

EBIC – European Banking Industry Committee (2005), 'EBIC Position Paper on the Proposed Capital Requirements Directive', Brussels.

European Shadow Financial Regulatory Committee (2003), 'Bank Supervisors' Business: Risk Management or Systemic Stability?', Statement No. 16, available at http://www.bis.org/bcbs/cp3/eushfireco.pdf.

Freixas, X. and J.C. Rochet (1997), *Microeconomics of Banking*, Cambridge, MA, USA: MIT Press.

Fritz-Aßmus, D. and E. Tuchtfeldt (2003), 'Basel II als internationaler Standard zur Regulierung von Banken', *ORDO – Jahrbuch für die Ordnung von Wirtschaft und Gesellschaft*, **54**, 269–88.

Froud, J., C. Haslam, S. Johal and K. Williams (2001), 'Financialisation and Shareholder Value: Consultancy Moves, Management Promises', *Economy and Society*, **29** (1), 80–110.

Genschel, P. and T. Plumper (1997), 'Regulatory competition and international co-operation', *Journal of European Public Policy*, **4** (4), 626–42.

Grahl, J. and P. Teague (2003), 'The Eurozone and financial integration: the employment relations issues', *Industrial Relations Journal*, **34** (5), 396–410.

Grossman, E. (2004), 'European Banking Policy between Multilevel Governance and Europeanisation', in A. Baker (ed.), *Governing Financial Globalisation. The Political Economy of Multi-Level Governance*, London: Routledge, pp. 130-146.

Hahn, F. (2003), 'Die neue Basler Eigenkapitalvereinbarung ("Basel II") aus makroökonomischer Sicht', *WIFO Monatsberichte*, **2**, 137–50.

King, M. and T. Sinclair (2001), 'Grasping At Straws: A Ratings Downgrade For The Emerging International Financial Architecture', Working Paper No 82, Centre for the Study of Globalisation and Regionalisation (CSGR), University of Warwick.

King, M. and T. Sinclair (2003), 'Private Actors and Public Policy: A Requiem for the New Basel Capital Accord', *International Political Science Review*, **24** (3), 345–62.

Lamfalussy, A. (2003), 'Creating an integrated European market for financial services', in P. Booth and D. Currie (eds), *The Regulation of Financial Markets*, London: Institute of Economic Affairs, pp. 105–20.

Larsson, B. (2003), 'Neo-liberalism and polycontextuality: banking crisis and re-regulation in Sweden', *Economy and Society*, **32** (3), 428–48.

Lordon, F. (2001), 'Finance internationale: les illusions de la transparence', *Critique Internationale*, **10**, 6–11.

Lütz, S. (1999), 'Zwischen "Regime" und "kooperativen Staat". Bankenregulierung im internationalen Mehr-Ebenen-System', *Zeitschrift für Internationale Beziehungen*, **6** (1), 11–42.

Lütz, S. (2002), *Der Staat und die Globalisierung von Finanzmärkten. Regulative Politik in Deutschland, Großbritannien und den USA*, Frankfurt/New York: Campus.

Mooslechner, P. (2004), 'The Transformation of the European Financial System – A Brief Introduction to Issues and Literature', Proceedings of OeNB Workshops, No. 1, 7–22.

Oatley, T. and R. Nabors (1998), 'Redistributive Cooperation: Market Failure, Wealth Transfers, and the Basle Accord', *International Organization*, **52** (1), 35–54.

Porter, T. (2004), 'The Significance of Changes in Private-Sector Associational Activity in Global Finance for the Problem of Inclusion and Exclusion', paper prepared for the Workshop on the Political Economy of International Financial Governance, 26 November 2004, Oesterreichische Nationalbank, Vienna.

Reinicke, W. (1995), *Banking, Politics, and Global Finance*, Aldershot, UK and Brookfield, US: Edward Elgar.

Resti, A. (2004), 'The Architecture of the New Basel Capital Accord. From Basel I to Basel II', in R. Ayadi and A. Resti, 'The New Basel Accord and the Future of the European Financial System', CEPS Task Force Report No. 51, Brussels, pp. 3–16.

Röttger, B. (1998), 'Gramsci und die Kritik des hegemonialen Neoliberalismus. Politische Re-Konstitution des Marktes und neoliberale Erweiterung des Staates', in U. Hirschfeld (ed.), *Gramsci-Perspektiven*, Hamburg: Argument-Verlag, pp. 134–55.

Sablowski, T. (2003), 'Bilanz(en) des Wertpapierkapitalismus. Deregulierung, Shareholder Value, Bilanzskandale', *Prokla*, **131**, 201–33.

Sanio, J. (2004), 'Keine Macht ohne Kontrolle', *Frankfurter Allgemeine Zeitung*, 2 May 2004.

Scharpf, F. (1999), *Governing in Europe. Effective and Democratic?*, Oxford, New York: Oxford University Press.

Simmons, B.A. (2001), 'The International Politics of Harmonization: The Case of Capital Market Regulation', *International Organization*, **55** (3), 589–620.

Sinclair, T. (2001), 'The Infrastructure of Global Governance: Quasi-Regulatory Mechanisms and the New Global Finance', *Global Governance*, **7**, 441–51.

Tsingou, E. (2004), 'Policy preferences in financial governance: public-private dynamics and the prevalence of market-based arrangements in the banking industry', Working Paper No. 131, Centre for the Study of Globalisation and Regionalisation, University of Warwick.

Weber, B. (2006), 'The Construction of the Single Market in Financial Services and the Politics of Inclusion and Exclusion', in this volume..

World Economic Forum (2002), 'Trust will be the challenge of 2003', press release, 8 November 2002, Geneva, available at http://www.weforum.org /pdf/AM_2003/Survey.pdf.

9. The Governance of Occupational Pension Funds and its Politico-Economic Implications: The Case of Austria

Stefan W. Schmitz*

This paper analyzes the efficacy of the governance structure of occupational pension funds (*Pensionskassen* – PKs) in Austria. Based on the results of the analysis, it further investigates the politico-economic implications for the political and legislative process regarding recent changes to the relevant act (*Pensionskassengesetz* – PKG).

The first section explains the exclusion of the beneficiaries' interests from the institutional interest of the PKs' association, i.e. the distribution of power, by the underlying governance structure of PKs. It focuses on the structural conflict of interest faced by PKs, namely between their beneficiaries and their shareholders (almost exclusively large Austrian banks and insurance companies). The shareholders' instruments to control the PKs are largely determined by the Joint Stock Company Act.[1] The PKG includes provisions which can be interpreted as means to counterbalance the shareholders' dominance and to ensure that PKs conduct their business in the interests of beneficiaries, but which were also motivated by the objective of selling PKs to beneficiaries and works councils. This section addresses the following question: How effective is the governance structure of PKs at the micro and meso level with respect to the objective of counterbalancing the structural dominance of shareholders? The notion of governance developed in the New

* The author thanks Daniel Gradenegger for his excellent research assistance and the members of the working group on financial governance for their very helpful comments. The usual disclaimer applies. The views expressed in the paper are those of the author and do not necessarily represent those of the OeNB.

[1] Potential agency problems between shareholders and PKs' management boards are not discussed in the paper as they are neither specific to PKs, nor do they affect the structural dominance of shareholders relative to beneficiaries.

Institutional Economics literature is employed in the analysis. It is demonstrated that the institutional arrangements in place are not effective in realigning the incentives of PKs with those of the beneficiaries in conflicts of interest between them and the PKs' shareholders. The shareholders' interests are likely to prevail in a conflict of interest with the beneficiaries. In this section, the institutional interests of PKs are determined by the governance structure at the micro and meso levels and by the interests of the stakeholders, in particular those of the shareholders, while the governance structure is treated as given.

The second section focuses on the empirical investigation of the politico-economic impact of the findings in the first section. It analyzes the role of the PKs and in particular the PK association (Fachverband der Pensionskassen) in the political process on the basis of a case study. In order to do so, a specific process is identified in which the interests of the beneficiaries and the shareholders are diametrically opposed – the passing of the 2003 amendment to the PKG. This section treats the governance structure at the micro and meso levels as endogenous and investigates the mutual interdependence of governance structures at the different levels (micro/meso versus political level). It finds that the interests of the shareholders do in fact prevail in this particular conflict of interest with the beneficiaries. It argues that the repercussions of the governance structure at the micro and meso levels on the political level can result in a vicious circle for beneficiaries, and that the political risks associated with long-term guarantees for beneficiaries of occupational pension funds are substantial and aggravated by the governance structure at the micro and meso level. It employs an actor-centered institutionalism.

A substantial quantity of microeconomic literature analyzes the optimal governance structure of occupational pension funds,[2] and there is a rich body of research on the political economy of pension reform.[3] These research areas consider either the political processes or the governance structure of occupational pension funds to be exogenous. This paper contributes to the literature by merging the two lines of research in an inquiry into the interdependence of the micro and meso level of governance in occupational pension funds and the political economy of reform in the relevant act. It also adds to the literature through its empirical focus on Austrian occupational pension funds (PKs).

---

[2] Rajan and Srivastava (2000); Ambachtsheer (2001); Besley and Prat (2003); Palomino and Prat (2002); and Deelstra, Grasselli and Koehl (2004).

[3] Inter alia Brooks and James (1999); Müller (2003); Ney (2003); Orenstein (2003); Weaver (2003); and the papers collected in Rein and Schmähl (2004).

The empirical investigation is restricted to Austria, as the governance of occupational pension funds throughout the OECD is quite diverse and an empirical assessment of its efficacy has to take into account the details of the relevant acts as well as the more general provisions governing joint stock companies and market structure.[4] The EU directive on the activities and supervision of institutions of occupational retirement provision (2003/41/EC), on the other hand, only contains very general provisions on pension fund governance. The relevant Level 3 committee (CEIOPS) has a consultative panel with 17 members, of which nine are representatives of financial industry associations, two represent consumers, and one represents trade unions.[5] This highlights the role of financial industry associations in the EU political and legislative process in the area of pension fund legislation and supervisory practice. As occupational pension funds are financial institutions, similar structural conflicts of interest can emerge at the EU level and in other OECD countries as in the Austrian case study, which calls for an investigation of the underlying governance structures. In a survey of pension fund governance, the OECD focuses on formal arrangements at the micro level without investigating their efficacy.[6] This paper contributes to this literature by focusing on an assessment of the efficacy of the formal arrangements based on a more detailed and at the same time broader perspective (micro and meso level) on governance. This is indicative of other systems in which occupational pension funds are organized as corporations (rather than as trusts or foundations)[7] in a comparative institutional approach.[8] In a recent report, the World Economic Forum (2005) finds that the transparency and accountability standards in pension funds and the beneficiaries' influence on strategic fund management provide cause for concern. The lack of proper governance and incentive structures that realign the interests of pension fund shareholders and management with those of the beneficiaries is regarded as a major obstacle for responsible long-term investment by pension funds, which would be in line with the beneficiaries' long-term planning horizon. The report recommends a voluntary 'Fund Governance Code' that ensures the representation of beneficiaries' long-term interests in intent, capability

---

[4] OECD (2004). The OECD Guidelines do not contain explicit provisions concerning the governance structure of occupational pension funds.

[5] http://www.ceiops.org (last visit: 25 November 2004).

[6] OECD (2001).

[7] According to OECD (2004), representation of beneficiaries in the governing bodies of occupational pension funds is common throughout the OECD, but substantially differs in detail.

[8] For a case study focusing on the UK trust system, see Clark (2004), who also argues that beneficiaries have very little effective influence on pension fund governance in the UK. Mahoney (2004) elaborates on the conflicts of interest in the funded pension system in the US.

and practice. These findings are particularly interesting as they emerged from a series of roundtables with representatives of fund management companies, investment banks, insurance companies and business networks, but largely excluded representatives of beneficiaries.

The paper is structured along the following lines: The first section presents the empirical analysis of the governance structure of PKs and focuses on the micro and meso levels. The second section contains the case study of the political and legislative process regarding the 2003 PKG amendment and presents a politico-economic investigation at the political level. The third section summarizes the paper.

1. THE GOVERNANCE STRUCTURE OF OCCUPATIONAL PENSION FUNDS IN AUSTRIA AT THE MICRO AND MESO LEVEL

The first section identifies the transparency problems and the principal-agent problems that beneficiaries face in PKs and addresses the question of how effective the governance structure designed to overcome these problems is at the micro and meso level.

Governance

The analysis in the first section is based on an *economic notion of governance*. It employs the methods of institutional analysis based on this notion, i.e. the New Institutional Economics approach to principal-agent problems.[9] The notion of governance refers to a set of institutional arrangements that address coordination problems resulting from incomplete contracts due to asymmetric information and opportunistic behavior. It comprises institutional arrangements at the micro level – such as corporate governance and contracts between sponsoring undertakings and PKs – as well as at the meso level, such as the regulatory framework and the market environment. PKs are not publicly listed, so the potential governance roles of the stock market and takeovers are not considered. The principal-agent problem between shareholders and PK management is not further analyzed, as it is largely governed by the Joint Stock Company Act and does not pose problems specific to PKs.

The principal-agent approach is particularly well suited for the current investigation due to the fact that beneficiaries are legally entitled to the

[9] Williamson (1985 and 1996).

funds invested in PKs, while the PKs operate under the formal, legal mandate to administer them in the beneficiaries' interest. The approach highlights the role of incentives and sanctions and thus provides an appropriate conceptual framework for the empirical analysis. The latter focuses on empirically observable sanctions and incentives (e.g. legal provisions) rather than important but less observable factors (e.g. social norms, social status of PK managers).

Nevertheless, the New Institutional notion of governance has a number of drawbacks: The approach is focused on economic incentives and sanctions. It is less suited to taking into account societal conventions, habits, and altruistic behavior as motives to conduct the business of pension funds in the sole interest of beneficiaries. In principle, it takes the benefits of delegation of long-term investment decisions to managers due to superior expertise as given. The approach presumes that the only problem in the relationship between the parties is one of asymmetries of information rather than asymmetries of power between large financial institutions and beneficiaries. The second section exemplifies the substantial repercussions that these asymmetries of power have on governance at the micro and meso level. Finally, the approach interprets policy choices with respect to the governance structure of PKs from a functionalist perspective (namely to counterbalance the structural dominance of shareholders) and does not *prima facie* assume that they were solely motivated as symbolic policy measures to legitimize political change.

At the micro and meso level, the regulatory framework for PKs is predetermined and treated as given, as are some of the determinants of market competition, such as barriers to entry, market transparency, asymmetric information and opportunistic behavior, in addition to technological characteristics of the production function (e.g. economies of scale and scope).

Transparency and Principal-Agent Problems

PKs are financial intermediaries incorporated as joint stock companies, which brings about a structural conflict of interest between beneficiaries and shareholders. This raises a *principal-agent problem* (i.e. *moral hazard problems)* between the beneficiaries and the PKs.[10] The principals

[10] Besley and Prat (2003) emphasize the principal-agent problem between beneficiaries and sponsoring undertakings in pension funds and analyze their governance structure in an incomplete contracts framework. To keep the model tractable, they restrict their focus to two periods, to a moral hazard problem between sponsors and beneficiaries, and to governance at the micro level. The three areas of control rights they take into consideration are funding decisions, asset allocation and asset management. They find that in defined

(beneficiaries) mandate the agent (the PK and in particular its management) to reach a certain objective, but they cannot directly observe the agent's effort. An optimal contract would provide incentive compatibility by relating the agent's payoff to his/her effort. However, the agent's effort is unobservable, and an information asymmetry prevails. If the beneficiaries could observe the output of the agent's behavior ex post, a contract that relates the agent's compensation to the ex-post observable output would improve the incentive structure for the agent. However, there are two problems involved: First, the output of investment decisions in an environment of uncertainty is not a deterministic function of the agent's effort. Consequently, the agent's effort can only be inferred with considerable noise from ex-post performance; it is difficult to separate effort from good or bad luck.[11] Second, the *lack of transparency* of financial institutions often makes it very costly for their customers to observe and analyze their performance ex post.[12] Even if ex-post performance could be observed cost effectively, it would pose additional problems for beneficiaries. Some risks can cause large losses in very short periods of time, such that it might be too late to react when they are detected. Others can result in small losses over long periods, but are very hard to detect at all. The OECD (2001) lists examples of these risks for beneficiaries arising from the moral hazard problem, such as outright fraud, abuse of funds to support issues of securities underwritten by shareholders, churning of portfolios, and suboptimal effort levels.

Substantial losses cannot always be offset by increased effort in the following periods and can result in long-term welfare losses for beneficiaries in the form of lower pensions. That implies that the individual and the ensuing societal welfare losses (in the form of old-age poverty) of a purely market-based ex-ante enforcement of prudential investment are potentially very high and can induce substantial

---

contribution schemes funding is usually constant, control rights should be allocated to beneficiaries, and trustees should be caring insiders chosen by and accountable to beneficiaries (e.g. trade union officials rather than outside finance experts). Under limited liability the sponsors have an incentive for excessive risk-taking following from the 'gambling for resurrection problem'. See also Rajan and Srivastava (2000) and Palomino and Prat (2002).

[11] In fact PKs invest about 95 per cent of their assets in investment funds, which gives rise to an additional principal-agent problem between the PKs and the investment funds with the corresponding monitoring costs. As many of the investment funds are administered by the shareholders of the respective PKs, the problem is partly internalized and not further analyzed in this paper.

[12] The analysis of the transparency problems in PKs focuses on the observability of performance and costs, rather than on broader notions of transparency such as procedural transparency, transparency of the capability to absorb risk, or market transparency.

uncertainty. Societal welfare losses might give rise to another *moral hazard problem* – this time between the public authorities (government/legislature[13]) and a coalition of beneficiaries and PKs – providing incentives for beneficiaries and PKs to regard the potential socialization of financial losses as implicit insurance against substantial losses in PKs, which could lead to excessive risk-taking.[14] This paper only focuses on the principal-agent problem between beneficiaries and PKs.

In addition, beneficiaries' room for maneuver to sanction disappointing ex-post performance crucially depends on the governance structure of the occupational pension fund and the intensity of competition in the relevant market.

The proponents of the PKG in the Austrian parliament recognized the sensitive social role of occupational pension funds and attempted to address the potential lack of transparency and the principal-agent problem between beneficiaries and PKs in a number of specific rules.[15] This does not preclude the possibility that these provisions were also motivated by the objective of selling PKs to beneficiaries and works councils. These rules contain provisions to increase the transparency of PKs, to ensure the beneficiaries' participation in the governance structure, and to restrain the set of admissible actions (i.e. investments) of the agent ex ante. In addition to presenting these and assessing their efficacy, I will discuss the extent to which market forces and competition among PKs, i.e. the intensity of competition in the market for occupational pension funds, might function as a governance mechanism.[16]

The Market

At the end of 2004, 13 single-employer and seven multi-employer Pensionskassen (PKs) were licensed in Austria. In the year 2004, their total assets increased from EUR 9.12 billion to EUR 10.13 billion (+11.1 percent). Household claims against PKs amounted to about 3 per cent of

[13] While the coalition of PKs and beneficiaries is clearly defined, their counterparty in this principal-agent problem is less so. Most bailouts do require actions to be taken by the executive and the legislative branches of public authorities due to the rule of law in the Austrian constitution.

[14] Public bailouts of beneficiaries and PKs can take various forms, such as softening regulation rather than enforcing it under distress (e.g. reducing own funds requirements in periods of financial distress), capital transfers to PKs under distress, and direct social transfers to beneficiaries hit by old-age poverty.

[15] Stenographic Record of the 143rd Session of the National Council of the Republic of Austria, Legislative Period XVII, Thursday, 17 May 1990, Nos. 16581–16620.

[16] To some extent, the assessment is intrinsically subjective, thus the presentation of findings is intended to make the assessments comprehensible.

their total financial assets.[17] At the end of 2004 about 10 600 contracts between sponsoring undertakings and PKs were established covering 413 000 beneficiaries, of which 44 000 were pensioners. Between 1990 and 2004 the nominal performance of PKs averaged 6.9 per cent p.a., while PKs faced losses in 2001 (–1.6 per cent p.a. in nominal terms) and 2002 (–6.3 per cent p.a. in nominal terms, or EUR 379 million).[18] The following section refers to occupational pension funds that administer occupational pension schemes for more than one sponsoring undertaking (multi-employer PKs). In a small number of areas, the PKG stipulates special provisions concerning single-employer PKs, which are not further considered in this paper. The vast majority of pension schemes of multi-employer PKs are defined contribution schemes (DCS), thus the paper focuses on these.

Legal Foundations

The legal foundations for the emergence of occupational pension funds and occupational pension schemes were laid in 1990 with the *Pensionskassengesetz* (PKG – Federal Act on the Establishment, Administration and Supervision of *Pensionskassen*) and the *Betriebspensionsgesetz* (BPG – Company Pension Act).[19] The BPG was motivated by the objective of safeguarding company pensions in Austrian labor and social law by offering the opportunity to transfer the accumulated entitlements to future pensions from the employer to a PK. In addition, the entitlements are vested after a maximum period of five years even if the employee leaves the company before the pension is due. Vesting was supposed to guarantee a high degree of security for prospective pensioners by decoupling the stability of the pension scheme from the stability of the employer, the sponsoring undertaking. Furthermore, it was expected to increase the mobility of labor, as employees – under the previous legal regime – usually lost their pension entitlement if they changed jobs.[20]

The objective of the PKG was to establish the governance structure of PKs and to introduce the relevant regulatory regime. Legislators coupled the objective of channeling savings to institutional investors in order to

[17] Source: OeNB.

[18] Source: Fachverband der Pensionskassen.

[19] The paper is based on the legal foundations in force before the amendment, as the case study refers to 2003.

[20] These objectives of the BPG and the PKG were explicitly put forward by the sponsors of the bill at the parliamentary debate in May 1990 (Stenographic Record of the 143rd Session of the National Council of the Republic of Austria, Legislative Period XVII, Thursday, 17 May 1990, Nos. 16581–16620).

promote the Austrian capital market with the social objectives of the bill and thus generated potential conflicts of interest between these two often incongruent sets of objectives. One of the proponents of the PKG in 1990 pointed out that pension funds play an important role on financial markets in many western countries: 'Therefore, PKs enjoy considerable prominence in economic policy, and we believe that, if they develop reasonably well, we will be able to establish the long missed large investors, so-called institutional investors, in our country'.[21] The Minister of Finance, who promoted the bill as well, highlighted the fact that institutional investors would serve the promotion of Austrian capital markets and provide considerable support for industrial initiatives.[22]

The business of PKs is defined in Art. 1 (2) PKG as a legally binding commitment to grant retirement benefits to prospective pensioners (referred to as beneficiaries in the PKG) or to pay retirement benefits to pensioners (referred to as beneficiaries [recipients] in the PKG), as well as accepting and investing the respective contributions to the fund. The PKG further stipulates that PKs have to conduct their business in the interest of the beneficiaries with specific regard to the security, profitability, liquidity and the diversification of the assets (Art. 2 [1] PKG). Thus the beneficiaries act as principals and the PKs as agents, which leads to a principal-agent problem. PKs are incorporated as single-license credit institutions.

Legal Provisions Addressing the Transparency Problem at PKs

The PKG requires PKs to obtain a license from the Financial Market Authority (FMA) (Art. 8 [1] PKG),[23] which also acts as supervisory authority (Art. 33 [1] PKG), and stipulates a *single license principle* for PKs (Art. 2 [3] PKG), which implies that PKs are financial intermediaries but must limit their activities to the business of occupational pension funds.

In addition, *PKs are required to notify the FMA* on a number of issues: PKs have to report changes in the composition of the board, any circumstances that could endanger the pension obligations of the PK, any violation of the capital requirements, and significant changes in the composition of the shareholders (Art. 36 PKG). As of 31 March 1997, a

---

[21] Josef Taus, Stenographic Record of the 143rd Session of the National Council of the Republic of Austria, Legislative Period XVII, Thursday, 17 May 1990, Nos. 16587.

[22] Ferdinand Lacina (Minister of Finance), Stenographic Record of the 143rd Session of the National Council of the Republic of Austria, Legislative Period XVII, Thursday, 17 May 1990, No. 16597.

[23] Before the establishment of the FMA in 2002, the license had to be obtained from the Ministry of Finance.

regulation on quarterly reporting requirements stipulated that the assets of each investment and risk-sharing group and their composition must be reported to the FMA, exceeding the requirements of Art. 36 PKG. PKs are required to provide a detailed business plan which contains the types of benefits offered and a presentation of the circumstances significant for the safeguarding of the beneficiaries' interests (including details on the bases of the relevant calculation as well as the type and management of volatility reserves (Art. 20 PKG). PKs have to appoint an actuary responsible for preparing the business plan and monitoring compliance (Art. 20a PKG). In addition, PKs appoint an independent auditing actuary to audit the business plan (Art. 21 PKG). The FMA has to be notified regarding both appointments. The business plan has to be approved by the auditing actuary and the FMA. The audited annual accounts of each PK and the audited report on the activities of each investment and risk-sharing group have to be submitted to Austria's central bank (Oesterreichische Nationalbank, or OeNB) and the FMA.

Furthermore, *beneficiaries have the right to obtain information* via various means: The beneficiaries and the competent works councils (representing them) have the right to request copies of the audited annual accounts and the audited report of activities (Art. 30a [2] PKG). The beneficiaries are represented in the advisory committee of each investment and risk-sharing group; this committee has the right to obtain information concerning the business of the investment and risk-sharing group (Art. 28 [2] PKG). In addition, the beneficiaries are represented at the supervisory board and have the right to attend the general meeting, where they have the right to obtain information concerning their investment and risk-sharing group. PKs have to keep an account for each beneficiary (Art. 18 PKG). Each year, the beneficiaries are to be informed in writing about their current claims and all changes in their employer's contribution to their pension benefits. The beneficiaries are also entitled to yearly information from PKs about their expected benefits (Art. 17 BPG). As of 1 January 2005, minimum standards for information provided by PKs to beneficiaries[24] entered into force. These standards are intended to increase the transparency of PKs for beneficiaries and contain provisions concerning yearly information on the yield and volatility of assets, investment policy and expected benefits. The information has to be comprehensible for beneficiaries and provide a realistic scenario of future developments based on the FMA parameters regulation (e.g. *Rechnungszins*, *rechnungstechnischer Überschuss*)[25]. In defined contribu-

[24] http://www.fma.gv.at/de/pdf/041216_m.pdf (last visit: 13 June 2005), GZ: 9 080 110/05-FMA-II/1/04-Pensionskassenaufsicht

[25] http://www.fma.gv.at/de/pdf/rechnung.pdf (last visit: 4 November 2004). The term '*Rechnungszins*' refers to the necessary future average rate of return (after costs) of the

tion schemes the PK has to make it clear that the beneficiaries bear the relevant market risks. In addition, the regulation contains information requirements vis-à-vis beneficiaries upon joining the PK, upon retirement or at the moment the beneficiaries leave the sponsoring undertaking.

The legal provisions addressing transparency problems in PKs are effective in increasing transparency for the supervisor and for the beneficiaries with respect to the performance of the relevant PK on a regular basis. They do not address and are not effective in increasing market transparency or transparency with respect to the PK's capacity to absorb risk. However, the question remains which actions beneficiaries can take in response. This in turn depends on the governance structure of PKs and the intensity of competition in the PK market.

Provisions Addressing the Principal-Agent Problem: 1. The Governance Structure of PKs

The governance structure of PKs constitutes a prominent means of addressing the principal-agent problem between the beneficiaries and the PKs. It comprises the following components: (*i*) supervisory board, (*ii*) advisory committee, (*iii*) management board, (*iv*) internal auditing unit, (*v*) general meeting.

The PKG requires that beneficiaries be represented on the *supervisory board* of multi-employer PKs,[26] but also states that the representatives of the shareholders outnumber them by two, unless laid down otherwise in the articles of association (Art. 27 [1] PKG).[27] In fact, the supervisory boards of the PKs are to have a minimum of six and a maximum of 14 members. The representatives of the shareholders outnumber those of the beneficiaries in all but two PKs, one of which is a single-employer PK. In addition, the works councils of employees of PKs are entitled to delegate a representative to the supervisory board. The chairperson of the supervisory board needs to be approved by both the majority of total members and the majority of shareholder representatives, which usually ensures the election of a representative of the shareholders. The

---

Pensionskasse, such that future pension payments can be fulfilled. The term '*rechnungstechnischer Überschuss*' refers to the future average rate of return (after costs) which the Pensionskasse expects to reach.

[26] 'This is the first time, according to my knowledge of Austrian law, that beneficiaries are represented on a board such as the supervisory board' (Josef Taus, Stenographic Record of the 143rd Session of the National Council of the Republic of Austria, Legislative Period XVII, Thursday, 17 May 1990, No. 16586; author's translation of the verbatim record).

[27] In the supervisory boards of single-employer PKs, the representatives of the beneficiaries are ensured at least the number of seats of the shareholders minus one, unless it is arranged in an agreement between the PK, the sponsor undertaking, and the beneficiaries that the regulation for multi-employer PKs applies.

representatives of the beneficiaries are elected at the annual general meeting. These representatives are frequently experts from the Austrian Trade Union Association (ÖGB).[28] In addition to the general regulations applying to supervisory boards for joint stock companies, [29] the supervisory board's consent is required on certain investment decisions and the establishment of investment and risk-sharing groups. The most effective means of governance at the disposal of the supervisory board are the rights to information on the business of the PK, the approval of strategic decisions, and the appointment as well as the potential termination of contracts of members of the management board. The sponsors of the PKG argued that pension commitments are to be considered a component of wages and that, therefore, beneficiaries' participation in decisions concerning the administration and investment of the respective funds was necessary.[30] However, due to the fact that the beneficiaries are outnumbered in the supervisory board, they cannot sanction management for perceived underperformance. In potential conflicts of interest, they can be voted down by the representatives of the shareholders.

PKs can, but are not obliged to, set up an *advisory committee* for each investment and risk-sharing group (Art. 28 PKG). This committee has the right to make proposals concerning the investment policy of the respective investment and risk-sharing group, to examine its annual accounts and the report of activities, to obtain information concerning its business from the management and from the supervisory board, to report to and table motions at the general meeting, and to make proposals to the supervisory board. Its members are to be appointed by the supervisory board based on nominations in equal parts by the management board and the representatives of the beneficiaries in the supervisory board.

The PKG does not include specific provisions concerning the *management board*, meaning that only the Stock Corporation Act (Art. 70 AktG) applies. The management board is responsible for conducting the business of the PK and has to pay due attention to the interests of the

---

[28] Control rights allocated to a large dispersed group of beneficiaries give rise to a multilateral, non-individually attributable positive externality that leads to the suboptimal exercise of control rights ('free rider' problem). Their delegation to representatives is intended to overcome this problem and to ensure the necessary expertise to exercise the rights effectively. The accountability of representatives in general meetings addresses the ensuing principal-agent problem.

[29] According to the Stock Corporation Act (Art. 95 AktG), these include the obligation to supervise the management board, the obligation to convene a general meeting if deemed necessary for the company, to obtain information from the management board, and access to the accounts and assets. In addition, a number of decisions of the management board require the consent of the supervisory board.

[30] Ewald Nowotny, Stenographic Record of the 143rd Session of the National Council of the Republic of Austria, Legislative Period XVII, Thursday, 17 May 1990, No. 16589.

shareholders, the employees as well as the public. This provision conflicts with the general provision in Art. 2 (1) PKG, which states that the PKs shall operate their business in the interest of the beneficiaries. In this regard, Farny and Wöss (1992) argue that the management board is obliged to harmonize the structural conflict of interests of the shareholders and the beneficiaries. They conjecture that the objective of PKs is to reach a sustainable return on capital rather than profit maximization, so that dividends above the market average should lead to a reduction in the costs of the PK to the beneficiaries. Schiemer, Jabornegg and Strasser (1993), on the other hand, argue that the very general provisions of Art. 2 (1) PKG cannot serve as an effective basis for deducing the concrete duties of or rights vis-à-vis the management board.

The management board is the most important component of corporate governance of PKs, as it holds the exclusive right to represent the PK and to manage its business affairs. Its decision-making monopoly is only restrained by the competences of the other bodies of the PK, in particular by the supervisory board. The supervisory board's main instrument to realign the managers' interests with its own is the power to (re-)appoint members of the management board as well as the potential termination of their contracts.

Every PK has to set up an *internal auditing unit* (Art. 32 PKG) which reports directly to all members of the management board and focuses exclusively on the continuous and comprehensive audit of the business and the operation of the PK with respect to lawful, proper and expedient conduct. The unit must dispose of resources commensurate to its duties. Since it reports directly to the management board, it does not effectively contribute to the resolution of the structural conflict of interest between beneficiaries and shareholders of PKs.

The PKG confers the right to attend the *general meeting* also to the beneficiaries (Art. 29 [1] PKG), whereas the Stock Corporation Act reserves that right for the shareholders (Art. 102 AktG). The election of beneficiaries' representatives to the supervisory board has to take place at the general meeting. Due to the fact that 'the beneficiaries have an immediate interest in the performance of the PK',[31] they are granted rights to information in the general meeting (Art. 29 PKG) otherwise reserved for shareholders (Art. 112 AktG). The management board is obliged to disclose information relevant to the agenda of the general meeting upon request. The information has to be truthful, complete, and

[31] No. 1328 of the Addenda to the Stenographic Records of the National Council, Legislative Period XVII, explanatory notes to Art. 29 PKG.

comprehensible; violations of these requirements can be sanctioned (Art. 255 AktG).[32]

In addition to the relevant provisions in the PKG, employees' participation in the selection of a PK should be further secured by the provision that any contract of a sponsoring undertaking and a PK must be based on a *collective* or *works council agreement* (Art. 3 [1] BPG), which must contain the claims of beneficiaries against the PK and the participation of the beneficiaries in the administration of the PK (Art. 3 [1] BPG). At the *political level*, the PKG prescribed an advisory council for company pension funds at the Ministry of Finance (Art. 35 PKG), which was abolished in 1997 due to a lack of interest among all parties involved. Subsequently the relevant provision was deleted from the PKG. The performance of capital markets in the 1990s resulted in relatively stable returns to PKs, so that substantial conflicts of interest did not emerge.

The governance structure of PKs provides means for the beneficiaries and their representatives to monitor the performance of the PK ex post. However, the governance structure does not enable the beneficiaries to effectively sanction the perceived underperformance of PKs (i.e. the management board). Thus it is not effective in providing ex-ante incentives for agents to realign their objectives with those of the principals and to tackle the moral hazard problem between beneficiaries and PKs.

Provisions Addressing the Principal-Agent Problem: 2. Investment Rules, Guaranteed Minimum Yield, and Own Funds Requirements

In order to address the specific risks associated with funded pensions, the sponsors of the bill (PKG) emphasized the important role of investment rules[33] and of the guaranteed minimum yield.[34]

---

[32] Schiemer, Jabornegg and Strasser (1993).

[33] 'And now the most important question: We have introduced investment rules, which attempt to combine a high degree of security with a high degree of investment opportunities . . . ' (Josef Taus, Stenographic Record of the 143rd Session of the National Council of the Republic of Austria, Legislative Period XVII, Thursday, 17 May 1990, No. 16586; author's translation of the verbatim record).

[34] 'What seems particularly important to me [Johannes Bauer] in this context [the specific risks of funded pensions relative to public PAYG systems], however, is that the legislator . . . requires a minimum yield of two per cent [at the time it was about 2.8 per cent p.a.]' (Stenographic Record of the 143rd Session of the National Council of the Republic of Austria, Legislative Period XVII, Thursday, 17 May 1990, No. 16611; author's translation of the verbatim record).

The *investment rules* for PKs are stipulated in some detail in Art. 25 PKG. The admissible investments are limited to claim rights (basically bonds), shares, and profitable land and buildings in an OECD member country. Euro-denominated bonds must amount to at least 35 percent, while investments in shares are limited to 50 per cent of the assets of an investment and risk-sharing group. Investment in funds issued by an investment company in the OECD are admissible unless they conflict with other investment limits included in Art. 25 PKG or imply cost disadvantages for beneficiaries. In fact PKs invest more than 90 per cent of their assets in investment funds. Since 1990 the investment limits have been adapted frequently; the minimum share of bonds has decreased, while the admissible maximum proportion of shares and that of foreign currency assets have increased steadily. With the revision of the PKG in 2005, the 'prudent person' principle was introduced and investment constraints were further relaxed. The FMA has to issue a directive concerning investment constraints, but in doing so it considers not only the beneficiaries' interests but also the general economic interest of a smoothly functioning PK system. The liberalization of investment constraints substantially increased the room for maneuver for PKs and their management and, hence, it increased monitoring costs as well as potential risks for beneficiaries in the principal-agent relationship and aggravated the principal-agent problem.

The sponsors of the bill (PKG) intuitively recognized the role of the *guaranteed minimum yield* as a mechanism to provide incentives for PKs and to internalize the costs of underperformance. The requirement to pledge own funds against the guaranteed minimum yield is referred to as a 'liability of the own funds of the PK and, thus, the PK itself for a certain minimum yield'.[35] The provisions concerning the guaranteed minimum yield were changed substantially in 2003 at the expense of the beneficiaries. The political economy of this reform is discussed in detail in the case study in the second section of this paper. In this section, I focus on the provisions put in force by the 2003 amendment (Art. 2 [2] and [3] PKG).

The minimum yield is defined as at least half of the average monthly secondary market yield of government bonds over 60 months, minus 0.75. If the average annual investment income of an investment and risk-sharing group does not equal at least the minimum yield, the beneficiary's (recipient's) pension shall be credited with the superannuation of the deficit in the following year from the PK's own funds.

---

[35] No. 1328 of the Addenda to the Stenographic Records of the National Council, Legislative Period XVII, explanatory notes to Art. 2 (2) PKG.

Beneficiaries do not receive compensation if the minimum yield is not reached over the past 60 months. In that case, a reference value for the respective assets is calculated using the hypothetical asset value based on the minimum yield. The time period for the calculation of the reference value is extended by 12 months for each consecutive year the minimum yield is not reached. Effectively the period over which the minimum yield must be reached is also extended. Each year the deficit (calculated over a five-year period) and the reference value (calculated over the extended period) are compared, and the superannuation of the higher value is credited to the recipients' pensions in the following year. For beneficiaries who have not yet retired, both values are computed until either of the two following cases materializes: First, the minimum yield is reached again, meaning that the actual value exceeds the reference value again and no further action is taken; or second, the beneficiary retires at a moment the actual value is still below the reference value and his/her pension is credited with the superannuation (in addition to the pension resulting from the actual value of his/her claim) corresponding to the difference between the reference value and the actual value from the PK's own funds.[36]

At all times, PKs must hold sufficient *own funds* to cover their risks and at least 1 per cent of the premium reserve (Art. 7 PKG).[37] In addition, the reform in 2003 introduced a minimum yield reserve which may only be used for obligations arising from the guaranteed minimum yield requirement. Each year, 0.45 per cent of the total value of the premium reserve has to be allocated to this reserve until it reaches 3 per cent of the total value of the premium reserve.

The direct costs of PKs for beneficiaries largely consist of an administrative fee which is calculated as a share of regular contributions. In addition, PKs charge an investment administration fee which is calculated as a percentage of assets under administration. Does this cost component provide positive incentives for PKs? Unlikely, as these fees mostly reflect the expenses of PKs for the investment funds in which they invest almost 95 per cent of their assets, meaning that they hardly influence the maximization problem of PKs.[38]

The provisions concerning investment rules are to some extent effective in addressing the principal-agent problem. By restricting the set of admissible actions for the agent (PK), they reduce the costs of monitoring for the principal (beneficiaries) and limit the beneficiaries'

[36] An amendment to the PKG in 2005 introduced the option to waive the minimum yield guarantee in the contract between the sponsoring undertaking and the PK.
[37] Investment and risk-sharing groups for defined benefit schemes in which the sponsoring undertaking bears capital market risks are exempted.
[38] Source: OeNB.

maximum risk exposure and their potential maximum losses. Their liberalization has reduced their effectiveness by enlarging the set of admissible actions of the agent and increasing monitoring costs.

The provisions concerning the guaranteed minimum yield are only partially effective in realigning the incentives of the PK with those of the beneficiaries.[39] The instrument of a guaranteed minimum yield internalizes the costs of suboptimal effort by the PK up to the minimum yield, but not beyond that level.

The provisions concerning the PK's own funds do not affect the incentives of PKs, as they are to a large extent independent of the actions taken by the agent at the margin (i.e. independent of the investment policy and the performance of PKs). PKs are required to hold own funds commensurate with their risk exposure, which would make an increase in risk exposure costly at the margin. However, experience shows that supervisory authorities do not enforce this provision, which is rather vague and subject to various interpretations of the phrase 'commensurate with risk exposure'. Consequently, the own funds requirement is reduced to the provision to hold at least 1 per cent of the premium reserve and is effectively independent of PKs' decisions concerning the risk characteristics of the portfolio at the margin. Nonetheless, it does play an indirect role as the minimum yield requirement has to be met from the PKs' own funds.

Intensity of Competition in the Multi-Employer PK Market

The sponsors of the bill (PKG) were well aware of the role of competition in contributing to the realignment of incentives for multi-employer PKs[40] with those of the beneficiaries and thus introduced explicit provisions that enable sponsoring undertakings to cancel PK contracts.[41]

If an employer and/or a PK cancel a PK contract, the beneficiaries' assets have to be transferred to another PK for the cancellation to be

---

[39] How their effectiveness was influenced by the 2003 PKG amendment will be discussed in the second part of this chapter.

[40] The relevant market for the analysis of competition consists of the market for the seven multi-employer PKs only, as by definition single-employer PKs are part of the sponsoring undertaking. Competitive conditions in the multi-employer PK market, however, can influence the 'make or buy' decision either to establish a single-employer PK or to join a multi-employer PK.

[41] 'Another important regulation and provision which increases competition, it seems very important to me that the cancellation of the contract is possible, as otherwise competition would be restricted' (Johannes Bauer, Stenographic Record of the 143rd Session of the National Council of the Republic of Austria, Legislative Period XVII, Thursday, 17 May 1990, No. 16611, author's translation of the verbatim record).

admissible and legally effective (Art. 17 PKG). The notice period is one year. The minimum value of the assets to be transferred is 98 per cent of the premium reserve and of the volatility reserve. The PK contract and the underlying collective or works council agreement have to contain the share of assets to be transferred (Art. 15 [3] PKG and Art. 3 [1] BPG). The cancellation of a PK contract and the transfer of assets usually induce losses for the beneficiaries, thus the transaction costs cannot be considered negligible.[42]

The PK contract is concluded between the PK and the sponsoring undertaking (Art. 15 PKG). The beneficiaries are only involved to the extent that the PK contract must be based on a works council agreement (Art. 3 [1] BPG).[43] It must contain the claims of beneficiaries vis-à-vis the PK, the participation of the beneficiaries in the administration of the PK, and the detailed conditions for the cancellation of the PK contract by the sponsoring undertaking. Other important provisions of the PK contract for the beneficiaries – e.g. the choice of PK, the admissible forms of investment, and the principles of investment policy – do not require the participation of the beneficiaries. As the latter are not party to the PK contract, they cannot cancel it in response to perceived underperformance of the PK. Potential exit cannot substitute for a lack of voice in the governance structure and cannot realign the incentives of the PKs with those of the beneficiaries. Beneficiaries would have to convince the sponsoring undertaking to sanction the PK for a perceived lack of effort. According to one interviewee, the selection criteria of the sponsoring undertaking concern not only the interests of the beneficiaries, but also the PK's relationship to the sponsoring undertaking's main bank (Hausbank).[44]

The PK market appears to be quite concentrated. The top three multi-employer PKs control 66.14 per cent of the market in terms of total contributions and 70.32 per cent in terms of total premium reserves.[45] Competition for existing customers seems limited. Despite the negative performance of PKs in 2001 and 2002, only two sponsoring undertakings switched multi-employer PKs in 2002, ten in 2003, and twelve in 2004.[46]

---

[42] Farny and Wöss (1992, p. 313).

[43] If the beneficiaries are not represented by a works council, an agreement between the beneficiaries and the sponsoring undertaking must be based on a model contract. The latter must be approved by the Ministry of Social Affairs.

[44] Otto Farny, Austrian Chamber of Labor (telephone interview, 29 September 2004).

[45] Source: Annual Reports of PKs. Data refers to end of 2003.

[46] Source: FMA. Until 2001 the Ministry of Finance (BMF) acted as supervisory authority but did not document the data. According to the BMF, the numbers were negligible and amounted to about two sponsoring undertakings switching PKs per year between 1990 and 2001.

These numbers are rather low compared to a market size of about 9 500 PK contracts with multi-employer PKs[47] at the end of 2003.[48]

Due to the low intensity of competition for existing customers in the PK market, the non-negligible transaction costs, and the fact that the beneficiaries are not party to the PK contract, the efficacy of competitive pressure to address the principal-agent problem between beneficiaries and PKs is low. Competition has no direct effect on transparency for the purpose of monitoring performance ex post.

The central results of the first section of the paper are that (i) the governance structure of PKs at the micro and meso level (corporate governance, regulatory regime, and market competition) are effective in ensuring transparency to monitor performance of PKs ex post, (ii) the internal governance structure of PKs does not provide an incentive structure that addresses the principal-agent problem between beneficiaries and PKs, and (iii) the competition in the PK market cannot substitute for the shortcomings of the governance structure in realigning the incentives for PKs with those of the beneficiaries.

In summary, the investigation shows that PKs are involved in a structural conflict between the interests of their shareholders and the interests of the beneficiaries. The governance structure at the micro and meso level is not sufficient to ensure that PKs administer the beneficiaries' assets solely in their interest or that the beneficiaries' interests prevail in an actual conflict of interest with the shareholders or the management. On the contrary, PKs – as joint stock companies – are legally required to act in the interest of their shareholders.

2. THE POLITICO-ECONOMIC IMPLICATIONS OF THE GOVERNANCE OF OCCUPATIONAL PENSION FUNDS AT THE POLITICAL LEVEL

This section presents an empirical investigation of the findings of the first section and their politico-economic impact. It analyzes the role of the PK association (Fachverband der Pensionskassen) in a case study in which the interests of beneficiaries and shareholders are diametrically opposed. This analysis identifies the political process and legislative process in the case of the 2003 amendment to the PKG as a relevant empirical example and addresses the following questions: *(i)* What is the empirical evidence

[47] Source: Fachverband der Pensionskassen.

[48] Market transparency is low, meaning that no data on the relative performance of PKs is available. If all PKs experienced similar losses, beneficiaries would not profit from switching.

concerning the structural conflict of interest between shareholders and beneficiaries in PKs? Whose interests prevailed in this particular conflict of interest, and whose interests did the PKs actually represent? Are the empirical results in line with the derivations of the first section? *(ii)* What are the politico-economic consequences of the findings of the first section? How do the governance structures of PKs at the micro and meso level influence the political process? What are the repercussions of the political process for the governance structure at the micro and meso level?

The empirical inquiry rests on primary sources such as drafts of the respective proposals for the relevant PKG amendment and the enclosed explanatory notes, the records of the parliamentary debate, the report of the parliamentary Social Committee, the official opinions submitted during the legislative process, and interviews with the politicians, experts and civil servants involved.

Political Economy and Actor-Centered Institutionalism

Underhill (2001, p. 7) defines political economy as the investigation of 'the relationship between the market (and the private interests and prerogatives it includes) and political authority at various levels of governance (and the notions of public interest which we like to presume are inherent in politics)'. He points out that the market cannot be conceptualized without the state. They are often complementary, interdependent institutional arrangements that govern social relations within societies.[49] Consequently, politics and market forces constantly interact, reinforce and constrain each other. Sometimes they act in accordance with each other, sharing common beliefs, objectives and strategies. Sometimes they are antagonistic, representing conflicting interests, visions and approaches. In this section, the interaction between political and economic actors in shaping a specific political process is investigated and related to their institutional interests.

The power to define what is public and what is private interest constitutes one of the most effective instruments of power in shaping governance. The notions of public and private interests are themselves subjective and have strong ideological connotations. Therefore, we analyze which institution is most effective in presenting its own institutional interest as the public interest. At the political level, the governance structure of PKs is considered to a large extent endogenous.

[49] See also Cerny (2002).

The case study focuses on an amendment that reforms this governance structure.

The analysis employs *an actor-centered institutionalism,* which focuses on the ways in which actors influence policy change and attempt to further their institutional interests within the prevalent setting of political institutions. The analysis has to identify the relevant political process, the respective actors, their institutional interests, their power resources and their strategies. The latter, in turn, are influenced – but not determined – by the prevalent setting of political institutions.[50] It is regarded as the appropriate method to investigate the role of the PK association as one of the actors in the political and legislative process. In the first section, the institutional interests of PKs were endogenized. It was demonstrated that they are shaped by the governance structure of PKs and the interests of the parties at the micro and meso levels. In this section, the actors involved (including PKs and their association as well as the representatives of the beneficiaries) are regarded as agents pursuing their institutional interests. In the particular conflict of interest investigated, their homogeneity and coherence is interpreted as substantial enough to justify their treatment as coherent actors. Actor-centered institutionalism assumes that agents intentionally act rationally, which 'suggests that rationality is a social practice subject to cognitive limits and the vagaries of the environment in which decision making takes place rather than a universal once-and-for-all state of mind'.[51]

Case study: The political economy of the 2003 amendment to the PKG

The case study focuses on the 2003 amendment to the PKG and further restricts the analysis to changes in the provision concerning the guaranteed minimum yield. In this particular case, the interests of the individual parties to the process and the allocation of costs can be identified clearly, and the ensuing conflicts of interest are pronounced.

[50] Scharpf (2000). The relevant actors are the PKs, their association, their shareholders (mostly banking and insurance companies), the bodies representing beneficiaries and certain proponents of the government (Ministry of Finance) and parliament. Political institutions are defined as reducing the complexity of underlying conflicts of interest and increasing the political capacity to actually attain a solution by excluding some of the interests at lower levels, such as legal and political procedures, routines, socially constructed perceptions of society, etc. (March and Olsen 1989).

[51] Clark (2004, p. 241).

The Effects of the Guaranteed Minimum Yield Reform in the 2003 PKG Amendment

The 2003 amendment to the PKG induced financial losses for beneficiaries. Instead of crediting the asset accounts with the deficit that resulted from performance below the guaranteed minimum yield, the pension resulting from the reference value is paid out from the PK's own funds. The value of the assets remains unchanged. The pensioners experience a (potential) financial loss induced by the amendment, as they forego potential investment income on the credited deficit. The (potential) loss occurs if the investment income exceeds the minimum yield in the following periods. The loss corresponds to the (potential, positive) difference between the investment income from the deficit in the periods following the underperformance of the minimum yield and the hypothetical investment income based on the minimum yield.

The PKs' shareholders profited, as the provision requiring the PKs to credit beneficiaries' asset accounts from the PKs' own funds (shareholder equity) was abolished at a time when the guarantee was expected to be invoked. As the PKs' own funds were insufficient to cover the (potential) deficit, shareholders would have had to provide additional capital. Furthermore, the likelihood of underperforming the minimum yield in the future was reduced by two measures: (*i*) The scope of the guarantee was reduced to the superannuation for recipients rather than the value of assets for all beneficiaries, and (*ii*) the relevant averaging period was extended from five years to the entire period of membership in a PK until retirement. According to the FMA, the potential gains for shareholders (and the beneficiaries' potential financial losses) at the time of reform were in a range of about EUR 300 to 400 million.[52]

In addition, the amendment had a negative indirect effect on beneficiaries in the long run. By reducing the potential losses for the owners of PKs related to the minimum yield requirement, the governance mechanism addressing the principal-agent problem between beneficiaries and PKs was weakened.[53] Furthermore, the amendment had negative repercussions for the stability of the financial system and for systemic governance. The forbearance of supervisors and regulators as well as the ensuing 'ad hoc' legislation reduced the incentives for shareholders and PKs to comply with financial regulation and to engage in proper risk

---

[52] Austrian Press Agency, APA0375 5 WI 0597, 13 June 2003. Gains and losses can be estimated only roughly, as problems stemming from the guaranteed minimum yield requirement did not materialize in 2003, but were expected for the years 2004 onwards.

[53] No. 1328 of the Addenda to the Stenographic Records of the National Council, Legislative Period XVII, explanatory notes to Art. 2 (2) PKG. The important role of the minimum yield guarantee was discussed in detail in the first section.

management. This can have negative repercussions for the reputation of the governance structure of the Austrian financial system. Thus it did not contribute to financial stability.

The amendment caused financial losses for beneficiaries and did not contribute to financial stability. It was in the interest of the PKs and their shareholders, who avoided covering (potential) financial losses for beneficiaries using own funds.

The Political Economy of the 2003 Amendment

The interests of the shareholders and the beneficiaries were diametrically opposed in the reform process. If the PKs had represented the interest of their beneficiaries, they would have had to oppose the amendment, according to the provision requiring them to operate their business solely in the interest of the beneficiaries (Art. 2 [1] PKG). Whose interests did the PKs and their industry endorse? Which role did the latter play in the political process? Whose interests did the government endorse and why?

The government's institutional interests

The government's institutional interest is to actively promote institutional investors.[54] In addition, the government frequently pointed out that it wanted to actively promote the second (i.e. PKs) and third pillars of the Austrian pension system.[55]

If shareholders had refused to provide additional capital for PKs in order to enable them to cover the (potential) deficit, the PK system in Austria would have faced a crisis. It could be argued that the government's institutional interests would incline it to endorse the shareholders' interests, as a crisis of the PK system would have had negative implications for the Austrian capital market and the prospects of private pensions. However, that conclusion is not unambiguous. First, it was highly unlikely that the shareholders would actually allow PKs to go bankrupt.[56] Second, it could be maintained that the 2003 PKG amendment

---

[54] The Action Plans of the Government Envoy to the Capital Market 2002/2003 and 2003/2004 highlight the role of institutional investors in the second and third pillars of the Austrian pension system in promoting the Austrian capital market (http://www.bmf.gv.at/Finanzmarkt/Kapitalmarktinitiative625/aktion.pdf, November 2002, and http://www.bmf.gv.at/Finanzmarkt/Kapitalmarktinitiative625/pkkapitalmarkt.pdf, August 2003; last visit: 9 November 2004).

[55] E.g. the Government Declaration 2003 , 6 March 2003 (last visit: 9 November 2004), http://www.bka.gv.at/2004/4/20/regierungserklaerung.pdf

[56] Nevertheless, it was highly unlikely that the shareholders would have actually allowed PKs to go bankrupt and to destabilize the PK system. The market for private pension products is expected to expand rapidly in the near future. New products such as the tax-subsidized retirement savings and severance payment funds as well as cuts in the public

was not in the government's interest, as it hampered the growth of the second pillar by reducing its appeal to (prospective) beneficiaries and could have a negative impact on financial stability (by reducing incentives for compliance with financial regulation) and the reputation of financial governance in Austria. In addition, about 400 000 beneficiaries (and voters) were negatively affected by the amendment. Therefore, it was likely to be costly for the government to endorse the shareholders' institutional interests.

The institutional interests of beneficiaries' representatives

The representatives of the beneficiaries issued formal expert opinions on the amendment and strictly opposed it. The Trade Union Association and the Chamber of Labor both argued that the guaranteed minimum yield formed part of the entrepreneurial risks of PKs since their introduction in 1990, and that PKs were obliged to take the appropriate measures (i.e. own funds corresponding to their risks under Art. 7 PKG).[57] Sophisticated financial institutions should have factored these risks into their business models, charged the related risk premiums, and built up reserves corresponding to these risks or applied the appropriate risk-mitigating techniques available. The representatives of the beneficiaries maintained that the problems, which had arisen due to falling asset prices on financial markets, were aggravated by management errors. The parameters underlying the pension projections (i.e. *Rechnungszins*, *rechnungstechnischer Überschuss*, *Sterbetafeln*) were chosen incautiously in order to forecast higher expected returns for beneficiaries and to boost demand.[58]

The shareholders' interests

There are no documents officially stating the shareholders' interests. The Banking and Insurance Division of the Chamber of Commerce did not

---

PAYG system will ensure a growing market. The shareholders of PKs are usually involved heavily in the other market segments as well and would hardly allow insolvencies to undermine their reputation in the market. Consequently, neither concerns about the instability of the system nor about the potentially ensuing fiscal burden would have credibly motivated the government to endorse the shareholders' position.

[57] Verzetnitsch and Leutner (2003), Tumpel and Kubitschek (2003).

[58] In response to management errors at PKs, the supervisor FMA restricted the choice of technical parameters in 2003 (Austrian Press Agency, APA0078 5 WI 0607 II, 24 April 2003, and FMA parameters regulation, http://www.fma.gv.at/de/pdf/rechnung.pdf, last visit: 4 November 2004). In response to the insufficiency of own funds, the 2003 amendment requires PKs to allocate 0.45 per cent of the premium reserve to a statutory minimum yield reserve until it reaches 3 per cent of the premium reserve (Art. 7 [3] PKG). The PK association announced that the beneficiaries would have to bear the costs in the form of higher fees for the administration of investments (http://www.iwm.co.at/inflist.asp?p=3&sec=2&1=de&owner=-3&idl=de&inf=1601, last visit: 20 July 2004).

issue an official expert opinion on the first draft of the amendment. From the implications of the amendment, one can infer that the shareholders aimed to reduce their implicit obligations (from an estimated EUR 400 million to an estimated EUR 100 million, which could be spread over several years) vis-à-vis beneficiaries by promoting the amendment. In a press conference on 13 June 2003, the chairperson of the Banking and Insurance Division of the Chamber of Commerce, which represents the largest shareholders of PKs, welcomed the 2003 PKG amendment. The shareholders argued that the (potential) solvency problems of the PK system constituted an unforeseeable, exogenous shock (namely falling international equity and bond prices). Consequently, neither the beneficiaries nor the government could expect them to bear the ensuing costs.

The institutional interests of the PK association

The PK association represented the shareholders' interests. 'Cui bono' considerations are indicative but not sufficient to demonstrate the link between the interests of the shareholders and the PKs. This, in turn, is necessary to demonstrate the politico-economic repercussions of governance of PKs at the micro and meso level and the governance of the PK system at the political level. The press statements of the PK association are indicative of the PKs' interests. In two press conferences (13 June and 24 June 2003), the PK association explicitly welcomed the 2003 amendment. It argued that the obligatory additional contributions from PKs' own funds would be reduced to EUR 100 million (from EUR 400 million) and that the obligation could be spread over several years (rather than being due in a lump sum).[59]

The government's official considerations

The government's official considerations regarding the amendment reflect the PK association's position. The first draft of the amendment was sent out for consultation by the Ministry of Finance on 28 March 2003.[60] The ministry argued that against all expectations prices on

[59] http://www.iwm.co.at/default.asp?p=3&sec=2&1=de&owner=3&inf=1167 (last visit: 15 April 2004), http://www.iwm.co.at/default.asp?p=3&sec=2&1=de&owner=3&inf=1168 (last visit: 15 April 2004), and Austrian Press Agency, APA0375 5 WI 0597, 13 June 2003. The PK association did not issue an expert opinion during the consultation process following the presentation of the draft amendment issued by the Ministry of Finance, which it usually does if it opposes an amendment.

[60] The draft was changed during parliamentary negotiations to come to the resulting minimum yield guarantee described above with the additional adaptations which further benefited the PKs' shareholders at the expense of the beneficiaries. The draft contained an averaging period for the guaranteed minimum yield of 84 months for pensioners and of the

international capital markets had substantially decreased over the period 2000 to 2003. Without capital injections by the shareholders, the ministry expected that the PKs' own funds would not correspond to their risks.[61] The situation emerged despite the legal obligation of PKs to hold own funds corresponding to their risks (Art. 7 [1] PKG). Rather than enforcing the regulation to ensure that PKs would hold sufficient own funds to cover their legal obligations, the government decided to change the law to bail out the PKs.[62] The supervisor FMA defended the draft amendment, as shareholders would otherwise face the burden of additional contributions to own funds of up to EUR 400 million. According to FMA, these would by far exceed the PKs' own funds (about EUR 60 million at the time), thus, pointing to the inadequacy of own funds.[63]

What role did the PK association play in the political process?

Members of parliament, their staff, representatives of the institutions representing beneficiaries and the PK association, and civil servants involved in drafting the 2003 amendment were interviewed in September, October and November 2004.[64] All but one of them stated that the draft compiled by the Ministry of Finance as well as the changes during the

---

entire contribution period for beneficiaries. It stipulated an obligatory credit to the assets of beneficiaries and pensioners in cases of underperformance of the required minimum yield. The final amendment reduced the averaging period for pensioners from 84 to 60 months, but abolished the obligatory credit to the assets of beneficiaries and pensioners.

[61] 'Therefore one has to assume that in the following years [after 2003] PKs might have to credit the accounts of a number of investment and risk-sharing groups according to the minimum yield guarantee. This obligation will pose a substantial financial burden for PKs, which will presumably not be covered by their own funds'. Draft Amendment to the Federal Act on the Establishment, Administration and Supervision of *Pensionskassen*, GZ, 040010/7-Pr.4/03, 28 March 2003, Vienna, explanatory notes, General Part (author's translation). See also Okresek (2003).

[62] '[By the initial lengthening of the averaging period for recipients from five to seven years], the stabilization of the system will be supported with due attention to the enormous volatility of capital markets' (Draft Amendment to the Federal Act on the Establishment, Administration and Supervision of *Pensionskassen*, GZ. 040010/7-Pr.4/03, 28 March 2003, Vienna, explanatory notes to Art. 2 (2) PKG, [author's translation]).

[63] Austrian Press Agency, APA0078 5 WI 0607 II, 24 April 2003.

[64] Interviews with National Council Member Sigisbert Dolinschek (FPÖ), sponsor of the amendment in the Social Committee and of the final motion in the plenary (face-to-face interview, 8 September 2004), Oberrat Friessnegg, Ministry of Finance (telephone interview, 8 September 2004), Ministerialrat Abteilungsleiter Peter Erlacher, Ministry of Finance (telephone interview, 29 September 2004), Otto Farny, Chamber of Labor (telephone interview, 29 September 2004), Fritz Janda, managing director of the PK association (telephone interview, 29 October 2004), Erich Holnsteiner, expert at the SPÖ Club in Parliament (face-to-face interview, 5 November 2004). The main proponent of the amendment for the ÖVP in the Finance Committee, Günter Stummvoll, refused to give an interview. Representatives of the Green Party were not available for interviews.

ensuing parliamentary debate can be traced back to the initiative of the PK association and the shareholders of PKs.[65] According to all of the interviewees, the shareholders argued that they would not be willing to inject further capital to keep PKs in operation if the obligations arising from the guaranteed minimum yield took effect.

How did the PK association and the PKs' shareholders manage to convince the government to endorse the shareholders' interests?

The authors of the bill in the Ministry of Finance and the sponsors of the motion in parliament presented it as a public-interest initiative. The amendments to the guaranteed minimum yield were motivated by the need to stabilize the PK system. This is consistent with the PK association's interpretation of the main objectives of the amendment. The State Secretary of the Ministry of Finance argued that the objectives of the amendment were ' . . . the long-term security of occupational pensions and the long-term security of the PK system'.[66] He made this statement during a press conference on 13 June 2003, which he attended together with the chairperson of the Banking and Insurance Division of the Chamber of Commerce and the chairperson of the PK association.[67] This evidence shows how effective and convincing the PK association was in presenting its institutional interest as the public interest and in convincing the government to side with the PKs' shareholders in the conflict of interest concerning the guaranteed minimum yield.[68]

The powerful position of the PK association and the PKs' shareholders stemmed from the threat of the shareholders to allow PKs to become insolvent, meaning that the amendment could be postulated as the only means of securing the stability of the PK system – a public-interest motive. The control over the financial capital of PKs leverages the PK association's and the shareholders' politico-economic power at the political level. The power in public discourse stems from constraining the public perception of the nature of the problem and the set of available

---

[65] The representative of the PK association argued that it was involved in the negotiations to change the draft and achieved improvements for the beneficiaries. He refused to comment on the motives of the Ministry of Finance and the initiative of the shareholders and the PK association in preparing the draft amendment.

[66] Press statement of the PK Association on 13 June 2003, http://www.iwm.co.at/default.asp?p=3&sec=2&1=de&owner=3&inf=1167 (last visit: 15 April 2004), http://www.iwm.co.at/default.asp?p=3&sec=2&1=de&owner=3&inf=1168 (last visit: 15 April 2004).

[67] The PK association is a subsection of the Banking and Insurance Division, as most of the shareholders of PKs are banks and insurance companies and PKs are themselves incorporated as credit institutions.

[68] That, however, does not imply that the structural dominance of shareholders was the only cause for the amendment.

policy alternatives.[69] In particular, the PKs and their shareholders managed to posit the potential collapse of the PK system as an exogenously determined objective fact, i.e. independent of the PKs' and their shareholders' actions (i.e. management errors, the wrong parameters employed in the past, and insufficient own funds relative to risk), and as a consequence of unforeseeable financial market developments. Consequently, neither the beneficiaries nor the government should expect the shareholders to bear the costs of the shock. The PK association managed to reframe the distributional (political) conflict as a technical (non-political) problem of financial stability.

How did the electoral dimension influence the decision of the government to promote the amendment, given the fact that beneficiaries dominate PKs' shareholders in terms of voting power? The final motion was tabled as part of the *Budgetbegleitgesetze 2003*, a substantial package of legislation that covered budgetary issues as well as a large public pension reform and the purchase of Eurofighter jets. These issues attracted substantially more attention in public debate than the highly technical changes in Art. 2 PKG, thus the electoral dimension would pose very limited disincentives for the government to endorse the shareholders' position.

The incorporation of PKs as credit institutions has repercussions for governance at the political level beyond the structural dominance of shareholders in the governance of PKs. According to one sponsor of the bill, the changes to the guaranteed minimum yield were not negotiated in the Social Committee but in the Finance Committee of the Austrian parliament. The logic and the policy network of the Finance Committee further strengthen the influence of the PK association and the shareholders of PKs – mostly banks and insurance companies, which are quite influential in the policy network of the Finance Committee. This further increases the PKs' and their shareholders' power resources at the expense of those of the beneficiaries' representatives, who are more influential actors in the policy network surrounding the Social Committee.[70]

In summary, the evidence indicates that the PK association and the PKs did not represent the interests of the beneficiaries, namely by

---

[69] According to one interviewee, the PK association opposed alternative solutions which would have decreased the immediate costs to shareholders, spread the costs arising from the guaranteed minimum yield over up to 20 years, preserved the rights of the beneficiaries and prevented damage to the credibility of financial market legislation.

[70] Talos and Kittel (2001) provide an analysis of the policy networks in Austria. They demonstrate that the banks are influential actors in the policy network in the area of financial legislation, while the Trade Union Association and the Chamber of Labor, as well as the Chamber of Commerce and the Federation of Industry, are influential actors in the policy network in the area of social policy.

preventing the effective dismantling of the guaranteed minimum yield, but rather that it actively promoted the amendment in the interest of its shareholders. This corroborates the evidence in the first section of a structural dominance of the shareholders' interests in the governance structure of PKs and of the likely prevalence of the shareholders' interests in actual conflicts of interest with beneficiaries. It further demonstrates that shareholders also employ their micro and meso-level dominance at the politico-economic level to further strengthen their position in the governance structure of PKs, and that both levels of governance are mutually interdependent.

3. CONCLUSION

The central results of the paper are: (*i*) Neither the internal governance structure of PKs nor market competition provides an incentive structure that effectively addresses the structural dominance of shareholders' interests in PKs at the expense of beneficiaries; the shareholders' interests are likely to prevail in a conflict of interest with the beneficiaries; and (*ii*) in an actual conflict of interests concerning the governance structure of PKs, the PK association and the PKs acted in the interest of the shareholders, as predicted in the first section; consequently, the governance structure at the micro and meso level has considerable politico-economic consequences at the political level, which can result in a vicious circle for beneficiaries. It subjects the governance arrangements in place (designed to protect beneficiaries in conflicts of interest with shareholders) to substantial political risk, which in turn is aggravated by the structural dominance of shareholders in the governance of PKs. Asymmetries of power at the political level have substantial repercussions on the governance structure at the micro and meso level.

The structural dominance of shareholders in PKs is a consequence of the fact that PKs are credit institutions and must be incorporated as joint stock companies. This, in turn, is motivated by the institutional interests of previous and current governments to promote the Austrian capital market by strengthening institutional investors.

The PK association played an important and effective role in initiating the 2003 PKG amendment and in shaping public discourse about the amendment. The association managed to construct the public's perception of the problem of insufficient own funds in such a way that it was interpreted as an exogenously determined objective fact and as a consequence of unforeseeable financial market developments independent of the PKs' management errors. The amendment was postulated as the only means of securing the stability of the PK system and, therefore, as a reform in the public interest.

In the short run, the policy options are limited. In order to increase the transparency of processes at the political level and to ensure the participation of beneficiaries, an instrument of meta-governance[71] should be re-introduced. In 1990 the PKG instituted the *Pensionskassenbeirat*, an expert committee advising the Minister of Finance in all matters relating to PKs (Art. 35 [1] PKG 1990). The committee consisted of five members nominated by the Chamber of Commerce (to which the PK association belongs), five members of the Chamber of Labor (which represents the interests of the beneficiaries), one member nominated by the Ministry of Labor and Social Affairs, and one nominated by the Ministry of Finance. The equal representation of shareholders and of beneficiaries would at least ensure that the advice provided for the Minister of Finance also reflected the interests of the beneficiaries. A comparison of pension fund governance in OECD countries seems to indicate that the organizational forms of trusts and foundations ensure better formal representation for beneficiaries.[72] This comparative analysis is restricted to a comparison of formal representation but does not analyze the efficacy of specific arrangements and is rather narrow in its scope on internal governance structures. An analysis of the efficacy of the formal arrangements in the UK suggests that beneficiaries have little influence in UK pension trusts as well.[73] This area warrants further comparative institutional research.

In the long run, the structural dominance of shareholders in PKs calls into question whether the privatization of old-age provision to credit institutions and its coupling with the promotion of capital markets optimally serves the beneficiaries' interests.

REFERENCES

Ambachtsheer, K.P. (2001), 'Public Pension Fund Power', *Journal of Portfolio Management*, 27, 61–4.

Besley, T. and A. Prat (2003), 'Pension Fund Governance and the Choice Between Defined Benefit and Defined Contribution Plans', Discussion Paper, STICERD UBD-LSE Pensions Program, London School of Economics.

Brooks, S. and E. James (1999), 'The Political Economy of Pension Reform', paper presented at the World Bank Research Conference, 14–15 September.

Cerny, P.G. (2002), 'Webs of Governance and the Privatization of Transnational Regulation', in D.M. Andrews, C.R. Henning and L.W. Pauly (eds),

[71] Jessop (1999, p. 16) defines meta-governance as mechanism to '. . . conform and coordinate several sites and objectives of governance'.

[72] OECD (2001).

[73] Clark (2004).

Governing the World's Money, Ithaca and London: Cornell University Press, pp. 194–215.

Clark, G.L. (2004), 'Pension fund governance: expertise and organisational form', *Journal of Pension Economics and Finance*, 3, 233–53.

Company Pension Act (Betriebspensionsgesetz – BPG), Federal Legal Gazette 282/1990.

Deelstra, G., M. Grasselli and P.F. Koehl (2004), 'Optimal Design of the Guarantee for Defined Contribution Funds', *Journal of Economic Dynamics and Control*, 28, 2239–60.

Farny, O. and J. Wöss (1992), *Betriebspensionsgesetz, Pensionskassengesetz, Gesetze und Kommentare 150*, Vienna: Verlag des ÖGB.

Federal Act on the Establishment, Administration and Supervision of *Pensionskassen* (Pensionskassengesetz – PKG), translation of the current version of the Act as of September 2004, Vienna: Financial Market Authority (FMA).

Jessop, B. (1999), 'The Governance of Complexity and the Complexity of Governance: Preliminary Remarks on some Problems and Limits of Economic Guidance', Department of Sociology, Lancaster University.

Mahoney, P.G. (2004), 'Manager-Investor Conflicts in Mutual Funds', *Journal of Economic Perspectives*, 18, 161–82.

March, J.G. and J.P. Olsen (1989), *Rediscovering Institutions – The Organisational Basics of Politics*, New York: Free Press.

Müller, K. (2003), 'The Making of Pension Privatization in Latin America and Eastern Europe', in R. Holzmann, M. Orenstein and M. Rutkowski (eds), *Pension Reform in Europe: Process and Progress*, Washington, DC: The World Bank, pp. 47–78.

Ney, S. (2003), 'The Rediscovery of Politics: Democracy and Structural Pension Reform in Continental Europe', in R. Holzmann, M. Orenstein and M. Rutkowski (eds), *Pension Reform in Europe: Process and Progress*, Washington, DC: The World Bank, pp. 79–110.

OECD (2001), *Pension Fund Governance*, Paris: OECD.

OECD (2004), 'Guidelines for the Protection of Rights of Members and Beneficiaries in Occupational Pension Plans', *Financial Market Trends*, 87, 199–219.

Okresek (2003), *Entwurf eines Gesetzes, mit dem das Pensionskassengesetz geändert wird*, Expert Opinion of the Federal Chancellery, 603.454/002-V/A/8/2003, 28 April 2003, Vienna.

Orenstein, M.A. (2003), 'Mapping the Diffusion of Pension Innovation', in R. Holzmann, M. Orenstein and M. Rutkowski (eds), *Pension Reform in Europe: Process and Progress*, Washington, DC: The World Bank, pp. 171–94.

Palomino, F. and A. Prat (2002), 'Risk Taking and Optimal Contracts for Money Managers', Discussion Paper, STICERD UBS-LSE Pensions Program, London School of Economics.

Rajan, U. and S. Srivastava (2000), 'Portfolio Delegation with Limited Liability', Working Paper, GSIA Carnegie Mellon University, Pittsburgh.

Rein, M. and W. Schmähl (eds) (2004), *Rethinking the Welfare State – The Political Economy of Pension Reform*, Cheltenham, UK and Northampton, MA, USA: Edward Elgar.

Scharpf, F.W. (2000), 'Institutions in Comparative Policy Research', MPIfG Working Paper 00/3, Cologne.

Schiemer, K., P. Jabornegg and R. Strasser (1993), *Kommentar zum Aktiengesetz* (3rd edition), Vienna: Manzsche Verlags- und Universitätsbuchhandlung.

Talos, E. and Kittel, B. (2001), *Gesetzgebung in Österreich*, Vienna: WUV.

Tumpel, H. and M. Kubitschek (2003), *Entwurf eines Gesetzes, mit dem das Pensionskassengesetz geändert wird*, Expert Opinion of the Chamber of Labor, MagAch/CB, 27 April 2004, Vienna.

Underhill, Geoffrey R.D. (2001), *States, Markets and Governance*, inaugural lecture at University of Amsterdam, 21 September 2001.

Verzetnitsch, F. and R. Leutner (2003), *Entwurf eines Gesetzes, mit dem das Pensionskassengesetz geändert wird*, Expert Opinion of the Trade Union Association, SR-GSt/F/Bi, 22 April 2003, Vienna.

Weaver, R.K. (2003), 'The Politics of Public Pension Reform', WP 2003 - 06, Chestnut Hill: Center for Retirement Research at Boston College.

Williamson, O.E. (1985), *The Economic Institutions of Capitalism*, New York: Free Press.

Williamson, O.E. (1996), *The Mechanisms of Governance*, Oxford: Oxford University Press.

World Economic Forum (2005), *Mainstreaming Responsible Investment*, Geneva: WEF.

Index